SMALL-HEADED FLYCATCHER.

Seen Yesterday.

He Didn't Leave His Name.

SMALL-HEADED FLYCATCHER.
Seen Yesterday.
He Didn't Leave His Name.
And Other Stories

Pete Dunne

Drawings by Louise Zemaitis

UNIVERSITY OF TEXAS PRESS, AUSTIN

Requests for permission to reproduce material from this work
should be sent to Permissions, University of Texas Press, P.O.
Box 7819, Austin, TX 78713-7819.

⊗ The paper used in this publication meets the minimum
requirements of American National Standard for Information
Sciences—Permanence of Paper for Printed Library Materials,
ANSI Z39.48-1984.

LIBRARY OF CONGRESS
CATALOGING-IN-PUBLICATION DATA

Dunne, Pete, 1951–
[Essays. Selections]
Small-headed flycatcher ; Seen yesterday ; He didn't leave
his name : and other stories / Pete Dunne.
    p.   cm.
    ISBN 0-292-71600-1 (paper : alk. paper)

1. Bird watching. 2. Birds. I. Title. II. Title: Seen
yesterday. III. Title: He didn't leave his name.
QL677.5.D85   1998
598'.07'234—dc21   97-43354

To Beth Van Vleck,
who watches birds too.

CONTENTS

ACKNOWLEDGMENTS

Writers are helped by a support force whose ranks are filled by just about everyone they know. It includes coworkers whose concentration is habitually broken by queries like "Hey, does *Phragmites* have one *t* or two?"; friends whose calls to finalize dinner plans are considered invitations to use them as editorial sounding boards; dogs that wait by the back door until the urgency of their whining finally cuts through a writer's trance; and overnight delivery people who understand that an unanswered knock at the front door means go around to the back door, leave the envelope . . .

And let the dogs out.

Broad-based support (and broad-brush gratitude) notwithstanding, it is impossible *not* to single out a few individuals whose contribution during the working of these essays has earned them special thanks. These include editors Richard Roberts, Fletcher Roberts, Tim Gallagher, Victoria Irwin, Jane Crowley, and Eldon Greij, whose friendship and counsel are worth any writer's envy, as well as Sheila Lego, Marleen Murgitroid, and Beth Van Vleck, whose talents as proofreaders were gratefully accepted and are even more gratefully acknowledged.

Of course, nothing I attempt could come to fruition without the patient indulgence of my wife, Linda, or the support of the Cape May Bird Observatory staff.

PREFACE

"I guess I'll be a writer someday," I said in response to one of the stock questions asked of, and by, people who are destined to become friends. This assertion, uttered on the north lookout of Hawk Mountain Sanctuary in 1975, elicited no response from hawk counter Michael Heller. Only years later did Michael confess that he didn't place much stock in my disclosure at the time.

"Everybody," he recalls thinking, "thinks that they are going to be a writer someday."

Today Michael is a plantation manager with the Chesapeake Bay Foundation. I am the director of the New Jersey Audubon Society's Cape May Bird Observatory. But back in the winter of 1975–1976, when Michael and I enlivened evenings by knocking back dark beers and reading the passages of favorite authors to each other aloud, I was still searching for my niche and hoping that the hawk migration study I was going to conduct for the New Jersey Audubon Society come spring would lead to something . . .

A job. A career. Maybe even an avenue to express the cauldron of thoughts and observations that boiled inside me—and have since been forged into essays, stories, and articles:

In magazines like *Audubon, American Birds, Bird Watcher's Digest, Birder's World, Birding, Living Bird, Natural History, Nature Conservancy, New Jersey Audubon, WildBird, Wildlife Conservation.*

In the biweekly column I penned between 1986 and 1995 for the New Jersey Sunday section of the *New York Times,* titled "In the Natural State."

In the *Peregrine Observer,* the newsletter of Cape May Bird Observatory, which served as the first vehicle for my stories and from which the essays of my first book, *Tales of a Low-Rent Birder,* were drawn.

Followed by *Hawks in Flight,* followed by *More Tales of a Low-Rent Birder,* followed by *The Feather Quest, Before the Echo, The Wind Masters* . . .

And now this book.

Yes, I guess I became a writer—a pretty prolific one too, if the volume of essays discarded while selecting favorites for this collection is any measure. In fact, I do *so* much writing for *so* many publications that readers sometimes ask *how* I can I write so much and not go dry. There are three reasons, I think.

First and foremost, I really love watching birds and delight in sharing my passion with others, whether in the field or in print.

Second, the focus and tone of the columns I write are thematically apportioned so each is approached with a different mind-set. For example, essays written for "The Catbird Seat," my regular column in *Living Bird,* trade heavily upon the foibles of birders and birding. They are short, whimsical, and sassy. By comparison, essays drafted for "American Birding," the column I once penned for now defunct *American Birds,* tend to be longer, more situational, and more philosophical.

Articles drawn from my "Beak to Tale" column in *Wild Bird News* are terse and people-oriented. Those crafted for "Birder at Large," which appears in *Birder's World,* are nostalgic and focused primarily upon birds themselves.

So each column's essays have a different style, a different perspective (offering a refreshing difference for writer and reader alike).

And the final reason to account for how I can draw from the

writer's well so freely and not run dry? I'm half-Irish, genetically linked to the planet's greatest race of storytellers.

That's how.

You may be curious about the title: *Small-Headed Flycatcher. Seen Yesterday. He Didn't Leave His Name.* It is the title of the book's longest essay, but a piece distinguished more by origin than length. Unlike the other thirty-three essays in this collection, "Small-Headed Flycatcher" was initially crafted to be spoken, not read. The audience was the American Birding Association members on the occasion the association's 1992 convention in Mobile, Alabama.

I'm too sly a storyteller to steal my own thunder (meaning I'll not unravel the story line here), but, as readers must know, stories are not spun from thin air. Behind every story there lies another: the story of the story's crafting. So for readers who would like a peek behind the writer's slate, here is the story behind the story— the story behind the writing of "Small-Headed Flycatcher."

In 1991, one year before the ABA convention, I was asked to be the banquet speaker at the Texas Ornithological Society's annual dinner. The invitation was tendered by then president, and friend, Dr. Bill Graber—a straight-shooting, straight-talking Texas gentleman.

My program, an audiovisual-augmented accounting of the year of birding and travel that was the substance of my book *The Feather Quest,* went well. Later, over drinks, I asked Bill how he enjoyed the program, and in a Texas-tempered baritone he replied, "Why, Pete, that was a *fine* program. A *fine* program," which is, of course, precisely what a guest speaker wants to hear.

"You know," continued the person whose love of honest truth would have earned a handshake from Diogenes, "that was *almost* as good as a story I once heard Peter Matthiessen give to us, several years ago, about his rediscovering heath hens on some tiny island off the coast of Massachusetts . . .

"Now that," said my gracious, truth-loving host, "was a *fine* story."

No storyteller, not even one who appreciates truth, likes to be told (even when it is true) that *their* story isn't as good as somebody else's story. And while I am a frank admirer of Peter Matthiessen's writing, I felt brazenly confident that I could tell a better *story* than Peter Matthiessen because . . .

Because like I said, I'm Irish!

So picking up Bill Graber's unmindfully dropped gauntlet, I cold-bloodedly set out to craft a better birding story than the one spun by Peter Matthiessen, using, for comparison's sake, the same basic story line—the rediscovery of a bird believed to be extinct—but drawing from and weaving in a different set of historic events: those relating to the finding of a bird whose discovery was independently claimed by rival artists John James Audubon and Alexander Wilson.

I threw everything I had into it. Every storyteller's trick. Every wordsmithing skill. All the Irish that was honestly mine to draw upon and even a measure that was not, that came from some vast depth, beyond the reach of my skill.

And at one marvelous moment during that inaugural telling, before an audience of five hundred listeners, I held a pregnant pause to the painful limit and was rewarded by the gratifying sound of *silence.* Utter silence.

"Got you," I thought quietly to myself. And I did have them too, an audience empathetically bound to the teller by the telling—had them right to the story's uncertain end.

No storyteller hopes for or garners more.

It just so happened that my friend Bill Graber was reigning vice president of ABA at the time and presiding over the banquet. So after the program. After the applause. After all the well-wishers (and the gainsayers) had had their say, I sashayed over to Dr. Graber and asked (oh so very casually) what he thought of the program.

"*Pete,*" said the man who didn't have a shred of memory concerning our earlier conversation, "I've got to tell you, that was a *fine* story, a *fine* story."

"You know," he continued after a moment's thought, "*That was as good* a story as one I once heard Peter Matthiessen tell at a meeting of the Texas Ornithological Society about . . ."

So I guess what I'm telling you is that I tied.

I hope you enjoy "Small-Headed Flycatcher."

Pete Dunne
Cape May, New Jersey

SMALL-HEADED FLYCATCHER.
Seen Yesterday.
He Didn't Leave His Name.

Part 1

STORIES

ABOUT

FAMILY

GIFT OF SEED

The house smelled of turkey and echoed with the sound of grand-children. We opened arms and hugged.

"Hello, Dad," I said.

"Solstice cheer!" he exclaimed. "Hurry up. There's something I want to show you."

My father turned, and a grimace twisted the smile from his face. He started toward the glass doors that open onto the deck, and though his legs are long, his steps were pained and short—a result of the Lyme disease that had taken much of his agility and very nearly his life.

We gained the doors and, like a child peeking around the cor-ner on Christmas morning, he leaned forward, studied the bird feeders with binoculars, then relaxed.

"He's not there now," he whispered. "Wait."

We did wait. Father and son. Watching chickadees and spar-rows, waiting for the new bird that had joined the ranks of my fa-ther's feeder regulars.

I saw my mother in the kitchen, working her usual culinary magic. Our eyes met, and we exchanged greetings along visual pathways. In response to my cocked eyebrow, she nodded in the direction of the feeders and smiled.

It was good to see the smile. It had not been there the last time we'd been together.

"We have to find something to catch his interest," she had im-plored more than urged back in October. "He can't get around like he used to. He can't use his hands very well. If he just sits in a chair all day, we're going to lose him."

"What about putting up some bird feeders out back," I suggested. "A couple of tube feeders filled with sunflower seeds for chickadees and finches. A platform feeder with millet for sparrows. A thistle tube to keep the goldfinches fat and sassy and— maybe some suet. Mom, a feeding station offers more color than a fish tank and more action than a meat counter when ground beef goes on sale."

"It's perfect," I continued. "Hours of entertainment. You get to know all the regulars and itch for each new arrival. You cheer on the chickadees, laugh at the nuthatches, and chastise the evening grosbeaks for hogging all the sunflower seeds."

"Besides, if keeping Dad sharp is the key, wait till he tries matching wits with squirrels. It's easier to keep the kids out of your pies than to keep squirrels out of your feeders."

"All right," she agreed. "Let's try it." That was two months ago.

"It was here just a minute ago," my father promised. "It likes the thistle feeder," he added to hold my attention.

"*There!*" he shouted as a bird flew in, claiming a perch. "That's it! Is that a redpoll?"

"That's a common redpoll," I affirmed, studying the puffy ball of feathers with the crimson cap. "Great bird!"

When he turned in triumph, I saw that the smile was back on his face, and the gleam in his eyes would have rivaled that of any child in the room. To look at those eyes, you'd never guess they'd ever known pain.

BROTHER MIKE'S RETREAT
FROM BIRDING

You've never met my brother Mike. He's what you'd call normal. Wife, kids, house in the 'burbs. Plays a little golf. Watches football on the tube. Lives for his lawn.

You've never met my brother Mike—but you probably know people like him. So you'll understand why I was having such a tough time convincing him that birders are normal.

We were standing on the hawk watch platform at Cape May Point State Park. I was looking at hawks. Mike was looking at the hawk watchers.

"You mean people come and stand here of their own volition?" he whispered (not wanting to hurt anyone's feelings).

"Travel hundreds, even thousands, of mi . . . *Peregrine over the bunker!*" I yelled as one hundred pairs of binoculars swiveled with the precision of a parade ground maneuver.

"How'd you get them to do that?" he demanded. "It's like some kind of totalitarian cult ritual."

"Hardly," I replied. "Birders are pretty independent."

"I'll say," he said, looking down the ranks, taking in an assortment of outerwear that ranged from Abercrombie and Fitch fine to Salvation Army discard (but leaning heavily on the side of Salvation Army). That's when someone produced a road-killed Virginia rail and started passing it around. Mike didn't say a word, but his eyes, looking squarely into mine, spoke volumes.

I guess to people whose keenest ambition is a close-cropped lawn, the antics of birders must appear odd. Normal people work like crazy for the privilege of sleeping in on Saturday until after the sun stops casting shadows. Birders get up *before* the sun casts shadows.

Normal people find a bird dropping on the hood of their newly washed car and go ballistic. Birders look up to see what's nesting on the overhanging limbs.

In my efforts to paint a palatable picture of my avocation, I have avoided telling brother Mike about some of the more suspect adventures birding has led me to. I never told him about the midnight encounter on that elevated railway two miles out in a marsh. There wasn't enough room on the tracks for the train *and* the members of my Big Day birding team, so we, being gallant, elected to step into the marsh.

I never told him about the time Patty H. skidded to a halt on an iced-over and totally blind I-95 exit ramp to point out my life hawk owl, or the time Bob B. and I canoed an ice-choked Delaware River on the Walnut Valley Christmas Bird Count just to add bufflehead to the count.

"It's okay," I explained to the near apoplectic park service ranger who met us at the landing. "We didn't dump, and we only had to chop ourselves free twice."

I've never told Mike about winter pelagic trips—how people will pay money and throw up all day for the chance of seeing a great skua or about the liquid-purging walk down Sycamore Canyon whose prize is a drab-looking sparrow that defines its territory vertically.

And I certainly never told Mike about Attu. How could you hope to explain (to a normal person) why people are willing to pay the price of a luxury cruise to spend three weeks in a building that doesn't meet the federal government's minimum standards for a homeless shelter and brave weather conditions that would freeze an eider to see birds that don't belong there?

Or how it is perfectly normal for a student living on a budget that wouldn't sustain an anorexic cat to brandish fifteen-hundred-dollar binoculars.

Or why a doting, loving father will risk a daughter's heartbreak (and a wife's wrath) and get to the church (after the fact) convinced that getting the bird constitutes pragmatic absolution.

It was all I could do to explain why a bunch of people passing a dead bird around constituted normal behavior.

"It's an opportunity to study a rarely seen bird," I explained. "It's the same as keeping a collection of study skins but better, since the plumage is fresher."

"You people keep dead birds?" he asked.

"Just the skins," I explained. "Until we're ready to prepare them, we store them in the freezer."

"You keep dead birds in the freezer?" he asked, believing me even less.

"Sure," I said, discreetly avoiding mention of the dead otter that was also vying with the frozen vegetables for freezer space. "We've got permits. It's legal."

The fact that there were laws governing such behavior seemed to comfort Mike. If birding was regulated (like everything else), maybe birding was indeed normal.

That's when someone yelled "*Wheatear!*" and several hundred people stampeded to the far side of the parking lot, where they proceeded to clamber atop the roofs of cars (in some cases not their own). It was the only way to see the bird perched on the roof.

"Want to see it?" I asked (I encouraged).

"I don't think so," he replied.

"Well . . . I'll see you later," I said, edging away.

"Later," he affirmed, edging the other way.

The next time we saw each other was Christmas. The subject of birding never came up.

THE WISDOM OF SISTERS

"Peter! Come to the window. QUICK!" I took the steps two at a time, reaching the kitchen window at a speed commensurate with the urgency in my sister's voice.

"Look," she said, directing my attention toward the backyard. "A hawk or something and it's killing a bird." I followed the line drawn by her finger and absorbed the scene.

"Cooper's hawk," the analytical portion of my brain deduced. A superb predator. A cruise missile of a raptor that can move through woodlands like smoke and match the movement of fleeing prey the way a mirror mimics.

"And a starling," I added, studying the bird pinned to the lawn—waiting for and absorbing the jolt of pity that comes of witnessing another creature's demise.

"It's still alive," my sister shouted.

"Yes," I said.

We've got to do something," she declared, starting for the door.

"No," I said, not loudly but convincingly. My sister returned to the window, absorbed the scene again, then turned and put all her anguish into a question.

"Why?" she demanded of her older, bird-learned brother whose feeders had drawn both the bird that was pinned and the bird that pinned it. *Why* should we, as thinking, feeling creatures not impose ourselves between a predator and its prey? As the starling struggled and its life ebbed, I tried to formulate an answer that would do at least small justice to the truth.

I thought of telling my sister that predation is a natural process—one that unites two species in a ritual of recycling, where both are moved toward higher levels of evolutionary perfection.

I thought of telling her that nature is profligate—always creates more than she needs—and that Cooper's hawks are just nature's way of cleaning house.

I thought of inviting her to study the young hawk and see it with my eyes. A streak-breasted bird of the year. Thin, probably starving. Chances were it would die before spring. Most of the Cooper's hawks born in any given year do not live to maturity.

I even considered being flippant and obtuse, telling her that the hawk was just another bird coming to the feeder.

But I did none of these things. I simply told her the truth as I knew it.

"Because we have no standing," I said. "I don't like everything I see in nature, and I don't understand it either. But I'm not smart enough or wise enough to second-guess nature, so I don't."

I thought that this disclosure would be enough to stay my younger sister's compassionate impulses, but I was wrong.

"Well, I may not be as smart as you are and I may not know anything about birds, but I'm going to save that bird," she said, turning, running.

And she did too.

KALEIDOSCOPE EYES

Our car rolled to a stop in front of the copse of trees. Northwest winds whipped the outer leaves, giving branches the properties of tentacles.

"Ready?" I asked.

"In a minute," wife Linda insisted, barely keeping her exasperation in check.

It was Sunday and early. Tomorrow was Monday and a school day. The semester's first exam was imminent, and my sudden intrusion into what had promised to be a day of study had not been greeted enthusiastically. In fact, initial efforts to pry Linda from her desk—to show her "something incredible"—had met hard resistance.

But as respectful as I try to be of my spouse's time, *this* time "No" was not an acceptable answer. This time she had to come with me.

Because I had found something incredible that morning, you see. In the trees. At the end of an old road leading out onto open marsh. Something wide-eyed, marvelous, and heart-stoppingly beautiful.

It was a spectacle so spectacular that it stripped away adult reserve and made me gasp like a child. It was the perfect example of why, after forty-four years, I still reside in this overpopulated and environmentally stressed state and why I have no thought but to continue to do so.

It was imperative that Linda see this spectacle too. Why? Because eight years of residency has not been time enough to pry the horizon from Linda's mind. Her roots and standards are still set in the unencumbered riches of the American West. To her mind, every day she wakes in the East is a day that begins with compromise.

You cradle-to-grave easterners who have never lived anywhere else may be confounded, even affronted, by Linda's attitude. You may not understand how a woodland differs from a wilderness or why a person might prefer the latter.

Well, I understand a little, barely. I have felt the power of the Rockies—the mountain range whose afternoon shadow once fell on Linda's doorstep. I have floated in the self-dissolving calm of Prince William Sound—the body of water that Linda once called her playground.

I know how, after just a few days or weeks in places like these, human souls expand to encompass them and how returning to an environment where human activity patterns are plotted around peak traffic periods is stifling.

I can only guess how a person raised by the open standards of the West must feel when they move East. It has been eight years since Linda left Wyoming and moved to New Jersey. And while she no longer cries whenever our eastbound plane circles for a landing, her eyes, fused to the landscape below, are clouded with disquiet.

I'm different, of course. Born into compromise; a seeker of beauty when and wherever I can find it. There are many wonderful natural treasures housed in New Jersey. But you have to know how to find them.

I've tried to explain this to Linda. "Nature in New Jersey," I tutor, "is like the contemplation of a bonsai garden or peering into a kaleidoscope. Focus on the beauty in front of you; block out the world around you. That's the trick.

"Don't think like a westerner," I counsel. "You'll go crazy with loss. The eastern old-growth forests are cut and gone. The rivers are sullied. The cities and people are here for keeps. Forget these things.

"Think *small,*" I counsel her. "Think eastern. When you see a stand of bloodroot blooming in the spring, absorb the wonder of it. When you round a corner and find a valley uncompromised by corporate headquarters, love it."

But I was brought up in New Jersey, and this discipline comes easy to me. Looking small and looking close and overlooking the things she does not care to see is something Linda does not do easily or well.

I recall a morning spent in the New Jersey highlands, on a marginally traveled highway named Clinton Road. We'd gone to look for northern breeding birds—warblers and vireos and thrushes whose songs fill Canadian zone woodlands.

It was in my estimate a terrific day, one filled with encounters. But over the course of the morning, Linda's enthusiasm ebbed, and silence closed around her like a shroud.

"What's the matter?" I finally asked.

"It doesn't even trouble you, does it?" she asked, gesturing toward the side of the road.

"What doesn't trouble me?" I asked, genuinely puzzled.

"That," she said, pointing directly at a pile of roadside trash—the cans, bottles, and product wrappings discarded by motorists. "That," she said, not even wanting to honor the stuff with a name.

I never even saw the trash. I was wearing my New Jersey blinders and had looked right past it.

Another time we were engaged in a Christmas bird count. Our territory in northern Morris County was a coveted patch—an overgrown gravel pit that habitually produced unusual birds for the count: assorted owls, lingering half-hearty songbirds, even a great egret on one momentous occasion, a first for the count.

As we picked our way through one of the trash heaps that abound in woodlands adjacent to heavily suburbanized areas, and as I stepped between sixty-gallon drums that may or may not have contained their original contents, I realized that Linda wasn't beside me anymore. I turned to find her on the far side of the dump, and she was crying angry tears.

"How can you stand to be here?" she wailed. And after she pointed it out, I found that she was right. I couldn't stand it either. We left, and since that morning in December we've never gone back.

We donned binoculars, got out of the car, and walked toward the trees. The grove was dome-shaped and hollow. Once there must have been a house within it, and the trees had served as a buffer against the winds that whipped across the open marsh.

But the house, even the foundation, was gone. Only the trees remained, and at the end of the road on that open marsh, they served as sanctuary to hosts of migrating things.

Even before stepping through the portal cut into living trees, even before the contents of the grove were unveiled to our eyes, we could see myriads of migrating birds. Redstarts fanned their tails in the leaves, and their wings flickered like flames. Black-and-white warblers moved along limbs like wind-up toys, and assorted flycatchers made acrobatic swoops through the foliage.

But it wasn't the birds I wanted Linda to see. It was something else, another migrant that had taken shelter in the grove. Covering the vegetation in blossomlike clusters were roosting monarch butterflies—hundreds of them. They made the branches bow beneath their weight. They carpeted the earth with cold, numbed bodies that came to life with the warmth of a hand.

Now that the sun had risen and warmed the interior of the grove, many of the insects had taken to the air. Avoiding the windy world beyond the trees, they swirled beneath the canopy.

Shards of sunlight falling through the leaves flickered and fled. Warblers and flycatchers darted and danced. And all around us, like bright orange leaves tumbling in a vortex, the monarchs swirled.

"It's like being inside a kaleidoscope," Linda breathed, taking my hand.

"Yes," I said. "That was my thought too."

Outside the grove there was another world and other people.

Outside the garden there were ugly things and discouraging things and painful things too.

But inside the grove there was beauty to rival the splendor of the Rocky Mountains and maybe Prince William Sound too. And for a little while, for lucky eyes that had been brought to see, there was wonder enough to fill even the most western soul.

THE BIRDIN' OF KINDNESS

I'm a reserved person—take pride in my ability to face disappointments stoically. But when I opened my third straight birthday card displaying an insipid cartoon canary and the announcement "A little bird told me it was your birthday," I put my face in my hands and wept.

It's not that I mind getting older. Heck, I've been doing that all my life. What vexes me is the unmindful cruelty of nonbirders. Ever since it became known that I'm a birder, nonbirding friends and relatives have been demonstrating their support by showering me with bird-related junk.

And I'm sick of it.

"Why another bird card?" I said to my open hands. "Why not a card depicting some incontinent old drooler welcoming me to the forties or some scantily clad vision promising earthly delights beyond the reach of my years?"

"*I'm normal!*" I wanted to scream. "*I pay taxes . . . cut the lawn . . . cheat on my diet, just like normal people!* Why don't I ever get anything but bird stuff?"

What is it about birdwatching that makes mothers think that the ugliest lamp in the history of porcelain will make a splendid gift so long as the lamp shade boasts an impossible assortment of tanagers, Old World buntings, and warblers standing in the snow? What is it about our avocation that turns tasteful, decor-sensitive people into the gift-buying equivalent of Roller Derby fans?

In anticipation of my upcoming birthday, I inventoried our living room and took stock of my unwanted stock, to make room for a new wave of kiln-fired kiwi toothpick holders, bluebird of happiness paperweights, music boxes that play "Yellow Bird," and coaster sets emblazoned with all the birds that John James Audubon managed to bend into a figure eight.

Standing upon my deerskin thunderbird rug, I cast my eye over an accumulation of wealth whose most prominent treasures included a throw crocheted by my sainted grandmother depicting a bird-draped Saint Francis of Assisi, a beer stein shaped into the likeness of a kori bustard, a turkey cleverly constructed out of porcelain vegetables, and a wood stove humidifier that looks like a muscovy and warbles like a canary.

Bear in mind that these are the keepers. The stuff we've relegated to the attic would make even the most tasteless Victorian pack rat long for the release of curbside pickup.

Of course, not all the bird-related stuff I get is useless or tasteless. But what's a person supposed to do with four copies of *Gone Birding?*

One Christmas (via my brother's secretary) I even received a gift copy of my book *The Feather Quest.* "Merry Christmas to my birdwatching brother," the inscription read. "I saw this book and thought of you."

I know that I'm not the only birder singled out for persecution. I have a naturalist writer friend named Diana whose friends also convey their affection with an avalanche of avian knickknacks. After the holidays we compare notes—a sort of birding bric-a-brac Big Day competition.

"So how many goldfinch/painted bunting/cardinal dish towels did you get this year?"

"Four."

"Beat you there. I got five. How about salt-and-pepper shakers with bluebirds feeding nestlings on them?"

"Two."

"Ooooh, tied score. What about lacquered pieces of driftwood boasting hand-painted kinglets?"

"If you let me count the goldcrest/firecrest combo along with the ruby-crowned and golden-crowned ensembles, three."

I used to think that the books that ended up on the bookstore bargain tables were publishing blunders—books whose sales simply could not realize an optimistic overprinting—but no longer. Now I believe that those half-priced coffee-table bird books are printed specifically to get people who know nothing about birds to buy them for friends who do.

And I've got an attic full of them.

"Oh, why," I pleaded to my hands, "can't I just once receive a normal present? A juicer. A breadmaker. Whatever happens to be in vogue this season. Why am I condemned to bear the brunt of so much misbegotten kindness?"

A single envelope remained on the table, one addressed in colored crayon, bearing the brand of a favorite niece. Bravely I opened the flap, withdrew a homemade birthday card, and stared at the lovingly drawn illustration. An illustration that replicated the outline of a child's hand. An illustration that resembled, not the expected bird, but—beyond all hope—a long-limbed, long-necked turtle.

"Oh blessed child," I whispered as tears flooded my eyes. "Favorite of my heart. You can count on a big fat check from Uncle Peter for the holidays."

Only then did I realize that "Happy Birthday" was written upside down. When righted, what had been a long-limbed turtle became just another turkey.

JUDGMENT DAY

The trail climbed where it should and dipped where it always has. That's one of the advantages of investing part of your youth in a 280-million-year-old ridge—long-term security in the futures market. Memory could not pinpoint the spot where I was supposed to leave the trail. But my feet knew the way. They veered and I followed. The place, when I came to it, was unmistakable.

In my mind I could see him standing there, that younger version of a much older man—the same man who was now surveying the spot where the avenue of a lifetime began. It was on this ridge, in the spring of 1976, that I stood for fifty-eight days—for 454 hours—counting the migrating hawks that passed. It was the project that gave me the skills and the standing that led to a career in the environmental field.

For 364 days a year, I have leave to look back and contemplate all that has transpired since that time—the privilege and perspective of age. But once each year, if I can, I go back to the ridge and let that person who was pass judgment on the person that is. I do it for perspective. I do it because a 280-million-year-old ridge offers a fixed point of reference to measure a life.

I wonder sometimes whether people whose lives are not anchored in the natural world have this advantage. I wonder, for instance, whether Bruce Springsteen ever goes back to the Asbury Park boardwalk. Whether the smell of cotton candy ignites memories. Whether the noise and crowds and flashing lights anchor perspective, offer haven, give counsel. I wonder whether in the noise and turmoil he can find himself honestly reflected and whether he likes what he sees.

I can see how this might be so. But boardwalks wear out and are replaced over time. Arcades trade hands, rides change theme music, people dress differently, talk differently. And boardwalks, unlike the natural world, are not neutral. They cater to the young. Would an aging rock star even want to go back to the boardwalk of his youth—particularly a rock star who now lives closer to the brighter lights of Vegas?

I looked at my old spot, at the boulders that had not moved in ten thousand years, at the view that remains unchanged—the perfect spot for a meeting of then and now.

I could see my younger self standing there. Wearing a sun-bleached 60/40 cloth jacket. Eyes hidden behind a pair of brand new Leitz 8×40 binoculars. Attention focused down-ridge as if nothing in the whole world mattered except finding that next bird of prey.

And do you know what? Nothing did.

"You're late," he said, not looking.

"You were always too early," I admonished, which was true. The kid was usually there before seven, even though hawks rarely went aloft before eight.

"You're a *year* late," he said. "You missed last year."

"Oh," I said, somewhat ruefully. "Couldn't get away."

The kid glanced my way, not even trying to hide his displeasure. Nothing, as far as he was concerned, was more important than hawk watching.

"New car," he noted, pointing to the parking area seven hundred feet below and a mile away.

"Same color as the Bug," I said, referring to the '72 Beetle the kid drove.

"Can you still pack all your worldly goods into it?" he demanded.

"No," I admitted, "I can't." The kid once asserted that he never wanted to own more things than he could stuff into a VW Bug and drive away with—a milestone he passed (and a promise he broke) in 1979.

"Getting kind of porky, aren't you," the kid challenged, with appalling candor and absolute accuracy. I was packing about ten more pounds than I was when we'd last met. Fact is, never again was I in the physical shape I was in when I first stood on this ridge.

"Can you still identify a hawk?" he challenged.

"Let's see," I said, picking up the gauntlet, filling my binoculars with sky.

The air over the Walnut Bluffs was wavy with heat—the heat that migrating hawks seek, to gain lift. A bird was turning circles just over the ridge—an accipiter. A mile away there were no field marks visible, and at this distance a bird's identity projects itself by hints and clues. The kid would someday write a book based on the secrets he was learning. But that milestone was still a decade away.

"Bird over the bluffs," I announced.

"Got it," he said. "Accipiter," he concluded.

"Cooper's hawk," I promised.

The bird left the bluffs and started for us. As distance diminished, subjectivity was stripped away and replaced by discernable features—a projecting head, a white-tipped tail, wing beats that were arthritically stiff—the things that make a Cooper's hawk a Cooper's hawk.

"Nice call," the kid admitted but grudgingly. Nobody likes to be beaten to a call at their own hawk watch.

"Thanks," I said. "Takes practice," I couldn't help adding. What I didn't tell him was that probability played a large part in the identification. Our vigil was being conducted at the peak of the Cooper's hawk migration. Sharp-shinned hawks, a near look-alike species, wouldn't be migrating in numbers until later.

The kid didn't know this—but then, when the kid was a kid, few people did.

"Well, at least you can still identify hawks," he admitted. "How's work?"

"Good," I pronounced, pleased that it was so. "But I'm pretty desk-bound. Not much time for birding."

"How much time?" the kid demanded.

"Just a few hours a week," I admitted.

The kid dropped his head in his hands and moaned—not that I blame him. Sometimes I do that myself. Then I thought of something that would please him.

"I turned down a job offer recently."

The kid brightened. "Doing what?" he wanted to know.

"Marketing director for an optics company."

"How come?" he asked.

"I like what I'm doing now."

"Another bird," he said, shutting down conversation. "Another . . . Cooper's hawk?" he asked more than said.

"Nice call," I judged.

There was silence for a time. Silence as we waited for birds to appear; silence as we waited for the hard questions to come.

"How's the writing?" The kid aspired to be a writer.

"Some of it's pretty good," I assessed. "But I think word processors are destroying any artistry in writing."

"What's a word processor?" he wanted to know.

"A machine that makes it easy to patch without fixing." I explained.

"How's the marriage?" he demanded.

"Infinitely better than the writing," I was pleased to say. "Worth your wait."

Morning became afternoon, and one by one the questions I carried to the ridge found their answers—on the neutral grounds of a timeless ridge. But the young inquisitor withheld judgment until one key question was addressed.

"What kind of music you listening to these days?"

"Some alternative rock," I said to uncomprehending eyes. "Some R.E.M. . . . a little Indigo Girls . . . Gin Blossoms, Enya . . ."

"Enya?" he demanded.

"Enya," I affirmed. "Kind of Celtic. Strains of Renaissance. You'd like her." Then I thought of something else he might like.

"Pink Floyd's got a new release."

"You still listen to Floyd?"

"Yeah," I admitted. "Sometimes."

There was no mistaking the approval in his eyes. "Awwwl right!" he said.

On my way down, I made a mental note to stop at the mall on the way home and pick up a couple of CDs. And a promise, if I could manage it, to try and lose some weight before next spring.

Part 2

STORIES

ABOUT

FRIENDS

THE SOLDIER

This is a tribute to the Unknown German Soldier—the man who changed my life. I do not know his name. I do not know what part of Germany he came from. I do not even know if he was a birder or a naturalist—although he may have been. Most Germans, at least most of those it has been my privilege to meet, have an abiding love of nature.

The fact is I never met the Unknown German Soldier. I only know the man who met him, briefly, soldier to soldier. That man was my father, Corporal Dunne, an American GI in his early twenties who was playing a small part in a big war.

"I took them from a German who didn't need them anymore," was all my father said of the instrument I held in my hands—a pair of six-power binoculars. The device lived then in the drawer where all the tokens of my father's life were housed—chains attached to watches that didn't work, old coins that didn't shine, medals that proved my father was the hero every four-year-old knows his father to be.

But the thing I coveted most, the thing that I courted the risk of a spanking just to hold, was the magic look-through thing: the 'noculars. I had discovered that this sleek black instrument had the power to change the world.

If you looked through one end, it made the world smaller. But if you looked through the other end, the world got BIGGER and everything looked CLOSER.

The photos on the dresser . . . my mother in the kitchen . . . The birds! Feeding in the snow. Closer . . . and *alive.* They seemed, these sparrows and juncos and cardinals, more beautiful and more alive than anything in the whole wide world (whose limits lay just about where my parents' property line was).

Those magic 'noculars, taken from a soldier who didn't need them anymore, were the portals through which knowledge and discovery flowed, bird by bird. They were the catalyst that turned a suburban kid into a birder. They led me to a career as a New Jersey Audubon Society director and to the person I am today.

Fifty years after the war that brought the 'noculars into my hands, the instrument sits on my mantel, nestled amid the tokens of another man's life, my life. They are scarred by use and time, but they still function. I could take them out right now and filter birds through their prismed tubes, just as I did as a child—when the world was filled with undiscovered wonder and its borders were defined by my parents' property line.

Sometimes in the evening, when the fire draws down and my mind turns in upon itself, the 'noculars will catch my gaze the way they once drew my hands. Regarding them, I see once again the birds they brought to life and consider the strange fortune that brought them there.

At these times I find myself wondering about the Unknown German Soldier. Who he was. Whether he, like my father, had children. And if so, whether they have children now who are turning their eyes upon the world, seeking wonder.

Because if he did, and if they did, and if there was a way, I fancy that I would take those binoculars back to Germany and place them in their hands. To keep the magic flowing. To honor the man who was its source (though I do not know his name).

R.

The figure was standing beside the road, aware of my approach but not interested. He was looking off across a section of marsh, and he was looking for something specific. You could see this from a distance. You could see it from the body language projected by a birder on point.

The distance had narrowed to fifty feet before he turned his attention my way. I recognized him then, and the grin that creased his face showed that he recognized me. It was a sincere grin, but it did little to alter the balance of the face, which was a study in defeat.

"Oh hello, Pete," he said nodding, holding his heroic smile. "I figured I might see you around."

"Hello, R." I said, addressing him by name, grateful that I remembered it. "How's it going?"

"Oh," he said shyly, almost apologetically, "OK I guess."

And for a moment I let hope get the better of me. For a moment I thought that maybe R. and the world had come to better terms, but I was wrong.

"I'll be doing more birding now, 'cause I got laid off my job. I guess that's good news."

Of course, it wasn't good news, but as disclosures from R. went, it wasn't as bad as some. We'd met in 1979. R was seventeen and liked nature. I was ten years older and taught bird ID courses.

There was something tragic about R. even then, something that said his life would be stalked by hardship. But it had taken fifteen years of compounded defeats to craft the image of passive sadness I saw now. Fifteen years of plant closings, terminated apprenticeships, job layoffs, and a bout with alcoholism and its lasting consequence: life without driving privileges in a mobile society.

"What do you have out there?" I asked, to get him off the subject of life's latest setback and to demonstrate my support by inviting his assistance. A person is never destitute so long as they have something to share. And if that something is coveted by someone else, you will always have standing in their eyes.

"I don't really know," he said, bringing his focus to bear on the marsh again. "Some shorebird. I came out here to sort things out. And these two birds jumped and squawked and flew. I wasn't familiar with the call. I'm waiting for them to come back."

"Snipe," I surmised but did not say. "How long you been here?" I asked.

"Couple hours," he said. "Something to do," he explained, gesturing toward the marsh.

The explanation wasn't necessary, and it wasn't complete either. Fact is, I understand how important something to do is when life gets knocked off-balance. What R. left out of his explanation is that things to do don't happen unless there are places to do them. For me, for R., and for many other people, the places we turn to when life takes a hard tack are the natural areas of our state.

Natural areas. Places with woodlands that close around you. Places with ponds that can swallow a cannonade of tossed pebbles and beaches that are open, unpeopled, and invite long walks.

I know what some people are thinking. "Diversion! That's all a body needs when times get tough. Diversion, not nature." Workaholics can bury themselves in work. Physical fitness buffs go run twenty miles. Gardeners plant a thousand bulbs or trim the rose bushes or organize the shed. Nothing mystical about it.

And if natural history buffs want to go out in the woods and peel the bark off of twigs in the name of therapy, well, what of it?

I don't think it's that simple, and I don't think a retreat into nature is that esoteric. I believe that *everyone* has an innate need to interface with natural areas and that everyone responds to them. I believe that nature heals better and faster than diversion and that people understand this *naturally.*

Consider Mr. M. He was a neighbor, an electrician and father to a flock of kids who were childhood chums of mine. His interest in nature, near as I could tell, was zero. And I never, ever, saw him enter the woods flanking our suburban development— except once.

It was the day after his son was killed in a traffic accident. I was off on one of my daily forays. We met on a pond side trail.

Of course, I was surprised to see him, and of course I couldn't find words to match his loss. Nobody can. But he understood my problem. He reached out an arm, touching me on the shoulder, thanking me without words. Then he walked on.

What was most remarkable about this meeting was not his kindness or his presence of mind. What was remarkable was his *state* of mind—if such things can be read in a face (and I believe they can). His face was the picture of serenity, of peace—the face of a person who had suffered greatly and won passage through grief.

I have seen this look depicted on the faces of statues in churches, and in such surroundings it is not out of place. In fact, it is beautiful. And once, on a woodland trail, I saw it on the face of the father of a childhood chum. It was not out of place there either.

There is something about the rhyme and pattern of nature that is eternal. There is something about weather and seasons and tides and lunar cycles that offers permanence and confidence.

A coworker, Pat Kane, offers summer programs for children, many of whom come from single-parent homes—many of whom are still caught in the turbulence left by a hard divorce. Pat uses nature as an antidote.

Says Pat: "Nature is something children can count on day after day. The leaves emerge in the spring. They drop to earth in the fall. They don't go on strike. They don't break promises. They just follow the natural cycle, and this is nature's way of saying that change is natural; change is OK."

Change is *natural.* It's only coming to grips with it that is hard.

I recall another person, a woman, who showed up at a hawk watch I was orchestrating many years ago. She was very quiet and very distant and this, in the right person, is very alluring.

It was several days before we spoke, several hours before I earned her confidence, and what I learned was that her father had just died. Rather than seek solace in people, she had opted to take her grief and her bearings beneath the river of birds migrating south. There she hoped to come to some accommodation with the change that had shaken her life.

Unlike my hawk-watching acquaintance, R. was as grateful for conversation as he was for the challenge presented by the birds he could not identify. My schedule was not pressing, so I indulged him. Listened to his account of the birds he had seen. Made encouraging noises in response to his plans to reap a harvest of new bird sightings this winter.

I did not disclose the identity of the mystery birds that bound him to the marsh. It would serve no purpose but to break the bond that had given momentary mooring to his life. Nor did I tell him that, unlike other shorebirds, snipe, once they have relocated, are not likely to return. What would be the point?

We parted eventually, wishing each other good luck. I left to complete the circuit of the trail I walk almost every day. And R.? R. stayed where he was. Just because there was nothing to see didn't mean that there was nothing to find—or that he hadn't already found it.

HAROLD

If you never met Harold Axtell—former whiz-kid at Cornell University's Laboratory of Ornithology, former trombone player on the Cunard Line, former curator of ornithology at the Buffalo Museum of Natural History (and my friend)—you missed a historic opportunity. Harold, until his death, resided in Fort Erie, Ontario. But this living link between the ornithologists of yesterday and the birdwatchers of today called New Jersey his home in October and November. When the winds turned cold and northerly, the path of birds turned south, and Harold's did likewise.

My introduction to this remarkable man occurred October 2, 1976, at Cape May Point. I was then a brash young hawk watcher with little skill and less standing. Harold was, according to rumor, a ghoulish perfectionist who could take every species of bird in North America down to its feather edges and who used questions the way the Spanish Inquisition used implements of torture.

I had been warned of Harold's imminent arrival. I had been told that the extraordinary numbers of Cooper's hawks I'd been reporting at Cape May Point had brought the Inquisitor's mind to bear on me.

This was 1976, remember, and that was an age that lived in the long shadow cast by the biocidal poison DDT—an age when Cooper's hawk numbers were reduced to a vestige. And Cooper's hawks were then, just as they are now, about as easy to distinguish from the very similar sharp-shinned hawk as Mercury automobiles are from Fords.

"Oh, *really*," the impish-looking man fitting Harold's description said after I explained that I'd seen more than thirty Cooper's hawks the day before.

"My!" he exclaimed, studying my face. "Well!" he said, into the hand he'd raised to help support his chin. "I've been trying to learn how to tell Cooper's hawks from sharp-shinned hawks all of my life," said the man who knew more about hawk identification than Einstein knew about physics. "Would you mind very much if I stood next to you and studied every bird that you *believe* is a Cooper's hawk?"

I said no, but not because it was all right. I minded very much having the Inquisitor stand at my shoulder, second-guessing all my identifications. I said no because saying yes would have branded me a heretic, a liar, and someone *who couldn't tell a sharp-shinned from a Cooper's hawk* (surely the basest denunciation in all of hawk watching).

It was only seven in the morning, and the next two hours were the longest of my twenty-five-year-old life. Two thousand accipiters went past the hawk watch during that span, and *none* of them, as far as I could tell, bore the field marks of a Cooper's hawk.

I didn't know then, as everyone knows today, that sharp-shinneds are early risers and that Cooper's hawks like to feed before they fly, so during migration they are not commonly recorded in numbers until after nine. All I knew was that I was failing to back up my boastful record with evidence and that the Inquisitor's skepticism was growing.

Finally, around nine, a bird appeared that seemed to have a head larger than a sharp-shinned hawk's; a tail that was round, not square-tipped; and pale underparts that gave the face the appearance of being covered by a hangman's hood.

"How about that one?" I said, putting my own head squarely in the Inquisitor's noose.

Harold focused his binoculars on the bird and studied it in silence. Seconds mounted and still the Inquisitor held his judgment in check.

"Yessss," he said finally, and the word put a smile on his face that stayed. "That one seems to me to be a Cooper's hawk also."

I tallied nearly a hundred Cooper's hawks that day. And Harold? Harold saw nearly a hundred also.

Harold, of course, was not a ghoul—in fact, anything but. He was, very simply, a gentle man, driven by an exquisitely inquisitive mind, who loved truth and nature and found no need to distinguish between the two. He was *not* a ghoul—but as a man in his seventies, his features had taken a somewhat gnomish tack.

Harold's face sagged like a discarded mattress and was as wrinkled as an unmade bed. His clothing was equally weathered but eminently utilitarian. His workaday uniform consisted of iron gray trousers, a gray-green work shirt, and a fedora so shopworn that even the wind didn't want it. In the cherished image of the eccentric birdwatcher, Harold *always* wore rubber galoshes. Always.

There was almost always the hint of a smile tugging at the corners of Harold's mouth—as if he and the Creator were privy to some private joke beyond the grasp of mere mortals. But when conversation turned to the subject of birds, the mouth turned serious and the eyes followed suit.

It is no small understatement to say that Harold was a talker. He could pursue a subject for hours and chase digressions down trails that branched and branched. But no matter how many digressive paths Harold might investigate, he never failed to backtrack with skill and follow the mother subject to a conclusion.

Once during a lull in the migration, I asked Dr. Axtell how he became interested in birds. The reply consumed all of one day and most of the next.

You must understand that when a person asked a question of Harold, he felt honor-bound and duty-bound to offer as complete a response as possible. Harold loved truth—the whole truth—and I think he never quite understood how or why most people are content with less.

I recall a day, and never without pain, when Harold met a birding group led by someone he knew. Someone made the mistake of posing a question to Harold, a depthful one, one that demanded an answer that went on for more time than errant birders, visiting a birding hotspot at peak season, are accustomed to give.

First one member of the group grew antsy and slipped away . . . then another . . . and another until all were gone. Harold, who was concentrating on the answer and his feet, never noticed until he looked up and found himself alone.

I was over a hundred feet away, but the look of dismay that creased his well-creased face was unmistakable and it drove right to the heart. He seemed about to cry. Then he seemed about to leave. But he did neither. Instead he bowed his head once more, and he continued speaking until the full truth was spoken.

Even though no one except God and Harold wanted to hear it.

It was at once one of the saddest and greatest things I have ever witnessed. And I would give much, *much,* to know the substance of a truth so profound that it could master such hurt.

In late November, when migration nears its end, the air holds the morning chill. The sun rises late, and the hawks rise later. You can see all that there is to see of a flight by arriving at ten.

The birds spiral high. They gather in sunlight-colored clusters that shine against the sky. If the winds hold true (and you pray that the winds hold true), the flight may last till noon. That is when conversation on the hawk watch platform fills the void left by the departed birds. That is when Harold is most missed.

I have never told anyone this, and I hesitate to tell it now, fearing maybe that it will not be believed. But in November, the air that holds the chill also holds a sound. Sometimes it is like the murmur of distant geese. Sometimes it sounds like an orchestra playing a lively dance tune behind doors that are closed and locked.

But sometimes it sounds like the scuff of rubber-shod feet, falling on a gravel parking lot, that draw no closer and only fade until the sound exists only in memory.

COLVILLE DIARY

Day 1—We didn't wait for the plane to disappear before starting to portage our gear down to the river. The denizens of this unnamed (and probably unmapped) tundra pond—oldsquaw, glaucous gulls, greater scaup, and red-throated loons—didn't waste time getting back to the business of nesting, either. In summer, days may be endless on Alaska's North Slope, but seasons are short.

"Looks like we beat the mosquitoes," I said to Bob Dittrick, friend, companion, and cofounder of Wilderness Birding Adventures.

"Looks like the weather god isn't going to hammer us today either," he added, grinning.

Yes, we were pretty lucky—privileged, actually. Here we were in one of the planet's last great wildernesses, poised for a nine-day trip down the Colville, one of the grandest rivers in the Arctic. We had no schedule, no obligations, and no greater ambition than to savor everything.

"Arctic warbler," Bob said, nodding toward a nearby willow thicket.

"Got it," I said, completing the litany, training my binoculars on the only life bird the trip was likely to produce. "Nice," I said when my appraisal was over. "Now I can enjoy myself."

Day 2—We rose late, eight or so in the morning, and left later. Gray-cheeked thrushes were *everywhere*. I mean, EH-VREE-WHERE (almost as common as Arctic warblers). I decided to test the conventional wisdom that once you see a life bird they become dirt-common. I decided to test it by keeping a running tab of the Arctic warblers encountered on the trip.

Breakfast was cold cereal and French-roast coffee. We shared it with bluethroats, yellow wagtails, and four species of sparrow, all the while enjoying a duet offered by winnowing snipe and yodeling oldsquaws. Hunting rough-legs were a visual blight.

It took no more than an hour to put our canoe together, a folding fabric affair of Norwegian make and design. Fully loaded it rode like a grebe.

Our put-in point was the Ipnavik, a merry little stream that writhes like an eel and nips at riverside bluffs. The bluffs are the key. They host the nesting raptors that make the Colville and its tributaries one of the greatest raptor factories in the world.

As a graduate student, ornithologist Tom Cade had navigated the Colville and mapped the bluffs. We served up lunch at one of his single-digit sites, within easy scoping distance of a pair of tundra peregrines. Dinner—spaghetti, garlic bread, and salad with vinaigrette dressing—was prepared at the site that served up a white gyrfalcon.

"Only the second white one I've seen here," said Bob.

"Pass the sauce, please," I replied.

"I figured we did thirty-one miles today," Bob estimated.

"Good job on the dressing," I agreed. "Any bread left?"

Day 3—You will want to know the dates of our trip. There are no dates. You may want to know what time we rose. There was no time. There was nothing but the day, which was at once as long and as short as an Arctic summer. If the questions had been raised earlier in this accounting, I might have had an answer. But by Day 3, I had put the outside world behind. This was the day I took my wallet out of my pocket and put it in the bottom of my duffel bag, and my watch went with it.

We got up when we got up. We left when the last of the coffee was gone. The rhythm of the day was set by the stroke of paddles, the hiss of sand in the river, and the electric *zinging* of riverside redpolls.

Intervals were marked by lunch (hummus, cheese, and rye crisps) and dinner (chile and red wine). We found three peregrine nests, ten nesting rough-legs . . . and added ten more Arctic warblers to the *fifty-one!* tallied the day before.

Yes, it's true. Empirical evidence supports the premise that once you see a life bird, they become dirt-common.

Day 4—Still no mosquitoes and still no retribution from the weather god. The lenticular clouds that appeared last evening were probably a ruse.

It's warm too—fifty to sixty degrees, and the heat building in our tent is the prod that drives us out in the morning. There's little reason to hurry. Birds are everywhere, and our campsites are chosen to be within easy sight of any peregrine nest worth viewing. Today's birds are on a bluff across from a gravel bar the size of Key West.

After a cheese omelet, hash browns, and coffee, we climbed a nearby cliff and took stock of the world from the eroded saddle of the ridge—between the severed ends of a petrified log. We ate a candy bar, picked through assorted fossils, savored a grizzly bear and her two cubs, and watched while the male peregrine harassed the recticies off the neighboring rough-legged hawk.

Twenty-three miles (and twenty-three Arctic warblers) later, we parked for the night on a sandbar that was a mosaic of wolf tracks and (you guessed it) across from a peregrine nest.

"What's for dinner," I inquired.

"Jambalaya," Bob said, enunciating with relish. "Cheesecake for dessert. The weather god," he added, "loves cheesecake."

Day 5—Woke to fog in the distance and the whine of a mosquito in camp.

Uh oh.

"That fog is associated with eight degrees centigrade," Bob confided. We don't want to see too much of that!" Of course, we had a more immediate problem—an impending insect problem—so we went off to check the status of the hatch. The tundra pools were a wiggling mass of mosquito larvae, but at least they were still larvae.

There were pancakes and golden eagles for breakfast—first time for both on the trip. The eagle, a subadult, was intent on catching one of the local flock of white-fronted geese. A territorial rough-legged hawk finally drove the eagle out of the area.

We put twenty-two hard miles on the canoe, into head winds most of the way. Then, rushing to put up the tent before a shower caught us, I snapped a pole.

"What about just sleeping out?" I asked.

"That," said the co-owner of Wilderness Birding Adventures as he calmly repaired the pole, "is like dropping your drawers to the weather god with your hands manacled."

Day 6—It rained overnight and we woke to the sound of . . . *a mosquito in the tent!!!*

"GET IT!" Bob commanded.

I made a one-handed grab and missed.

"It's real bad luck to let the first one get away," Bob said. "That's our last night with the door open."

I'm not going to tell you that Bob is a superstitious man. I'm just going to tell you that he is a very successful guide who leads birding groups all over the Arctic while offering a level of comfort that clients find easy to accept but hard to believe. Far be it from me to question the foundation of his success.

It became abundantly clear that we were falling out of favor with the weather god as well as the Keeper of the Hatch. A squadron of thunderheads stalked us all day, and we had to play cat and mouse with one particularly tenacious cloud (probably their captain). We finally gave our shadow the slip by hiding out in an old river channel. That's where Bob spotted the cave with the pyramid of whitewash projecting from the floor—a pyramid surrounded by a two-foot pile of reincarnated ptarmigan who had come back to earth in the form of gyrfalcon pellets.

That evening we set up camp on a gravel bar across from . . . Well, you guess.

Day 7—Zero miles by canoe. After a bear mush breakfast, we decided to hike up the Oolamnavigovik River, a Colville tributary. The status of the river and surrounding sixty-three *million* acres, currently under the jurisdiction of the Bureau of Land Management, is under dispute. Bob was due to testify on behalf of wilderness designation, and he wanted fresh observations.

The first part of the hike cut through willow thickets boasting bushes fifteen feet high *and* a trio of gray jays, a bird whose established range (according to published range maps) stops south of the North Slope. Not at all unexpected but just as interesting, we stumbled upon a redpoll nest with five brown-spotted blue eggs. Gorgeous!

Atop a bluff that looked like a slag heap worked over with a blowtorch, we dined on reindeer sausage, cheese, and pilot bread and watched grizzly bears and caribou moving across the tundra. The wind was cool, the sun was warm. We stretched out like lizards, watching the sun through molten eyelids until the clouds came up and the world got colder.

Day 8—The world got real cold. And wet! The weather god was closing in, but he'd made a strategic error. He'd waited until we were in our tent.

Our arrangement with the pilot was for him to come look for us, so, not having a rendezvous site, we weren't in any hurry to get wet. Instead, we enjoyed some downtime in the tent—reading, sleeping, writing (sleeping), watching the local raven kids cutting up and the peregrine couple arguing over mealtimes.

About midafternoon the female peregrine set up a ruckus, which turned out to be directed at a dark brown critter the size and shape of a coffee table.

"Wolverine!" Bob shouted.

We watched from the tent as the Arctic weasel tried to avoid the peregrine's efforts to cut it down to the dimensions of a footstool.

It was clear that the wolverine wanted the eggs—but maybe not at the asking price, the price of getting flayed. The dispute was finally settled by outside arbitration. A Canada goose nesting below the peregrine's ledge flushed, exposing her clutch of eggs (and offering the wolverine an alternative it could live with).

"How 'bout breakfast . . . or dinner?" Bob invited.

I moved for dinner. Spaghetti, mushroom sauce, and the last of the wine. A fine way to celebrate life mammals—and the longest night of the year. Even the rain stopped.

After dinner we loaded up and traveled four miles downriver— away from the peregrine nest and astride a stretch of river that would take the plane easily. Around midnight a sucker hole opened in the overcast, giving us a glimpse of the midnight sun on the longest day of the year. From the thicket, an Arctic warbler broke into song—number 185.

Not a bad day.

Day 9—We couldn't sleep in, not on pickup day. Bush pilots keep loose hours, but when they arrive is when you're supposed to be ready. It wasn't even noon when Bob said, "I hear a plane." Then I heard it too. A distant hum that sounded like dread.

The sky was clearing. Sunlight was playing across rain-spattered hills and reaching for the river.

"Looks like it's going to be a nice day," I observed.

"Does," Bob agreed, sadly.

During our nine days in the Arctic, we had heard several planes but none that had intruded upon us. This one was different. And though there are many ugly sounds in the world, one of the worst is the sound of the bush plane that is coming to pick you up. In fact, I can only think of one sound worse. That is sound of the weather god laughing.

THE LAST BIG DAY

The robins were starting their evening song as our van turned off the macadam and onto the rutted lane. It had been fourteen hours since we'd first navigated this nameless pine barrens tract. The robins had been singing then too.

Branches raked the side of the vehicle, and puddles leaped for the safety of the underbrush. Our van bucked, and occupants had to use both hands to keep their seats bonded to the seats.

At the end of the lane, sandwiched between a field and a pig farm, we stopped. Almost immediately a large, soot-colored bird lofted out of the pen and into view. A burst of adrenaline cut through our fatigue, opening channels to the deductive centers of our brains—but to little avail and no gain.

"Turkey vulture," several voices intoned flatly. We'd already seen turkey vulture during the day. And on the World Series of Birding, every species found counts just once.

Another vulture joined the first, another TV. Then another, and another. It looked as though things were moving toward a repeat of our earlier, failed effort.

Just as disappointment was beginning to seem certain, another bird fled the pen. Its body jerked, its wings pumped, and white-tipped flight feathers flashed.

"It's a black [vulture]," someone shouted (and it might have been me).

"Got it," said Pete Bacinski.

"Got it," said Linda, my wife.

"Got it," said Rick Radis.

Bruce Cavey, our World Series of Birding team sponsor from Zeiss Optical (and a neutral observer), remained neutral.

All eyes turned toward the last member of our World Series team, a man whose face is as familiar to birdwatchers as Washington's profile on a one dollar bill—the man who in 1934 crafted a book that turned a scientific study into a populist pursuit enjoyed by millions.

Did he get on the bird before it disappeared? Could we count it as a unanimous sighting on our World Series list?

"Yes," he said, nodding. "Black vulture for sure," said Roger Tory Peterson, the dean of North American birding. It was the 160th species we'd tallied during our long day of birding, and it would be the last bird.

May 15, 1993, was not the first opportunity I'd had to bird with Dr. Peterson, who at eighty-four was the oldest participant in that year's World Series of Birding, an annual contest sponsored by the New Jersey Audubon Society. The author of *Field Guide to the Birds* was also a member of my team on the very first World Series of Birding, held in 1984.

I was thirty-two then, the director of the Cape May Bird Observatory and the instigator of an idea for a competitive event that would raise money for the environment based upon the number of birds seen. He was seventy-four and a legend.

It would have been unthinkable to contemplate a birdwatching competition and not consult the wisdom of birding's grand master. So one day, early in the planning process, I telephoned Dr. Peterson at his home in Connecticut to state my case and learn his mind.

Would he favor the idea? Would he give it his blessing? I needn't have worried.

"Whose team can I be on?" asked the man who pretty nearly invented birding. "Can I be on yours? We should start at Troy Meadows at midnight, don't you think? Then move on to the hills above Boonton for migrants at dawn. . . ."

In case you are not a birder, this is the birding equivalent of being invited to play a round of golf with Lee Trevino, jam with Eric

Clapton, or shoot hoops with Magic Johnson. It's like calling the Vatican for directions and having the pope ask whether he can go to church with you on Sunday.

And on May 19, 1984, Roger Tory Peterson marshaled the efforts of the Guerrilla Birding Team (as we called ourselves), carried us to a total of 201 species, and swept us to victory in the first annual World Series of Birding.

I recall well our dawn site on that morning of the contest. We stood on the old elevated railroad bed near Waterloo, New Jersey, sifting the sounds of a dawn chorus through our ears, filtering out and identifying each newly wakened songster.

I recall how Roger Peterson stood: with his feet spaced, his ear turned, and his white-frocked head inclined toward the woodlands and fields beyond.

Every bird adding its song to the chorus was identified by Dr. Peterson almost as soon as the notes left its beak. He punctuated each bird's identity—eastern phoebe, golden-winged warbler, northern waterthrush—with an index finger jabbed at the sky.

It was a glorious dawn and a wonderful day, and it set the pace for the World Series that followed. And the event grew—grew in measure with its success. Where thirteen teams took to the field in 1984, now there are more than fifty. Where once less than fifty hard-core birders participated, now hundreds take to the field.

But during a decade of growth, that first World Series maintained one singular distinction. It marked the only time that Roger Tory Peterson was a participant. This shortfall was remedied on May 15, 1993, when Dr. Peterson returned.

Ten years is a long time in the measure of human lives. Infants become spelling bee champions. Spelling bee champions grow up and become graduate students or fighter pilots or perhaps parents with future spelling champions of their own.

Older men with a lifetime of achievements already behind them get older, and it was an older Roger Tory Peterson who came to Cape May for the 1993 World Series of Birding.

The years, he was frank to admit, had fallen between his ears and the world somewhat. Many warbler songs had become discordant, and blackpoll warblers, whose ethereal notes barely brush the human registry, had grown disquietingly quiet in his backyard in Connecticut.

His eyes, too, were a concern to him. Two cataract operations had greatly improved his vision, but they could not give back the visual acuity of the twenty-five-year-old artist who published the field guide to the birds.

In 1984 we ran a World Series route that covered much of the state, but in 1993 our ambitions were more tempered. We elected to cover Cape May County alone. It would give us more time to bird and take hours off the day at both ends.

Frustration was our companion from the start. There was a screech owl that would not call, great-horned owls that refused our invitation to engage in a duet, and that clutch of black vultures already mentioned that missed their dawn appointment.

Fog prevented us from catching the morning flight of seabirds off Cape May Point, and a night without migrating birds left branches bare. Our list suffered accordingly.

But there were successes too. Like the maddeningly intermittent Louisiana waterthrush that sang a lusty greeting on the morning when it counted. Like the pomarine jaeger that sprang full-blown from the surf and the red-shouldered hawk whose screams reached Roger's ears first—having eluded all of ours.

And at the Sunday awards brunch, when the team captains rose to offer an accounting of themselves and their team's fortune, it was Roger Peterson who brought the room to silence with his recollections of Big Day birding in days gone by and of the Cape May he knew sixty years ago. Then the lines formed—the lines of autograph seekers that follow Dr. Peterson everywhere. People whose lives had been touched by the man in front of them and who wanted to affirm his gift with their thanks.

Despite his tiredness, despite the admonishing eye of wife Ginny, he accommodated them all, affixing his signature to the books and the World Series bulletins passed his way—the bulletins listing the names of those teams and those individuals who shared in Roger Tory Peterson's last Big Day.

Part 3

STORIES

ABOUT

BIRDS . . .

IN PRAISE OF JAYS

When I think of August, the first thing I recall is silence. The resident birds who greeted each morning with song in June and July are indifferent now, their need to sing rings around their breeding territories gone with the season. The passage birds too are reticent. A "chip" is all you'll get.

So it's silence (not the heat, not the baked earth smell) that I think of first when I recall August woodlands. But the second thing I recall is the sound of a band—a roving, brassy-voiced band of blue jays that move through the summer-tired trees like a crested wave.

They surround you. Taunt you. Jeer at you. Accuse you of trespass, premeditated passage, upright locomotion, and indifference to blue jays. They lean into your face like drill sergeants chewing out a bumbling recruit, screaming blue murder. Then turning on their branches, looking toward the forest for support, the harangue stops as quickly as it started.

The troop murmurs among itself for a time. Members scratch a few feather lice. Pick at a leaf or two. Sidestep down a branch and regard you slyly. "Just a joke," they seem to be saying. "Nothing personal." Then the troop flies off, seeking devilment and diversion elsewhere.

As they leave, I find it hard not to smile and thank both heaven and earth for blue jays.

There are eleven jay species in North America: blue, Steller's, gray-breasted, Florida scrub, western scrub, island scrub, pinion, gray, green, brown, and Clark's nutcracker. All are bold. All are brash. Most are flamboyantly garbed, and—with the exception of the gray jay of northern forests—the males, females, and young of the species are virtually identical. Only one is found in my home state of New Jersey, or has ever been found in New Jersey! *Cyanocitta cristata*—the "noisy coxcomb," in the words of Washington Irving; "beauty covering a multitude of sins," in the estimate of Neltje Blanchan, a turn-of-the-century bird lover.

"He is mischievous as a small boy, destructive as a monkey, deft at hiding as a squirrel," Blanchan goes on to say about the bird in her famous treatise *Bird Neighbors*. "He is unsociable and unamiable, disliking the society of other birds. His harsh screams, shrieks, and most aggressive and unmusical calls seem often intended maliciously to drown the songs of the sweet-voiced singers."

Me? I see another side to this strikingly plumaged, year-round resident of forests, parks, and suburban haunts. I see a flamboyant fraud, a cherub in truant's clothing.

I have had opportunity to hold blue jays in the hand—several nestlings and a larger number of adults that I had netted and subsequently banded. Bold-as-brass reputation notwithstanding, hold a blue jay in a hand and they become docile as lambs. They don't struggle like chickadees. They don't shriek like a starling. They just lie there, eyes glazed, bills agape, breath shallow. The brass doesn't show again until the bird is released.

During the nesting season too, the birds are reticent, furtive. One summer a pair of blue jays nested in a spruce in our backyard. The loose-stick nest with the woven rootlet core was placed deep in the branches and two-thirds of the way up the fifteen-foot tree.

The male never flew directly to the tree while Linda and I watched. He would sit in a cross-yard mulberry and wait until certain we weren't turned his way; then, launching himself, he'd fly silently to the bottommost branches of the spruce. After a moment's pause, he'd move up the tree, branch by branch, until the nest was gained. Then, his morsel offered and accepted, he'd leave—always by the back door.

The docile nature of blue jays has its limits (as many a neighborhood cat has learned). If not for its crest and striking plumage, the bird would be famous for its bill. Large and formidable, it serves as both weapon and tool, as well suited for poking holes in too inquisitive noses as into white oak acorns.

But nothing seems to earn the ire of blue jays more than the sight of a roosting owl. On scores of occasions I have been led to the location of roosting owls by orienting toward the screamed alarm calls of jays. They surround the bird, leaning perilously close, screaming insults and stooping toward the unfortunate owl's head. But why?

Some animal behaviorists say the motive is altruism. By mobbing the owl, scientists explain, the jays are warning other jays (and other forest birds) that a danger lies close at hand. Watch out! Mobbing may also serve to drive a predator away, thus removing the threat.

Me? I think it's just showing off. The way I translate "Jay, jay, jay," is "Nah, nah, nah." When I see blue jays taunting owls, it reminds me of a troop of youngsters taunting the playground bully. "Look at me. Look at me," the birds seem to be sassing. "See how close I can get. Betcha I'm braver than you are."

I've watched blue jays edge toward perched Cooper's hawks, stalk to within several feet of their mortal enemy. When the hawk charges, the jays retreat, scolding and screaming. It's like a game of tag, albeit a high-stakes game (as the number of feather blue fairy rings scattered about the forest floor attests).

I'm also convinced that the memory of blue jays is acute. On a number of occasions, I have followed the sound of scolding jays to a predator roost site where I have seen owls and jays interacting before, only to discover that the jays are engaged in pantomime. The birds are screaming—sometimes poking their heads into an empty cavity, sometimes hovering around an owlish-looking perch. But there is no predator, at least not in the present.

Does the location act as a visual stimulus, triggering a mobbing reaction? Or said another way, is it possible that the jays are *acting out* an old campaign for their amusement? I realize that the difference between acting in play and reenacting is no modest cerebral leap. But if any bird is capable of weaving legend and pageantry into its life, it's the "noisy coxcomb."

Even if the bird is not a mime, it is certainly a mimic, and a good one at that. I have heard blue jays imitate the calls of red-shouldered hawks with such accuracy that whole Big Day birding teams have fallen for the ruse. The birds offer a fair rendering of the calls of Cooper's hawks and red-tailed hawks too.

Though a year-round resident in my northern state, blue jays are migratory. In late September and early October, groups of birds can be seen moving along ridge tops. In Cape May, in October and in May, there are mornings when hundreds and perhaps thousands of jays can be seen.

They fly in loose globular flocks that occupy a horizontal plane. They flap more or less constantly and look toward the open water of Delaware Bay with no small amount of trepidation—and with good reason. Jays after all are forest birds. If danger threatens and the birds are out over the open bay, they have no place to hide, which they try and do whenever danger threatens.

Suddenly one of the troop calls the alarm—a single, strangled "Jay." As one the whole airborne troop executes a crash dive, plummeting straight down into the trees, a hundred (or two or three hundred) feathered darts in accelerated free-fall.

If the problem is a hawk, the birds wait until it goes by, then launch themselves from the trees and continue on. If the escape was triggered by a false alarm (i.e., if one of the members of the troop pulled the communal rip cord without sufficient provocation), it seems that the heads poking out of the foliage have an accusatory demeanor. It's as if each is accusing the other of being the whistle-blower.

Blue jays have their bad points to balance the good. Yes, they sometimes prey on the nestlings of other birds. Yes, they are aggressive at feeders and hog all the sunflower seed.

But when the days turn cold and all the brightly colored birds of summer have abandoned us, it's the jays who add color to the landscape. And when the summer heat steals the song from the mouths of birds, woodlands still ring with the cries of blue jays.

SMALL-HEADED FLYCATCHER.

SEEN YESTERDAY.

HE DIDN'T LEAVE HIS NAME.

I'm not asking you to believe the story you are about to read, not willing to compromise the bond of trust that binds one birder to another. Frankly, I'm not sure I believe it myself.

It's a story whose roots are buried in the origins of birding and whose branches rake the future. A story of discovery and wonder and achievement. A story of pride and selfishness and loss.

It's a birding story, and it began—as you will come to learn— nearly two centuries ago. But my small part began on a typical, lackluster morning in June—the time of year just after the last of the mourning warblers straggle through and before the lesser yellowlegs fly.

It was Monday, a workday. I ambled up the Cape May Bird Observatory steps, the sound of laughing gulls in my ears. I walked in, made coffee, wandered over to my office, and started leafing through several days' accumulation of Post-It notes, crumpling them as I read.

There were half a dozen reminders from a snarling pack of editors, advising that assorted drop-dead deadlines had passed. There were three messages from my mother and two from my boss, Tom Gilmore—all bound by a thematic thread that might be summarized "It would certainly be nice to hear from you again someday. Call."

One message was from Berny's Auto Repair Shop. Berny is the guy who keeps *Hawks in Flight* coauthor Clay Sutton's aging Toyota and my vintage Saab in repair. This is the same guy who bought a yacht and named it *Hawks in Flight* in our honor. That message read: "Sorry, Pete. It's not just the linkage." Kathy, my administrative coordinator, had drawn one of those insipid smile faces next to this one.

At the bottom of the mound was one final message—a cryptic one that made no sense. It read: "Pete: Small-headed flycatcher. Seen yesterday. He didn't leave his name."

Small-headed flycatcher! Small-headed flycatcher? You know, there is nothing like working in the old natural history racket for fielding crank calls. You name 'em, we get 'em. You can mark your calendar by them.

In March the phone lines are jammed with calls about the old kamikaze cardinals throwing themselves against the window. In April it's woodpeckers banging on drainpipes (and what are we going to do about it). May and June—the dreaded BBCs (the baby bird calls) start pouring in. And come July and August, the phone lines are flooded with SOS appeals for laughing gulls with busted wings.

You know, if there was one laughing gull left on earth and I was living in a cave in Tibet, the thing would fly into a telephone line and bust a wing, and someone would bring it to me.

And *then* it's October and . . .

Ring . . . ring . . . ring . . . "Good morning. Cape May Bird Observatory."

"Oh, I'm so glad you are there. Oh, I hope you can help me. We have this bird. And it is all brown with black spots, and it has a red spot on the back of its head and a great big black V on its chest. It's been sitting on our lawn all morning and . . ."

One day I even tried answering the phone with the greeting "It's a flicker," but it didn't make any difference. Callers still insisted on describing the bird.

But as for small-headed flycatchers . . . Well, *that* was one for the record book.

The name meant nothing to me. The message demanded no further action. The Post-It note joined the others in the wastebasket, and *that* would have been *that* except . . .

Except one week later a manila envelope arrived in the mail containing a colored pencil drawing and a handwritten letter.

The words were learned, florid—the product of a scholarly mind. The handwriting was bent, corrupted—the product of an aged, palsied hand. The letter described a bird of approximately five inches in length and what the writer judged to be "eight inches in extent."

I figured that meant wingspan.

"The upper parts," as he described them, "were dull yellow-olive; the wings dusky brown, edged with lighter; the greater and lesser coverts tipped with white; the low parts dirty white, stained with dull yellow, particularly on the upper parts of the breast; the tail dusky brown and two exterior feathers marked like those of many with a spot of white on the inner vanes; head remarkably small; bill broad at the base, furnished with bristles, and notched near the tip; legs dark brown; feet yellowish; eye dark hazel."

The drawing, though painfully done, replicated the description. It resembled a Nashville warbler with wing bars or maybe an immature yellow warbler with an outsized eye. Both the letter and the drawing were signed "John Hancock." The address: Greenwich (pronounced "green witch"), New Jersey.

Now I know most of the birders in New Jersey and I didn't know John Hancock—never heard of the man. But I did know Greenwich, a beautiful old shipping town astride the Cohansey River, a watercourse known in history books as the site of a "tea party" in league *with,* but less celebrated *than* the famous tax revolt in Boston Harbor. I returned to the letter and the drawing.

He said that the flycatcher lived in an "alba" cedar swamp not far from his home. He said the bird had *not* been there before. Not since his youth. And possibly, *possibly* not since "AMERICAN ORNITHOLOGY."

AMERICAN ORNITHOLOGY, underlined, all caps. I liked that part. Was this fellow Hancock trying to tell me that he'd discovered a new North American species or what? "A juvenile yellow warbler," I concluded, studying the drawing, considering the several discordant points but dismissing them. Swamp woodlands aren't exactly prime habitat for yellow warblers. And a fledgling yellow warbler in mid-June in New Jersey is about two weeks too early. But that's what the drawing depicted, and what else could it be?

Pine warbler? Uh-uh. Wing bars weren't prominent enough. Nashville warbler? Not nesting in South Jersey, no way. Philadelphia vireo? Even *less* likely—though still a heck of a lot more plausible than the scenario that this fellow Hancock was dishing up.

I drafted a quick reply, offered my opinion, *then* realized that there was no return mailing address. So I put the letters, mine and his, and the drawing back in the manila envelope. And set it in the top compartment of my work tray until I could deal with it. It was still there when I left Cape May Bird Observatory two months later to take another post, with New Jersey Audubon. And that was nine years ago . . .

But even so. Even *now* I can still see it sitting there. The most important ornithological document I've ever set hands on. And I have ransacked CMBO's files. Torn closets apart. Gutted a landfill's worth of bundled documents, searching for that envelope. But it's gone, lost. And it would have been lost beyond recall too, except . . .

Except that, several years ago, Linda gave me a present. Four framed lithographs drawn by famed bird artist Alexander Wilson. "For the new dining room," she explained. "Happy birthday."

Two were dominated by raptors. Another depicted marsh birds. The last, sparrows. Tucked in the upper-right-hand corner of the plate featuring the great horned owl. Sandwiched between hawk owl and barn owl was . . .

A small yellow bird.

A bird that shed any names experience could bring to bear.

A bird that I could not identify—but a bird I *knew* I had seen depicted somewhere before.

At the bottom of the plate, written in Wilson's frail script, was a name. That name.

Now, I'm not going to say I believed it. Believed that some old gomer from Backwash, New Jersey, had rediscovered a bird that is substantiated by *no* modern records. Is not backed up by a specimen in any collection. And whose very existence is clouded by controversy, denial, and doubt. Both Wilson and Audubon *claimed* to have discovered the species. The bird was then—and it remains today—the very epitome of the rivalry (yes, even enmity) that existed between these twin pillars of American ornithology.

It was Wilson who beat Audubon to press, who offered his account of the bird he claimed to have collected along the banks of the Schuylkill River in 1810 (maybe 1811—the account is unclear).

"It was remarkably active," Wilson says in his description, "running, climbing, and darting about among the opening buds and blossoms with extraordinary agility. From what quarter of the United States or of North America it is a wanderer, I am unable to determine, having never met with an individual of the species."

Wilson subsequently determined that the bird nested in the swamps of South Jersey. He collected, he said, "several individuals there, in June." *Muscicapa minuta,* he named the bird, a privilege accorded the discoverer of a new species.

"Not so," said Audubon, and, when his *Birds of America* was published a quarter-century later, he said a good deal more. "When Alexander Wilson visited me at Louisville," said John James Audubon, "he found in my already large collection of drawings, a figure of the present species, which, being at that time unknown to him, he copied, and afterwards published in his great work, but without acknowledging the privilege that had thus been granted him. I have more than once regretted this, not by any means so much on my own account, as for the sake of one to whom we are so deeply indebted for his elucidation of our ornithology."

This is how a gentleman called another gentleman a liar and a thief in those days.

No, I'm not going to say I actually believed this improbable scenario. That as I lay awake that night, staring at the ceiling, I gave it more than the ghost of a chance—thought of it as anything more than a story line worth pursuing.

I'm not going to tell you that the next morning when I walked into Arnold's General Store in Greenwich, inquired about John Hancock, and learned that at the age of eighty-seven he had died, that I was much more than *disappointed*.

Or that when I stood on the porch of the old brick house. Where six generations of Hancocks have lived and died. And talked my way past the brittle smile of the widow Hancock. That I thought this visit would actually come to, *lead to* . . .

Something that no one reading these words should ever believe.

Not when I entered the book-lined library. Not when I saw the pressed and labeled sedges . . . and mounted butterflies . . . and Indian artifacts . . . and stuffed birds . . . and original Audubon lithographs . . .

Not when I saw. In a glass-fronted bookcase. The ancient corner-thumbed copies of *American Ornithology*.

Not when I inquired. "About a *bird*." That her husband discovered a few years ago. "In a swamp." And did he ever mention it?

And received a curt, Quakerish nod.

Not even when I asked whether she knew where the swamp was and followed the line drawn by her finger to a distant wall of trees. No, not even then did I *dare* to believe that such a thing could be so.

It was windy when I left the house. A strong, early autumn cold front was coming through and rain was not far off. I had to shout my good-bye to be heard. "You better hurry," the widow Hancock said to my back, "if you're going to that swamp . . ."

There was more to that sentence, but the wind took the words from her mouth and scattered them.

"I've been wet before," I said, turning, waving. And before I reached the edge of the woods, I was wet again.

No, I didn't give the venture much hope; can't say I was even seriously looking as I navigated the old logging road that bisected the swamp. Until a small yellow rain-dampened bird, which must have been sitting on a branch right in front of me, flushed, flew, and disappeared behind a wall of Atlantic white cedar.

I don't know how many of you have ever seen a white cedar

swamp. The trees stand as thick as fur and the needles absorb all sunlight. The air is heavy and close; the water, tannin-stained and still. The bottom is *treacherous,* log-strewn. Slick with slime and the underlying muck has no equal this side of a basketball hoop.

I plunged in after the bird and jockeyed for two hours to get a look at the creature. Twice I caught a glimpse of a slim yellow form maneuvering around trunks. Once, from a distance, I saw it perched—or saw *something* perched that might have been, *must* have been, the bird.

Even from a distance, it was clear that it wasn't a flycatcher—not an empid flycatcher, anyway. The stance was more horizontal than erect. The silhouette slim. The tail twitchless. The head? Small, warbleresque, maybe vireolike.

You know, Wilson lumped vireos, flycatchers, and even some of the warblers together—calling them *all* flycatchers.

The bird never vocalized. Never.

I cannot tell you what this bird was. I can only tell you what it was not, and THAT is what brought me back the next morning—with chest waders and a camera and an optimism that could not be realized. The bird wasn't there—had probably gone with the front, migrated south. I went back several more times in the next couple of weeks, but it made no difference. The yellow bird that shed all the bird names I knew (except one) was gone.

Disappointed? Oh yes! Devastated. But you know the disappointment didn't last. It gave way to a secret, maybe a selfish, sort of elation. Because, you know, I *had* seen this bird. Really seen it! Not definitively. Not backed up by any evidence. But *seen* what the old Quaker gentleman had seen—and no one else since Wilson and Audubon. SEEN! What *had* to be. What couldn't be anything *but* . . . a small-headed flycatcher.

Why, it was the greatest ornithological rediscovery since Gurney's pitta (whatever the hell that is). Might be the ornithological discovery of the century.

My discovery (now that the Quaker was dead). Mine!

And to prevent hordes of people from descending on the spot and threatening the safety of the bird, I . . . uh . . . decided to say nothing about its existence or its whereabouts to anyone.

Anyone! Including, maybe *particularly,* the widow Hancock. Lord only knows who she might blab to.

Anyone!

Remember what happened between Audubon and Wilson: disputed claims, muddied glory. Remember what happened to the last great auks on the planet? They were collected. Remember what has happened to a host of birds from ivory gulls coming to feeders in New York State to assorted exotic hummingbird species along the Gulf Coast? Captured, banded, released, and never seen again.

So I decided not to take a chance—not to breath a word of the bird's existence to a living soul—until I could secure photographic evidence of my discovery when the small-headed flycatcher returned in the spring.

Listen. A digression. I hate to break up a good story line, but I've got to tell you this. A funny thing happened to me the day after I discovered the bird and went back again. I met this odd-looking kid about eight or nine years old. He was wearing grimy shorts and a Grateful Dead T-shirt. His face was dirty. He needed a haircut. He was sitting on the hood of my car.

At first I thought it was the dirt on his face that made him look so odd, but as I got closer I realized that it was the face *itself* that was odd. The features were crooked, out of place. The lips thin, almost absent. Nose small, pushed to one side. Ears large and asymmetrical—one sat high and forward, the other was low, trailing behind the jaw.

And the eyes? The eyes were wide and staring, and they seemed to be focused upon something far, far away.

You will understand that New Jersey's bay shore is an isolated place and that blood has been mixed here over and over again. Heredity thickens and clots in places like the Delaware bay shore—genes unravel and sometimes children are born whose bodies or minds are misshapen and bent, sometimes both.

"You need a haircut," I said, trying to sound friendly, trying to bend his gaze my way.

"I live in that house," he said, pointing, turning his head (but not his gaze) toward the sound of my voice.

The house was old, mantled by towering sycamores with trunks as rotten as the structure.

"That's a nice house," I said, putting a patch over the obvious poverty with a lie. "What's your name?"

"My dad's lame up," he replied.

"Oh, that's too bad," I said. "Did he have an accident?"

"Our yella lab just had pups, an' one is mine for keeps."

"That's terrific," I said (beginning to wonder whether the kid had even one oar in the water). "What are you going to name it?"

"We got a television," he replied—another digression, not the name of the dog.

"Ah, what's your favorite program?" I probed, but without much optimism. The kid was definitely on the outside looking in.

"What's them," he said, turning his face and a finger my way again. The finger fell on my binoculars.

"Binoculars," I said, but the name evidently meant nothing to him. "They make the world look bigger."

The kid didn't say anything for a while—nothing at all—and I thought, "I've lost him completely." Until I realized that the eyes that would not focus were fastened upon the binoculars. Then they went flat again.

"No," he said.

"Oh yes," I insisted. "Here, I'll show you." I held the binoculars up to his eyes, set them for infinity, and directed them across the marsh toward a cargo ship moving up the shipping lane in the bay . . . on past a series of duck blinds . . . over toward a harrier hunting the marsh.

He didn't move his hand to hold them. In fact, except for his head, he didn't move at all. And when I took the binoculars back he turned, and without another word he walked away.

Two days later, when I returned to search again for my fly-catcher, he was there waiting, and a week later he came running out as soon as my car came into view. We never did exactly hit it off conversationally. But he followed me around, offering me the benefit of his disjunct thoughts, and he looked through my binoculars every chance he got.

The last time I went to the swamp, sometime during the first week in September, I surprised him with a present. A pair of Swarovski 8×30 binoculars on loan to me for review. I was supposed to return them. I told the public relations people I lost them.

I gave him a field guide too. One of Roger Peterson's. I would have given him a National Geo guide, but I didn't think he was advanced enough for subspecies differentiation yet.

The kid just stood there holding the binoculars in one hand and the book in the other, staring at whatever it was that he stared at beyond the horizon. Then he said good-bye.

I wondered how he knew.

It was a long winter, a long time to wait for the ornithological rediscovery of the century. I gave Linda a new camera and telephoto flash system for Christmas (then played with the stuff through Christmas dinner, focusing over and over again on a Wilson lithograph hanging on the wall).

I spent countless hours staring at the ceiling in January, out the window in February, wondering where small-headed flycatchers winter. Wondering how the species had survived, *could have* survived, for so long undiscovered in a small, well-birded state.

It was the cedars, of course—that was the key! Atlantic white cedar is, as it was two centuries ago, a coveted wood: straight-grained, rot-resistant, easy to work, wonderfully scented. Decoys were carved from it, ships' masts fashioned, chests built, closets lined. The shingles of Liberty Hall in Philadelphia, home of the Continental Congress, were cut in Dennisville, New Jersey, you know.

And after the greed for white cedar had stripped the trees from the land, why, they mined for it. Plumbed the depths of clear-cut swamps, raising still-perfect logs from the muck, though some had lain there for centuries.

It was a perfect explanation—a flycatcher that lived in white cedar stands! The habitat was destroyed. The bird disappeared. And now, after a century of regeneration (New Jersey is 45 percent forested, you know), there were once again maturing stands of white cedar in the state . . . *and a small-headed flycatcher!* Somewhere, somehow, the bird had survived.

Over the course of the winter I read everything I could about Alexander Wilson, bored cocktail party guests to tears with the nuances of his life. I even wrote to Alex Trebek on *Jeopardy*, suggesting that they include an Alexander Wilson category on the show.

I hung Wilson's portrait in my room, studied the fragile face and tannin-dark eyes, and practiced in the mirror until I had the look down pat. Then in January I went to Bacharach's and had my portrait taken—you know, for press purposes, for when I broke the news of the discovery in the spring.

I could see it. Me and Al Wilson (and maybe J. J. Audubon too), side by side, front-page news. I could read the headlines . . .

In the *New York Times*: ORNITHOLOGICAL ENIGMA SOLVED IN SWAMPS OF SOUTH JERSEY: 180-YEAR-OLD RIFT BETWEEN ORNITHOLOGICAL GIANTS MENDED BY AUDUBON NATURALIST.

In the *New York Daily News*: DUNNE DOES IT: DISCOVERS DISPUTED DICKYBIRD.

In the *National Enquirer*: EXTINCT SWAMP CREATURE USES TIME WARP TO REAPPEAR IN 20TH CENTURY. "It turned my boy into a birdwatching zombie," tearful mother relates.

Then, early in March, on a day with southwest winds pushing clouds across the sky and daffodils poking through the shroud of last year's leaves, I journeyed to South Philadelphia, to Gloria Dei (also known as Old Swedes' Church), the place where the father of American ornithology lies.

I found the grave easily enough. Read the inscription on the monument. Ran my fingers over the letters of the barely legible name etched in stone and told the stone, and whatever spirit it housed, the secret I could not reveal to a living soul.

Then I journeyed uptown to the College of Physicians, the institution that George Ord, Wilson's biographer, companion, and friend, left his papers to. I went to the ancient card files, flipped through the names, wrote a stack number on a form, and turned it over to a librarian. Ten minutes later the sleeves of my sport jacket were smudged to the elbows with the dust and book mold of George Ord's copies of *American Ornithology*.

I didn't hurry my task. I leafed through the books, savoring the paintings, savoring them at random, savoring the genius of my secret sharer.

And in volume 6, plate L, figure 5, I found the painting that matched the one on our dining room wall, and on page 62 the text I sought *and the date*—the 24th of April—the day Wilson discovered the bird that was our bond.

The 180th anniversary of its finding was going to be a memorable one. Of this I was absolutely certain.

I don't remember what lies I told to free myself on that day. But I would have told anybody anything—anything but the truth, of course. And I don't remember anything of the ride—except for the last part. After I passed the Hancock House. And turned off the old Salem-Canton road. And rounded the corner. And saw the gaping hole in the wall of trees where the cedar swamp had stood. I can tell you everything that happened from that point on, which is strange because my mind was cold numb, and I remember it not as if it were something that really happened to me. I remember it the way you might recall a story told by a friend—the way you might recall this story to another.

The swamp was a sea of close-cut stumps; the water, thick with bark and branches. They'd cut it during the winter, of course, while the water was frozen. Cut all of it, just the way that people on the bay shore have cut timber for centuries.

There was a man. Wearing bibbed overalls and a John Deere cap. He was dragging logs with a tractor. I waved when he drew near, signaling him to stop, which he did by disengaging the clutch, leaving the engine running.

"Have you seen a small-headed flycatcher?" I yelled, trying to make my voice carry over the sound of the tractor.

"Ma Fly?" he said, looking down. Looking puzzled. Finding nothing amiss. Shaking his head to indicate he didn't understand. I tried again.

"Have . . . Have you seen a small yellow bird?" I pleaded, holding up two fingers. Hoping to offer dimensions (but I couldn't decide whether to show him the bird's length or its extent).

I'll give the guy credit. He tried. Leaned forward. Cupped a hand behind an ear. But it wasn't any use. He shook his head, pointed to his ear, grinned a toothless grin, and shrugged. Then he pointed to his watch, waved, and eased the tractor into gear.

I guess I stood there for a while. Just stood there. Then at some point I must have started walking. Thinking how it felt to let the ornithological find of the century slip through my fingers. Thinking that it could have been prevented.

Trying not to think of the fool I had been.

I don't know how far I walked—a mile, maybe two. And I don't know when the kid showed up, but suddenly he was there. Walking beside me. Being trailed by a yellow labrador retriever. And he was chattering about something. Some stupid bird or another.

"How are things at home?" I intoned.

"A big ol' bird," he said, sticking to the subject. "Bigger'n a crow, big as a hawk but . . ."

"How's your father's leg?" I interrupted, not caring one way or the other.

"*Black!* Not brown," he said continued. "*Real* black! And *white!* In the wings. Most especially when it flies an' . . ."

"Uh-huh. What'd you name the dog?"

"Its head's pointy and red on top," he continued, "(Least-wise, *one* of 'em is). An' the eye's all bright and shiny and butter-color . . . *like the bill.*"

"Mmmmm." I said. "Bill's a nice name for a dog. Seen anything good on TV lately?"

"An' they make *all* kinds o' noise," he said. "Bamming on wood and yappin' and everything. All the time! Especially near the tree they live in. In a hole. Down where the survey people were mea-surin'. For the new nuc-le-er electric plant they wanna build."

"Huh," I said. "I must have missed that program. Maybe I can catch it as a summer rerun."

The kid didn't say anything for a while. Just kept pace, looking up at me with those incredible blue eyes of his. Funny, you know I don't think I ever noticed the color before.

"I got to go now," he said suddenly, turning, waving, marching away. *Really marching.* He put his hand up to his mouth and started make tooting sounds—like he was blowing notes through a tin horn or something.

Cute kid. Nice dog.

That's about the end of the story. I wandered back to my car eventually. Drove to work. Went home that evening. When Linda asked me what was new, I told her the truth. "Nothing." Two hundred years had passed. Nothing had changed at all.

It did occur to me to write to the widow Hancock, to ask about any journals her husband might have kept. A couple of months later, I got a letter from a sister in Massachusetts, who told me the widow Hancock had passed away over the winter, that the estate had been sold, and that anything not salable, meaning paper and stuff, had been thrown away.

And no, I haven't been back to Greenwich, not since. Things like small-headed flycatchers, Bachman's warblers, heath hens, and . . . well . . . birds like these don't turn up every day. They are a once in a lifetime opportunity at best. I had my chance and I blew it.

But if *you* happen to be birding in South Jersey sometime soon, sometime next spring, you might want to wander on over to Greenwich and check it out. See what's around.

And if you happen to run into a blue-eyed kid with a faraway look in his eyes being followed by a good-looking lab the color of old ivory, Bill . . .

Tell him the guy who showed him how to make the world look bigger said "Hi."

DEEP POCKETS

When I was young, my wealth was stored in pockets. There was very little wealth in those days—not that much has changed—but what little I had fell neatly into those cotton-lined coffers. At bedtime the treasures would be extracted and lined up on the dresser so I could savor the favors of the day.

Some of this booty was perennial, the everyday objects that both distinguished me as me and bound me to the fraternity of pocket-packing youngsters. Principle among them was a wallet whose contents (a few photos and the odd letter or two) were mostly there for bulk. Prized was a Swiss Army knife whose array of accoutrements elicited wonder and envy among friends. Usually there was a pen, a Bic, and often as not it leaked.

Wedged between these perennial treasures were the special offerings of the season, the things picked up in my forays afield. In summer perhaps a good, smooth skipping stone found its way into pockets, or the shed skin of a garter snake. Winter forays might produce an owl pellet, a patch of rabbit fur discarded by a fox, or a bounty of praying mantis egg cases.

Important tip. If you go out collecting praying mantis egg cases, don't let them accumulate in the bottom drawer of your dresser. If you do, you'll learn something of insect development but more about a mother's wrath.

But spring and fall were the seasons when pockets ran full, the seasons when pockets fairly split at the seams. In April there were

Indian arrow points that germinated in newly plowed fields and, come May, a fresh crop of fishing lures dangled from overhanging limbs, challenging the most adventuresome hands.

Then autumn! With woodland trails marked with blue jay feathers and flicker feathers and hickory nuts and black walnuts and . . .

Acorns! Acorns so beautiful that they begged a hand to enfold them. Acorns so beautiful that every new one found eclipsed the beauty of the last and absolutely begged to join the others already crammed into pockets.

I am older now, and it strikes me as comfortably curious that in my forays afield I still measure wealth in terms of pockets. With binoculars and a stolen hour, I venture into a promising woodlot or an old familiar haunt in search of roving pockets of birds. In winter, these include perennials like chickadees and titmice, creepers and downy woodpeckers—birds I know I'll always find there.

But in spring and fall, other species fill out these woodland pockets, giving form to the season and impetus to the search. Yellow-rumped warblers and black-and-whites, animate redstarts and buzzy-voiced bluewings, Blackburnian warblers of the impossibly beautiful raiment and black-throated blues—my perennial favorite. Each seems more beautiful than the last, and they find a place in the pockets of my mind to be carried home.

In the evening, when the lights are out and I sink between the sheets, snug as a penknife in a pocket, I dig into the coffers of my mind and review the treasures of the day. Giving each treasured glimpse its due, anticipating the birds that may be gathered into pockets tomorrow.

EMBERS OF SPRING

Winter, when the Christmas counts have passed, when snow has lost novelty and turned to slush, recalls to me a fireplace after the logs have been reduced to ash. Walking through some landscape, I contemplate the essence of an extinguished season but find myself looking ahead toward the blaze of light and life called spring. Red-winged blackbirds are the embodiment of this season-vaulting exercise.

With their coal-colored bodies and smoldering shoulders, they seem like the embers I find when I sift through the ashes of yesterday's fire, searching for a spark to ignite another blaze. Their presence in December and January assures me that winter never quite conquers. Their display, on that first warm morning in February, proves that winter is finite.

The way I mark my calendar, spring arrives the day the epaulets flare.

You know the day the moment you step from the car. There is something in the air—some spark, perhaps, as opposing seasons are struck together. There is something about the way the birds comport themselves, something that sets them apart—or maybe it is just that the birds themselves are set apart, spread like ink spots across a muslin-colored landscape where before they'd gathered in flocks.

On wind-whipped shrubs or winter-beaten reeds the birds hitch themselves aloft. Bouncing in the breeze, holding their ground when approached, the birds return the question in your eyes with a beady stare.

For minutes on end, nothing happens. The birds stand like actors who have forgotten their lines, each waiting for the next to offer the cue. Finally one bird begins the ritual that breaks winter's spell.

Boldly it arches its back. Theatrically it drops its head. Imploringly it droops its wings. Then, chanting the magic incantation that turns winter into spring, it flares its epaulets, sending a red-and-yellow spark streaking across the landscape.

"Tur-a-ling."

A rival catches the spark and, mimicking its neighbor's movements, makes its own epaulets blaze. Another bird bursts into color and song. Another . . . another . . . until the whole marsh blazes with wind-fanned embers.

Other places boast other first signs of spring. Crows that stream north over snow-covered landscapes. Vees of waterfowl that drive a wedge into winter. Spiraling woodcock that dance themselves dizzy. Small frogs that force spring's door open with a resonant *"cre e e ek."*

But for me, for as long as I can remember, the herald of spring has been the coal-colored bird with the ember-colored epaulets. The blackbird that springs from an ash-colored world, igniting the coming season with an ember from the last.

Part 4

. . . AND

BIRDING

GETTING A LEG UP
ON BIRD-SIGHTING SHEETS

Without a sideways glance my dog, Moose, gained the fire hydrant and began his standard olfactory analysis. Starting low, working up along the hydrant's length, he reviewed the passing and the fortune of his fellow canines.

Sometimes his focus was arrested by a particularly poignant entry. His nose would pause and ponder. Sometimes his nose would interpret something that rated a derisive sniff, and he'd move on quickly. Finally, his analysis completed, Moose saluted the post with a raised rear paw, adding his name to the list.

That's when it hit me. I've seen this behavior before—and so have you. It's a near universal practice among birders. It's called checking the bird-sighting sheet.

It happens every day in open-air pavilions and visitor centers all across the country: set-jawed birders stalk toward the clipboard marked "Recent Bird Sightings" and study the entries. Starting with the most recent sightings, working back, they run their fingers along the list, gleaning the fortune of birders who'd passed this way before them.

Chancing upon a noteworthy sighting claimed by a birder whose pedigree is uncertain, they sniff. Discovering that some other top dog has beaten them to print on a good bird, they bristle.

And when the review is completed, the birders each get to make their mark. They raise a pen and sprinkle the page with hot new entries—to post notice of their passage, to offer testimony of their skill.

It's "D. Boone kilt a bar on this tree" with a birding spin. It's ritual posturing played out in the honest name of shared interest and free speech.

Most of the time these posturings are simple and straightforward.

"9/2/92. 5 buff-breasted sandpipers; 2 imm. Baird's Block C-5. B. Goodbirder."

"3/15/93. Ad. m. Eurasian wigeon feeding in mixed flock east side of Ocean. Dr. I. C. Furst."

Sometimes entries are elaborate—actual dialogues between birders debating the merits and antimerits of an identification. (I recall a stint at New York's Jamaica Bay National Wildlife Refuge that touched off a war of words that consumed pages.)

Sometimes sighting sheets set the stage for real-life drama. Several years ago, a verbal duel was played out on the pages of the bird-sighting sheet at a birding hot spot in South Texas. At issue was one of the most fundamental tenets of birding: shared information.

On one side of the issue stood several local birders who were logging directions to a roosting long-eared owl (a local rarity). They were exercising the right of free speech. On the other side was the individual who had, in fact, discovered the bird and who was leading people to the site for pay. He was exercising the right of free enterprise (and carefully excising written directions to the bird with a pen).

Free speech versus free enterprise, but the dispute was settled by an act of free will: the bird left (leaving the issue very much unresolved).

Not all the information imparted in bird-sighting sheets is informative or even valid. In fact, some of the things that find their way into print don't even relate to birds.

For example, the knee-jerk notations of people who can't distinguish bird-sighting sheets from visitor logs.

"John and Mary Pseudonym. Just visiting. Lovely park."

For example, the trite musings of feeble-minded individuals who use bird-sighting sheets to demonstrate how clever they are.

"Woody Woodpecker. Identified by call. Ha-ha-ha HA-ha."

Oh, I'll admit that some of the feathered fictions that find their way into sighting logs brush the limits of the clever registry. Despite its latitude, Cape May Point State Park, New Jersey, enjoys a rash of penguin sightings every summer. Visiting birders are startled by this—until they realize that the park's beach is adjacent to Saint Mary's by the Sea, a summer vacation retreat for Roman Catholic nuns.

Birding's ethic of honesty prevents *real* birders from resorting to creative chicanery of this nature—except, perhaps, during competitive Big Days when a "ghost" pectoral sandpiper, strategically plotted, can cause rival teams to waste lots and lots of time.

The ethic also does not extend to several wry-minded surrogates of my acquaintance who travel the country, attaching my moniker to sightings like "Canada goose" (a bird I actually like) and "Sea gull" (regrettably, a bird I've never seen).

Fact is, I only wish I could travel as widely as my name. Fact is, my signature is illegible. Hint to readers: if you can read the signature in the bird-sighting book, it's not me.

My favorite all-time notation in a bird-sighting log was anonymous. It didn't even relate to any particular bird. It celebrated an event.

It was a Memorial Day weekend, the closing days of spring. Migration had been poor, some said nonexistent, and mornings came and went without the fallout everyone dreamed of.

Then, on Saturday morning, birders up and down the eastern seaboard woke up to an avalanche of birds, a tidal wave of color and song. No mere list of sightings could do justice to that day. But one birder managed to summarize the spectacle that could not be itemized.

In letters that spanned two pages of the log, the birder wrote: THIS IS IT!

And that, so simply and eloquently put, was that.

CONFESSIONS OF
A LISTING HERETIC

Birding (like civilization) is founded upon adherence to common standards and practices. It's what distinguishes us from the savages: from golfers, from people who cheat at solitaire. It's what makes life lists and Big Day scores and Christmas bird counts possible, comparable year to year, team to team, person to person.

What would we have if some people went around spuriously counting red-legged black ducks as full species and other people just up and decided that black ducks and mallards were conspecific?

Anarchy. That's what.

Would you want to bring up a young birder in a world where some people counted green kingfishers seen on the Mexican side of the Rio Grande or even *lied* about the birds they counted on their life list?

You would not!

On the other hand, there's a lot of gray out there between the black and white. Some of the rules governing what and how birds are counted are hard and fast. Others are open to interpretation. And sometimes even the most conscientious birders have been known to hedge just a wee little bit in the name of a good bird or a good cause. In fact, some of my favorite birders have advocated positions with regard to the legitimacy of certain birds that are downright heretical.

Take, for example, Dr. Ernest Choate, who was for many years Cape May's birder laureate and the keeper of the Cape May bird list. For years, Ernie carried a Manx shearwater on the Cape May bird list, even though the bird was seen off the Lewes, Delaware, breakwater—twelve miles from Cape May. His rationale: "We can count anything on the Cape May list that can be seen from shore. On a clear day, we can see Lewes, Delaware. Therefore we can count the bird."

This same brand of logic has led my good friend Clay Sutton to practice a most convincing reinterpretation of the rules governing Christmas bird count circles. The northern limit of the Cape May count passes through Goshen. From Goshen an observer can see Jake's Landing three miles away, and if you are gifted with the eyes and skills of Clay Sutton, you can even see and identify hunting raptors at that distance. But for the sake of accuracy, Clay makes it a point to go over and "ground-truth" his observations.

Maybe it's the spirit of the season, but Christmas bird counts tend to bring out the loose interpretationist in us all. Nobody will ever know how many count circles are dotted with "pimples"— little bulges in those pure-hearted lines that sneak into key locations. Why, the venerable Barnegat CBC has half of Long Beach Island dangling off its southern rim—a veritable geographic hemorrhoid! And, in the best tradition of Christmas counts, some of the birds that get reported at the roundups would prompt Diogenes to blow his brains out.

I'm a practicing and self-avowed listing heretic myself, and this is what gives me standing to throw stones. Once, on the Walnut Valley Christmas Count, I went out for a bit of predawn owling. A heavy snow had fallen overnight, stopping just after two in the morning. Traveling down the road (of course, *in* the count circle!), my headlights picked up something lying on the road. Closer examination disclosed a dead screech owl. The bird was lying fully atop the snow. *Therefore* it had been killed after two o'clock. *And therefore* it had been alive and in the count circle on the count day.

Screech owl. Check.

And then there was the black vulture claimed by the Guerrilla Birding Team in the 1988 World Series of Birding. The bird was nesting in a cave well out of our route. A nocturnal visit was the only alternative, but there didn't seem to be any way to approach the cave without frightening and maybe flushing any adult within—something we patently refused to do. Midnight found me fifty feet from the cave entrance, playing a flashlight in the trees above the cave, hoping vainly to find the bird at roost. Just as I was preparing to leave, a loud "hisssss" emanated from the cave entrance. I left. With a smile.

Black vulture by call. Check.

This same spirit of concern is what led to an impromptu rule change in this year's World Series of Birding. A very accessible goshawk nest had become known to many of the event's participants, and concern for the bird's welfare mounted. To save the bird from harassment, a ruling was made. Any team that knew the location of the nest needed only drive to the grove, park, wait three minutes, then drive away. The bird would count, sight unseen.

But the finest example of creative counting I have ever heard of is credited to the venerable Floyd P. Wolfarth, who once while hawk watching saw a distant flock of brant suddenly break into two flocks, one of which disintegrated into chaos. His conclusion: only two birds could have precipitated such a reaction—a golden eagle or a gyrfalcon. An eagle would have been visible at that distance; a gyr, no. Therefore . . .

And at the end of the fall, when the Raccoon Ridge totals were posted. There it was too. In black and white.

FORMULA FOR

A WHITE-WINGED TERN

Seeing a white-winged tern, Old World marsh tern, and New World waif is not an easy matter, certainly not as easy as just heading for Delaware's coastal marshes in late July, scanning the flocks for *Chlidonias* terns, and picking out the one with the pale white rump. Oh no! Finding the white-winged tern takes luck or skill or perseverance—or, usually, all three!

But for white-winged tern aspirants who are neither lucky, skilled, nor patient, there is another way to get the bird. It relies on a sure-fire formula: a set of conditions that once met virtually guarantee success. In fact, so foolproof is this formula that practitioners might just as well (and just as legitimately) simply check off the bird and stay home.

To get the white-winged tern, pick a day when the temperature and the humidity make the air feel like chowder and the only shade around lies beneath a cloud of mosquitoes. You must be sure to wear shorts, so as not to encumber the catalytic chomp of greenhead flies, and to leave your baseball cap in the car (next to your water bottle, insect repellent, and lunch), so the biting deerflies can inject madness into your method.

The choice of vantage point is critical. You must stand on the far side of the largest impoundment pool—as far from the flocks of feeding terns as possible and still be able to count the bird in Delaware. Make sure that the sun is directly in your eyes. If you

can see color or distinguish shape through the glare, move to a
worse location.

It helps to have poor optics—binoculars so out of alignment
that they would induce eyestrain in a potato, a spotting scope so
internally fouled that the world looks like it's been lacquered with
mustard. It also helps to have a field guide that assures you that the
bird is unmistakable within *range* and *habitat*. (Since you will be
relying on "giz" to confirm your identification, you will certainly
be within range; and, since you followed the directions given on
the hotline, you will unquestionably be in the right habitat.)

It is also important to surround yourself with white-winged tern
aspirants who are as desperate for the bird as you are.

People who need it for their seven hundredth North American
life bird or who are trying to break the Delaware Big Year record.

People who own $3,400 spotting scopes and talk about how
they've seen *leucopterus* on three continents (yet are never seen to
scan).

People who flew in from California, have searched for three futile days for "the bird," and must fly out that night.

People who are "absolutely certain" that they saw "the bird"
earlier in the day but who came back hoping for a "better look."
Saw it . . .

"Here?"

"Right here?"

"Close?"

"As close as those birds are now. Close enough to count. But,
you know, I'm the kind of birder who really likes to study their life
birds, not just count them the way some people do—know what I
mean? That's why I came back, hoping . . ."

It helps to have a number of birders present who still need seaside sparrow for a life bird (to help inflate the confidence levels of
serious white-winged tern aspirants). It is essential that Kenn
Kaufman *not* be present, so that serious WWT aspirants will not be
intimidated by an expert presence.

If all the elements are as I have described them, then conditions
are conducive for finding a white-winged tern, *but* there is still one

element missing. The formula for finding a white-winged tern demands that you time your visit to coincide with that period when juvenile Forster's terns are capable of sustained flight—Forster's terns that show dark backs, white rumps, dark caps, and a shallow forked tail just like a basic plumage . . .

"WHITEWINGEDTERN! In the flock! Going right. Going left. Going right."

"Is it still going left?"

"Right!"

"*Got it!*"

"Got it!"

"Got *it!*"

"Got it!"

That's *definitely* the bird I had this morning."

So, if you follow this formula as stated, if you want to see a white-winged tern badly enough, success is guaranteed. It's either this or wait until a real white-winged tern passes close enough to note definitive field marks.

But like I said, that takes luck or skill. And who has time for that?

THE PRICE OF RESPECTABILITY

He was wearing a leprous white panama, lizard skin shoes, and a platinum-colored suit that glistened like a shark in a sauna. He was stepping out of a limo the color of a cherub's bottom and the size of a luxury liner.

"It's the fifty-pound sterling silver swan on the hood that makes it," I thought. But that was before I noticed the light-rimmed vanity plate that read (I swear I'm not making this up) "John."

While the gas station attendant rushed to fill it up, one of the planet's seamiest denizens began eyeballing my car, phonetically decoding the legend emblazoned across the hood that read "New Jersey Audubon Society." Fixing what I read to be a patronizing smile upon me, the man identified as John strutted to my open window, pointed to the New Jersey Audubon logo, and said more than asked: "You one of those *bird*watchers?"

"At last," I thought nostalgically. "A member of society who wants to demean me." It's been a long time since anyone has been disparaging about my avocation, and frankly I miss my old social misfit standing.

Half a lifetime ago, birdwatching was an interest you hid in the closet. If you were a kid, it wasn't cool; it was certain to get you picked last when they divvied up sides for sandlot baseball. If you were an adult, it made you tantamount to a commie sympathizer, might even have landed you in jail (particularly if you espoused a liking for prothonotary warblers).

I can remember my parents discussing my unnatural attraction to birds and wondering how to replace the binoculars in my hands with something more socially acceptable, like a baseball bat. I can remember telling a guidance counselor that I liked watching birds— and being called back for extra sessions.

Even after I grew up, went to college, started working for New Jersey Audubon, I *still* couldn't earn the social acceptance accorded your average mass murderer. When family and friends would ask my brothers what Pete was doing, they'd mumble something inaudible and change the subject. One poignant evening I described all the neat bird-related stuff I was engaged in to my sainted grandmother, only to be treated to her admonition: "You should have stayed in the carpet business—you'd be making good money now."

There was some stigma associated with being a birdwatcher, some shame (or pride) that divided the world up between us (birders) and them (society's rank and file). Birding made you an outcast, a renegade. Over time not only did I come to accept a measure of social severance, I grew to like it.

"Heck," I reasoned, "if everybody liked watching birds there'd be gridlock on the refuge auto routes and standing room only on the hawk watch."

That's all changed now. Suddenly everybody's into birding and everybody wants to know about it. When the whiskered tern set down in Cape May for a North American first, network newscasters were calling and begging for interviews. Now that it has become established that birders are an economic force, optics manufacturers are pleading for marketing tips, and every whistle-stop chamber of commerce is planning a birding festival.

Whenever I drive somewhere in the company car, people wave, flash membership cards in assorted environmental organizations, stop me in parking lots, and ask how to attract hummingbirds. Worried parents ask me how to get the video joysticks out of their kids' hands and replace them with binoculars.

Suddenly I'm not an outcast anymore. I'm a personality. An oracle. An avenue to spiritual enlightenment and economic development. Suddenly everyone wants to tell me about the house finch nesting over their hot tub, or the product they've developed that keeps squirrels off of feeders.

Suddenly, after a lifetime of being a social outcast, I'm normal. And I can't stand it. I feel like Dostoyevsky without his guilt, Ahab without out his whalebone leg, King Richard without his hump. That is why I greeted John's approach so gleefully. Here, I felt certain, was a man who could give me back my hump.

"Why, yes," I assured the lizard-shod gentleman. "I'm a birder."

"Oh, man, that's wonderful," he said, destroying all hope for a testy exchange. "I got a question for you. See, I love birds. And every morning I go to this parking lot to feed the sea gulls. Whenever my car pulls into the lot, the birds just crowd all around me. Now, what I want to know is, do you think they really recognize me or what?"

"Sir," I said, taking in both the figure and the car, "I'm confident they recognize you."

"Oh, that's just wonderful," he said. "By any chance does your organization accept charitable donations?"

"I should have stayed in the carpet business," I thought.

ETERNAL ERRORS

"Hello," the somewhat hopeful voice intoned. "I'm with the [she gave the newspaper's name], and I'm calling about . . ."

"The photo on the cover of your bird festival insert that's labeled a double-crested cormorant but is in reality a male anhinga?"

"Then it's true?" she asked.

"We've been laughing about it all morning," I said cheerfully.

"Oh NOOOOOoooo," the voice more or less wailed, and I could certainly appreciate the person's discomfiture. After all, a bird publicly misidentified is a momentary embarrassment. But boo-boos that get set in print—well, published boo-boos are forever.

Sometimes the root of these offset (mis)identifications is simple ignorance—like the anhinga photo signed off by an editor on the staff, or like the illustration that accompanied the ad for the Cordova Shorebird Festival in 1993.

Intrigued by the festival's choice of an apparent thick-knee, as opposed to a shorebird species more representative of coastal Alaska, I phoned the Cordova Chamber of Commerce to gain insight into the selection process.

"Oh, we have them here," a very friendly voice assured.

"I don't think so," I said.

Her assurance undermined, the chamber representative said she would talk to the ad's designer and get back to me, which she did.

"Yes," she announced. "We have them here."

"Have what?" I asked.

"Curlews," she said.

"Yes," I agreed, finally understanding. "Bristle-thighed curlews, 'Hudsonian' curlews, but not *stone* curlews. That's an Old World species."

"Oh," she said.

Sometimes the boo-boos are rooted not in ignorance but in a moment's carelessness. One of my favorite faux pas involved an article in an eastern Pennsylvania newspaper extolling the merits of the year's osprey migration at famed Hawk Mountain Sanctuary.

"One of the best migrations in memory," the columnist said. *"Evidence that the birds are making a comeback."*

All this was verifiably so. The discord had nothing to do with the copy but with the photo accompanying the article—a photo which I carefully (and gleefully) clipped and sent to my friend and then Hawk Mountain curator, Jim Brett, along with the observation that the year's osprey migration was probably among the latest on record as well as the finest—provided the head shot of the adult northern goshawk accompanying the article was representative of the "osprey" they'd been counting.

Funny, but until that photo I'd never really noticed how similar the facial patterns of adult goshawks and ospreys really are.

I've been party to a few printed indiscretions myself, of course. Among the finest was an article penned about the Salton Sea, in which I habitually referred to yellow-*legged* gulls instead of the indigenous yellow-footed gulls.

But my all-time prize-winning misprint was the mess-by-committee blunder committed against the first edition of *Hawks in Flight*. At the page proof stage, coauthors Clay Sutton, David Sibley, and I noted that the illustration covering large falcons—peregrine and prairie falcons—had been mislabeled, a problem we attempted to correct with a call to the publisher. The gremlins won anyway. When the book was published, not only were the prairie and peregrine falcons still mislabeled, so was the gyrfalcon.

Perhaps the most hilarious insult to accuracy I have ever witnessed related not to an article but to a video. A birdseed company, hoping to secure an endorsement from the American Birding Association, sent a promo tape that was aired at a meeting of the association's board of directors. At one pregnant moment, a point-blank male house finch was shown that, to everyone's astonishment, threw back its head and belted out a beautiful morning warbler song.

Needless to say, the members of the board almost collectively ruptured their diaphragms. Needless to say, the company did not secure an endorsement.

Back to the anhinga.

"It's no big deal," I assured the distraught young caller. "These things happen all the time."

"Oh, but it *is* a big deal!" she said. "The contest rules state that only photos taken in Cape May County [New Jersey] are eligible. And anhingas aren't found in Cape May County, are they?"

"Not commonly," I agreed.

"But sometimes," she said, grasping the short straw.

"Yes, sometimes," I confirmed. "There are several records for the county."

"Then the photographer *could* have taken the picture here?"

I didn't say anything for a moment. I thought about saying yes. Then I thought about saying nothing. Then I told her the truth.

"Not likely," I said. "The bird is sitting in a mangrove tree, and mangroves aren't native to Cape May either."

"OOOOoooo," she said.

PASSING SIGHTS AND SOUNDS

[*Scene: A small parking lot serving a popular coastal birding area best known for autumn migrants. It is midmorning. The cars are thinning. Parking spaces that would have been filled instantly an hour earlier now stand vacant.*

Two birders approach each other from opposite ends of the lot. One is in his early fifties. His walk is brisk, his manner relaxed, open, friendly. His clothes look like they were lifted right out of the pages of "Town and Country" magazine, and his 10×42 binoculars are so new that the strap squeaks. With the touch of a button on his key ring, a silver Range Rover blinks its lights and chirps a greeting. The other man is younger, in his early twenties. His face is intense but calm, his eyes translucent and alert. He needs a haircut. He is wearing old jeans and a faded World Series of Birding T-shirt. Around his neck hangs a pair of ancient binoculars held together with duct tape. His bicycle is chained to the fence next to the Range Rover. He bends down to unfasten the chain just as the other man arrives.]

OLDER BIRDER. Hello! How's the birding?

YOUNGER BIRDER. [*Looking up, nodding*] Hello. [*Pauses, listening or maybe just thinking before he answers*] The birding's fine.

OLDER BIRDER. Terrific. Great morning. Got three year birds today: merlin, Cape May warbler, and a gray-cheeked thrush. How about you?

YOUNGER BIRDER. [*Still bent over, spinning the dial on his combination lock*] A lot of early season neotropical migrants are still going through, but blackpoll and palms arrived in good numbers. Some middle-distance stuff turned up as well. Eastern phoebe, white-throats, kinglets. [*Pauses, thinking*] Lots of thrushes dropping in early.

OLDER BIRDER. Sounds great. Gray-cheeked is a real prize, you know. Couldn't have gotten it without these. [*Points to his binoculars*] Unbelievable bins. Crystal clear! Have you seen them yet? They're new.

YOUNGER BIRDER. [*Not looking up, still concentrating on his bicycle lock*] Yes.

OLDER BIRDER. [*Taking off his binoculars, offering them*] Go ahead. Try them. [*The younger birder stands, takes the binoculars, examines them, tries to hand them back.*] No. Go ahead. [*Smiles, encourages*] Look through them. You won't believe it. [*The younger birder obliges.*]

YOUNGER BIRDER. Nice. [*Starts to hand them back, hesitates. Looks up, searching the sky, then trains the binoculars on a trio of high-flying birds.*]

OLDER BIRDER. [*Looking up, squinting*] Swallows?

YOUNGER BIRDER. Two Nashvilles and a palm.

OLDER BIRDER. [*Not listening*] Probably tree swallows. Wonderful glasses, aren't they?

YOUNGER BIRDER. [*Handing back the binoculars*] Yes.

OLDER BIRDER. [*Beaming*] Thanks. Knew you'd like them. I'm getting another pair for my wife. When we went to Antarctica last July her bins kept fogging. Ever been to Antarctica? Hell on equipment. You spend that much on a trip, you should have first-rate equipment.

YOUNGER BIRDER. No.

OLDER BIRDER. [*Startled*] What?

YOUNGER BIRDER. No. I've never been to Antarctica. You asked me.

OLDER BIRDER. [*At ease again*] Oh, right. Well, when you get to Antarctica, remember what I said about equipment. Don't cut corners.

YOUNGER BIRDER. [*Suddenly alert, searching*] Yellow-bellied fly-catcher.

OLDER BIRDER. Did you say "Yellow-bellied flycatcher"? [*Younger birder nods but doesn't answer.*] Where?

YOUNGER BIRDER. I'm not sure. Somewhere in those trees over . . . [*Brings his binoculars up, a reflex as fast as a knee being assaulted by a hammer*] There it is. Perched in the sunlight . . . Flying now.

OLDER BIRDER. [*Bringing his binoculars up too late*] I didn't get on it. Why did you think it was yellow-bellied?

YOUNGER BIRDER. It called.

OLDER BIRDER. But you didn't see a yellow belly?

YOUNGER BIRDER. [*Hesitating*] No. It was an adult in very worn plumage.

OLDER BIRDER. [*Nodding sympathetically*] Too bad you didn't get a look at the belly. That's where quality optics really pay off. Like that gray-cheek this morning. Right in the shadows. Did you say you saw one too?

YOUNGER BIRDER. No. I said there were a lot of thrushes drop-ping in before dawn—mostly gray-cheeks and Swainson's.

OLDER BIRDER. It's tough telling gray-cheeks from Swainson's, isn't it?

YOUNGER BIRDER. [*Perplexed*] More from wood thrush, I think. Attenuation is sometimes a problem with distant gray-cheeks, but . . .

OLDER BIRDER. [*Breaking in*] Oh, wood thrushes are easy to tell from gray-cheeks. Much more spotting on the breast. Course, you need good optics. [*Looks at his watch*] Sorry, gotta run. Nice talking to you. Keep working on those thrushes. Takes practice.

[*The older birder gets in his car, closes the door, waves, then drives away. The younger birder watches for a moment, then bends down and finishes unlocking his bicycle.*]

MADE IN HEAVEN

The maitre d' stepped to our table, interrupting our exchange of greetings and introductions.

"The New York call you've been waiting for, madam."

"Please excuse me," the most beautiful woman in the world said, rising, leaving. She moved like a Roman goddess.

"What do you think?" Bob invited. "Isn't she wonderful."

"She is," I agreed. "But next time you meet a girl and decide to get married, give me and the airlines two weeks' notice or pick a best man on your side of the continent."

"What?" Bob said mockingly. "Not have the man who introduced me to birding supporting me at the altar. Unthinkable."

Bob and I go back a long way. Two bird-crazy kids who cut our teeth on Peterson. Though we hadn't seen each other since his move to the West Coast ten years earlier, it was clear Bob had lost none of his youthful exuberance. I knew, from correspondence and mutual friends, that he lived, breathed, and slept birding. Until now it had been his whole life.

"Where did the two of you meet?"

"At a desert rest area on I-10. There was a black-throated blue warbler reported."

"Sooo," I breathed in relief, "she's a birder?"

"A beginner," he affirmed.

"And you're her mentor."

"Sort of," he replied.

Bob must have noticed my look of perplexity because he added, "She doesn't know I'm a birder. When she backed into my car my binoculars were still under the seat."

"It wasn't her fault," he continued. "I sort of stopped behind her car when a *Dendroica* flew across the rest area."

"I see," I said, ignoring the chill running down my spine. "But she likes birds," I said hopefully.

"Of course!" Bob said (to my relief). "Why wouldn't she?" he added, ending that anxiety-free moment. My mind turned to the set of Stone's *Bird Studies at Old Cape May* I'd bought from an antique book dealer as a wedding present.

I was wondering whether it was too late to exchange them for a crystal punch bowl when Bob continued, "You don't think a Questar and Gitzo tripod combination is too heavy for someone weighing ninety-two pounds, do you? I'm afraid it might be," he added. "Especially when you add the weight of Sony TCD-D10 Pro II recorder and a Telinga parabolic mike."

"You bought her a Questar *and* a recording system for a wedding present!" I replied, trying to make it sound like a question (and failing).

"Of course," he said. "She's the love of my life. Besides, where we're going she'll need it. Go ahead," he demanded. "Guess."

"The Islands?" I offered.

"Island! Singular," he said.

"*The* Island?"

"The island," he affirmed. "Attu."

I tried to picture the moldy concrete bunker that houses Attu birders and apply the label "honeymoon suite," but without success. "Isn't Attu a little rustic for a . . . uh . . . beginning birder?" I cautioned.

"There's running water inside now," he said defensively.

"There's always been running water inside," I said.

"I mean in pipes," he said, piqued. "Anybody can go to Hawaii for a honeymoon. But how many people can say they went to Attu? Think about it."

I did think about it. And I blanched.

"Have you told her where you're taking her?"

"It's a surprise," he said.

"You are sure she's an outside sort of girl?" I ventured.

"I told you we met in a desert rest area. Stop worrying."

"Well, what's her profession . . . I mean does she . . ."

"She doesn't have to," Bob interrupted, clearly annoyed by my lack of enthusiasm. "She has family money generated by some international concern specializing in pharmaceuticals, entertainment, and transportation."

At this moment my questions were interrupted by the return of Bob's intended.

"What did your godfather say?" Bob asked anxiously.

The bride-to-be seemed momentarily unhappy—which, if anything, made her even more beautiful.

"I didn't speak with him," she said. "He's on a business trip to Central America. The call was from one of his, uh, lieutenants, who urged me to wait until Uncle gave his blessing before going through with the ceremony.

"But I said we are flying out tonight and that's all there is to it. I'm sure everything will be fine. I'm his favorite niece. He always says what makes me happy makes him happy.

"And," she giggled, reaching for her wine glass, looking into her lover's eyes, "what makes me unhappy, he makes disappear.

"Poof," she said, smiling secretly, tearing her eyes away from Bob and turning them upon me.

"Bob's told me so much about you, Pete. He said if there is anything not to like about him you are probably to blame.

"Incidentally," she added, "I gave my uncle's people your motel room in case there are any questions. I hope you don't mind."

"Excuse me," I said to the two of them. "I'll be right back." I lied.

FOR MELINDA
WITH LOVE AND SQUALOR

My biologist friend leaned across the car and opened the passenger seat door, dislodging an avalanche of Styrofoam cups, fermenting hoagie wrappers, pistachio shells, cassette tapes, and a well-seasoned, road-killed Virginia rail.

"So that's where that rail went," she said, grinning. "Just throw your gear anywhere," she invited, gesturing toward the rear—toward the pile whose components appeared to include half the contents of the library at Alexandria, elements of at least two mismatched tripods, a Bushnell Spacemaster spotting scope still being carried on some university's inventory, a cooler filled with benthic samples and long-neck bottles, a parachute, a sleeping bag, a pair of chest waders, the car's muffler, and two pairs of clogging shoes.

"Huh," I thought, hesitating, searching for an empty nook, "I didn't know Melinda was into clogging."

Melinda must have mistaken my hesitation for aversion. "Uh, sorry about the mess," she began, "but . . ."

"Don't mention it," I said, cutting her apology short, selecting a spot to toss my stuff that wouldn't topple the pile (or restrict access to the cooler). "My VW Rabbit is named Pig Pen," I explained.

"Oh," she said, smiling again, patting the dashboard of her Pinto sedan with obvious affection. "Pete, meet Detritus."

I'm not saying that all birders treat their cars the way Sherman treated Atlanta, or that the average birdingmobile looks like it was lifted off the screen set for *The Grapes of Wrath.* I've known birders whose vehicles were so spotless they could serve as operating rooms—birders who consider Windex and a portable vacuum as indispensable as binoculars and spotting scope.

But most birders (at least most birders who grudgingly give me access to their cars) have a more cavalier attitude about auto interiors, and a good many of these acquaintances are plainly indifferent to them.

Consider Rick, a Maryland birder whose VW Golf looks like it's been slept in—which it has, over and over again. During his years as Maryland's breeding bird atlas coordinator, Rick has probably logged more Z-time in his automotive steed than your average small-town graveyard-shift patrol officer.

Consider Judy, from Mississippi. Judy's spunky Honda Civic is a veritable automotive midden, filled with tokens and treasures enough to humble the efforts of the most avaricious pack rat.

Consider my venerable old Pig Pen, whose deposition of tracked-in debris was so thick come trade-in time that it had formed geological strata. The top several layers were dry, desertlike. But the underlying sediment, from middepth down to metal core, had characteristics consistent with your basic Pleistocene swamp.

My current steed, a Saab 900 (dubbed "Pete's Pit" by wife Linda), is the latest in a proud line of dumpsters on wheels. Everything—I mean *every*thing—I might ever need in the next five years is stashed in that car.

How do I know this? Because it has taken me five years to provision the Pit properly. Every time I went birding (shorebirding, pelagic birding, hawk watching) and put some important accoutrement (window mount, rain pants, lucky hawk-watching visor) into the car, well, it just *stayed* there.

Say I'm birding Brigantine National Wildlife Refuge in July and need an expedition-grade goosedown parka to save a fellow birder whose air-conditioned rental has brought him to the brink of hypothermia. Well, I've got one.

Say I run into Peter Matthiessen and want him to autograph a copy of *Shorebirds of North America.* Well, I've got one of those too. Found it just the other day while searching for a 40× eyepiece to fit the Balscope Senior I dropped off a jetty in 1974. It (the eyepiece) was located in the panel pocket of the 60/40 cloth jacket (I was wearing it the day I met Maurice Broun) that had unaccountably found its way into the duffel bag (containing my hiphugger bell-bottoms and work shirt embroidered with scenes inspired by *The Lord of the Rings*) instead of the old milk crate (that used to house my selection of eight-track tapes) where, of course, it belonged.

Small wonder it took so long to find it.

Now you are probably wondering why I just can't take all this stuff out of the car, store it at home, and draw upon it at need? Well, I certainly could! If I could predict when and where in July I was going to meet a hypothermic birder or run across a Balscope Senior in need of an eyepiece.

Or if home was a more orderly and organized place than my car—which it is not. As a matter of fact, if you *really* want to see chaos, you should see my office.

Makes what Sherman did to Atlanta look like urban renewal.

THE OLD MAN
AND THE PLOVER

He was an old man who birded alone, and he had gone eighty-four days now without finding a good bird.

"Cheer up," the boy had said. Before the fall term the boy had been his companion. Now they spoke only by phone.

"Remember we are in September," the boy continued.

"The month the good birds come," the old man said. "Anyone can be a birder in May—even you."

"Go suck an egg," the boy replied, but with humor. The old man had taught the boy to bird, and the boy loved him (even if the old man *did* still call northern harriers "marsh hawks").

"Tomorrow I will be at the dikes at dawn," the old man said. "To be there when the tide is full."

"Bitchin'," the boy replied. "Find something to make the members of the Records Committee commit suttee, old man."

"With luck," the old man replied.

He was there before the security gate opened. But he knew the trick of short-circuiting the electronic timer by placing a metal toolbox beside it so that it would open.

"I am an old man," he thought, "but I know many tricks."

He was well out on the dikes by the time the sun came up. With his binoculars, he scanned the pools.

"Just the usual stuff," he assessed. "Peep, yellowlegs, dows, stilts, and the odd pec." Then a falcon put the flocks up, and the old man saw the large dark-rumped plover for the first time.

"Yes," he said. "Yes." And he trained his scope on the place where the bird landed.

At first he saw nothing but the head, which was strangely shaped for golden plover. Then he saw the back, which was brightly spangled, and the underparts—black only to the legs and bordered by white.

"No," he said. "He can't be *that* good."

But he was that good, and the old man found a checklist, which was his only paper, and began sketching the details he could see.

"I wish I had the boy," the old man thought. The boy was an ornithology student who knew tertial talk and even the names of birds in scientific Latin.

Then he said aloud, "I wish I had the boy. To help me and to see this."

The old man had never seen a greater golden plover and could not recall all the field marks that distinguished it from the golden plovers of eastern North America. He illustrated what he saw, his hand cramping with the effort and his excitement, and was nearly finished when a falcon routed the bird for good.

"Have something?" a voice wanted to know.

The old man turned to see a stranger approaching. Everything about him was friendly except for the eyes, which were aloof.

"A greater golden plover in breeding plumage," the old man exclaimed. "You just missed it."

The stranger was silent, and his face now matched the eyes.

"Unlikely." he said. "There's one record for the lower forty-eight."

"Here," the old man offered, "my notes."

The stranger studied the sketch and handed it back.

"Looks like a *fulva*."

"What?"

"A *fulva*. Pacific golden plover. Don't you know that the lesser golden plover was split?"

The old man shook his head.

"Well, it was. You need to do some homework."

The old man was humiliated but not defeated, and he remembered the boy and how proud he would be, and so he resumed work on the sketch, recording the details now as he remembered them. It was then that he saw the next two birders approaching, members of the state Records Committee.

"*Ayy,*" he said aloud. There is no translation for this word, and perhaps it is just a noise such as a man might make, involuntarily, as his spotting scope goes over a jetty in a wind.

"Who else saw the bird?" the first one asked.

"Did you get photos?" the second one wanted to know?

"Did it call?" the first one demanded.

"Well, write it up anyway," they said before leaving.

"I should have brought a camera," he thought, sadly. "And I should have had the boy."

His hope was gone but not his pride. It wasn't until he returned to the refuge headquarters to log his sighting and was confronted by the assemblage of gripped birders that this, and all that was left of his happiness, was taken too.

"Did you notice the length of the legs?"

"Did you check the primary extension?"

"Did you note any signs of molt?"

"Did you see the color of the underwing lining?"

"Have you seen the species before?"

"Are you sure it wasn't just a black-bellied?"

In the end he did not log the sighting, and when the checklist with his diagram fell to the tarmac as he got into his car, he did not care.

Later a tourist couple taking a break from the casinos in Atlantic City made a wrong turn and wandered onto the refuge. The woman, seeing the paper, picked it up.

"What's that?" the man asked.

"A list of birds found on the refuge," the woman replied. "Someone's scribbled on it."

"I didn't know there were so many birds here."

"I didn't either," the woman replied.

"Maybe we should take up birdwatching. I'll bet it's fun."

"Maybe we should. It's got to be more fun than losing money."

At his home, the old man lay face down on the couch. He was sleeping without dreams and waiting for the boy to return his call. He wanted to say hello and to hear a friend's voice.

SEPARATING HOAGIES

We were sitting on the hawk watch eating hoagies—South Jersey subs. P.B.'s was a turkey and Swiss; mine was Italian with everything on it—not that you'd know this by simply looking at them. Hoagies are sort of the *Empidonax* flycatchers of the sandwich world.

"The Records Committee didn't accept your brown noddy sighting," P.B. confided, putting friendship ahead of procedure.

"Tooorifik," I said through a mouthful of salami/provolone/lettuce/tomato/pickles/hot peppers/extra oregano.

"You aren't upset?" he wanted to know.

"Nope," I assured, smiling grandly, going for another bite.

"Really?" he said.

"Really," I assured, savoring the last epicurean morsel.

P.B. paused, accepting the disclosure at face value. "Well, I wish other people were as understanding," he lamented.

I do too, for the sake of birders and records committee members alike.

Records committees have a difficult job. Their task: review sight records of unusual species and determine, on the basis of evidence, whether each record should or should not be added to the state's bird list.

The problem is, some birders regard records committees as judge and jury. The problem is, the acceptance or rejection of a sighting by a records committee is widely held to be a reflection upon the accuracy of the identification or the skills of the observer. It is not. It cannot be. All a records committee can do is weigh evidence and determine whether it is sufficient to support acceptance. If a committee assumes authority more than this, it is overstepping its jurisdiction. If birders assume more than this, they are demeaning their own skills and responsibilities.

Look. It's simple. From bird to record book, a sighting has four levels of reality. First and most fundamental is *what the bird actually was*. If you believe in genetic coding, if you subscribe to the structured regimentation of Linnaeus, then you must believe that at some level all living things relate to nothing but one of their own kind.

Next, but not necessarily related, is *what the bird looked like*— which may or may not be the same as what it was. Molting plumage can transmute horned grebes into eared grebes; distance, heat waves, and an elevated perch can transform an Iceland gull into a great egret.

Now comes the human variable and level 3: *what the bird was identified as*. It might have been an Iceland gull and it might have looked like a great egret. But if an observer is confident that the bill was spatula-shaped . . .

Then comes the written description, based on notes and memory. Then comes the review by committee members who bring their cumulative experiences to bear. Then comes *what the committee believes*.

An observer is two steps removed from reality; the committee, three. Your reality as observer is more fundamental than theirs. You win on points. And while they, acting responsibly, may elect not to include the record on a state bird list, that does not and should not preclude you from including it on yours.

I tried to explain this to P.B., who listened intently but wasn't entirely won over by my philosophical equanimity.

"OK," I said. "Let's put it this way. What kind of hoagie did you have?"

"Turkey and Swiss," he said.

"On the basis of what evidence?" I demanded.

"That's what it tasted like," he asserted.

"I didn't taste it. What other evidence do you have?"

"It's what I ordered," he explained.

"You might have picked up the wrong sandwich at the counter," I suggested. "I need more evidence."

"The wrapper has a number 9 written on it," he pointed out. "Number 9 is turkey and Swiss."

"Wrapper isn't sandwich. The counterperson might have made a mistake."

"Well, I could give you a piece," he mused, "but it's all gone."

"So you can't. It's gone. And I reject your identification of turkey and Swiss on the basis of insufficient evidence."

P.B. looked puzzled, then exasperated. He started to say something but I cut him off.

"How did it taste?"

"It tasted great!"

"Then it doesn't make any difference whether I believe it or not, does it?"

"Not a bit," he said, smiling, pausing, reflecting, bringing the conversation back to where it started.

"You know," he said in all seriousness, "your bird could have been a black noddy instead of brown. It's possible."

"It could have been sliced chicken and not turkey."

"I would have known the difference," he promised.

And he would too.

NOSING OUT AN IDENTIFICATION.
TAKING IT WITH SALT.

"Dr. Gesundheit to see you, Mr. Duster," the intercom intoned.

"Send him in," the editor of Hootin-Tootin's field guide series said, speaking into the book proposal clasped in his hands. Reaching the bottom of the page, registering no intrusion, he repeated the directive.

"I am in," a voice corrected.

"Oh," the editor replied, dropping the manuscript, fixing his eyes upon his guest, trying to determine whether the somewhat height-challenged individual was seated or standing. "Very pleased to meet you," he said, reaching across his desk, inviting a handshake. Instead of taking the extended hand, the visiting scientist crouched and began peering up into the editor's face.

Startled, the editor stooped in an effort to meet his guest eye to eye. This caused the doctor to drop to his knees, which triggered Mr. Duster to lie flat on his desk, which caused the ornithologist to go down on all fours. His concentration on the editor's face never wavered.

"Your nostrils are vunderful," he exclaimed.

"Thank you," the editor exclaimed. "Yours are nice too," he added (although, in truth, he had yet to see the dorsal side of the man's nose). "You study human nostrils as well as bird nostrils?" he assessed, juxtaposing the man's antics and subject of his book proposal—*A Field Guide to Avian Nasal Mites*.

"Nein," he said, drawing a magnifying glass from a jacket pocket, peering intently into the editor's left nostril. "Der nostril ist just der environment. It ist der mites dat I study."

"Of course," Mr. Duster said, drawing away, raising the book proposal between them in a successful bid to prevent the doctor from pursuing him across the desk. "And your premise is that all birds can be differentiated on the basis of nasal mites that are specific to that bird species?"

"Der ist no question," the scientist replied. "Every bird on der planet can be identified by der mites alone even better den der DNA."

"Fascinating," the editor exclaimed, considering the possibilities, growing excited about scooping the entire field guide industry. "So by using your system even look-alike species can be identified in the field?"

"Ya. Mit my field guide to der nasal mites, even der *Empidonax* flycatchers are as plain now as der nose on der face. Here, I show you," he said, taking the manuscript, flipping to a series of magnified photos showing creatures so ugly that they would induce sleeplessness in Steven King.

"Dis ist der mite from der least flycatcher. See how it ist small und gray mit a round head und stubby mandibles. Now der acadian flycatcher mite. See. Bigger und on der back greener, ya?"

"I, uh, well, I guess," the editor replied, "but . . ."

"A bad photo," the doctor explained. "An adult mite dat ist very worn. In der book, we use a better photo, ya?"

"Also," he said, "der habitat ist different. Der least mite ist always at der edge of der thick, hairy growth und only near to der wet places. Der acadian mite ist always where der hair ist thickest und der nostril wettest."

"Do they vocalize?" the editor wanted to know.

"Ya, der least mite says 'ah-CHOO,' der acadian mite 'AH-choo.' Ist very different."

"I see," said the editor. "How about western and cordilleran flycatchers?"

"Ah," the doctor said, warming to the subject. "Here," he said, flipping to the next page.

"I don't see any difference," the editor confessed.

"Der ist no difference," the scientist exclaimed triumphantly. "But der western flycatcher mite ist always found in der right bird nostril. Der cordilleran in der left."

"This is fantastic," the editor exclaimed. "This could revolutionize bird identification."

"Und der scientific study too. Here, der green heron." The scientist flipped to another page, one showing two ugly-looking creatures—one dark and labeled "Striated," the other pale and labeled "Green-Backed."

"These are *very* different," the editor exclaimed. "Clearly different species."

"Nein, nein, nein," the Doctor stuttered. "Der mites are der same just as der birds are der same. Only der views are different. In der North America bird der mites on der tummy lie. In der South America, always on der back."

"Remarkable," the editor exclaimed. "The only question I have is, how do you see the mites in the field?"

"Ah," the doctor exclaimed, winking. "Dat ist der trick, ya? You use der salt solution."

The editor didn't say anything for a moment. Then it occurred to him that perhaps the doctor was making a joke.

"You mean you have to be very close—close enough to put salt on its tail?"

"Nein," the Doctor explained. "You must squirt der saline solution into der bird's nostril und take a sample to study through der microscope. Ist only way."

"I see," the editor said.

"Vat I offer you ist right of first refusal," the doctor said, beaming.

"Exactly right," the editor replied.

Part 5

REFLECTIONS

THE FOX AND THE HARRIER

The harrier, an adult male, was sitting in the open marsh, half-hidden in grass. The bird was calm, nominally alert, but perhaps a little too preoccupied with its preening. This is how the fox managed to get so close.

The animal was stalking the harrier from behind, using the grassy lip of a tidal creek to best strategic advantage. From where the harrier sat, the fox was invisible. From my position I could see it all, and from my estimates I could envision only one outcome to the unfolding drama.

What should I do? I like foxes—because they are beautiful and intelligent, and because they are marvelously skilled predators. But I like harriers too, and for the very same reasons. In fact, among all of New Jersey's nesting birds, the northern harrier is my clear favorite.

The choices were these: I could interfere, cheat the fox out of its meal but save the harrier; or I could do nothing, gaining insight perhaps but at the expense of a favorite creature's demise. It was a dilemma.

This is going to be an odd essay, and maybe a boring essay, and maybe an irritating essay as well. But it is an essay I have a mind to write and the point it raises is one worth taking to heart. Its philosophical roots are buried in a life of wildlife observation, but its impetus was prompted by the juxtaposition of several disparate events.

These events linked up and framed an answer to an age-old question, one I now pose to you: What is our role in nature?

No, no, you can't take the high road, assume that lofty heroic stand that humanity has no role in nature. It's too late for the creature that fished out the Grand Banks, lubricated Prince William Sound, and blew a frog-scorching hole in the ozone layer to play Pontius Pilate.

As a member of the species that is usurping the planet and monopolizing its resources, I believe that it is our responsibility to know when to step in and intercede, or intrude, when nature gets into a bind. Thanks to the fox and harrier, the members of the North American Rehabilitators Association, and Tom, I think I've found an answer.

Tom is a hunter, an environmentalist, and a writer for one of the Big Three hook and bullet magazines. Tom was doing a column on hunters who are also environmentalists; he wanted my input and the subject of management came up. Many hunters consider conservation and management to be synonymous, but they are not.

Conservation is an ethic that opposes destruction, misuse, or erosion of natural resources. It is nonspecific and its essence is restraint.

Management is the manipulation of habitat and animals to benefit one species or group of species over others. It is a tool. It is specific. And its essence is action.

Conservation the ethic and management the tool both involve conscious choices with regard to the environment. The conservation movement started in the last century when overhunting and habitat destruction reduced much of North America's wildlife to a vestige of its former abundance. The solution was restraint *and* management—and it worked! Much of North America's depleted wildlife was restored.

In this century, management has been used primarily to keep the populations of assorted wildlife populations—principally game species—high. But management is selective. It benefits species that humans assign value. And while it is often tangentially beneficial to other, nontarget species, it may be and usually is detrimental to others.

Take the American woodcock, an upland shorebird and a popular gamebird. Woodcock numbers have been declining. Why? Because woodcock require open fields and new growth woodlands ("edge"). As forests in the Northeast have matured in the last half of this century, woodcock habitat has decreased.

The response of game management engineers has been to encourage landowners and refuge managers to cut swaths through mature woodlands, creating edge. Now here's the rub: creating edge benefits the woodcock, but it is detrimental to many species of woodland songbird. Edge is an open door for cowbirds, and cowbirds parasitize songbird nests, resulting in reduced nest productivity. Both woodcock and songbirds are declining, and the management policy is tantamount to stealing from Peter (and John and Matthew and Simon . . .) to give to Paul.

At least that's how I read it. At least this is the sort of institutionalized interference that led me to conclude, long ago, that too often wildlife management is biased manipulation predicated upon human interest, not natural diversity and broad-scope biological need.

And this is what early on in my writing career led me to profess that the best way to maintain an environment is to just plain leave it alone. Don't interfere. Don't manage. Just let nature strike her own, proper balance.

If anything should be managed, it's people, not wildlife.

This laissez-faire conclusion led to a hard-line conviction. When people called my office and said, "I've got this bird that has fallen out of the nest. What should I do?" I said, "Put it back." When someone tells me woodcock are declining because forests are maturing, I say, "Sounds natural enough to me."

Then, right after my conversation with Tom, while this management question was still fresh in my mind, I attended the Wildlife Rehabilitators annual meeting. It served to undermine my laissez-faire stance.

Good folks, these rehab people. As concerned about stressed and injured wildlife as the founders of the conservation movement were concerned about the wildlife heritage of a continent.

Wildlife rehab people are the ones that get to go one-on-one with preschoolers with twenty grams of baby robin clutched in their hands and tears down both cheeks. Wildlife rehab people are the ones conservation officers turn to when the peregrine falcon is found in the marsh with a wing half torn off by shot—because some fool can't tell the difference between a falcon and a duck, or because some brigand disguised as a hunter puts his perverted vanity above the law of the land.

And wildlife rehab people are the ones that get called in when vessels rupture and oil casts trouble upon the waters, causing death and injury to hundreds and thousands of birds and animals. Rehab people use their skills and they direct resources to salvage what can be salvaged and redress a wrong committed against nature. They *interfere* because a wrong has been done, and it is up to responsible people to set it right.

Just as those founders of conservation once did.

So I came to modify my position about management. I'm still very much of the opinion that an environment is maintained best when it is juggled least. I am still of the opinion that it's people who need management, not wildlife.

But since our species cannot be part of this world and not part of the environment—since our encroachments are bound to have impacts and these will have to be redressed—then this is how I view humanity's role in nature.

As the custodians of the planet, we are obligated to restore nature when some action of ours threatens or degrades it. But as creatures who are not all-knowing and cannot foresee all ends, we are wise to let nature establish her own order and limits without imposing preferences or biases.

I decided to do nothing. I decided not to warn the harrier or deflect the fox, and although I did not *like* my decision I was comfortable with it.

The fox crept near. The harrier suspected nothing. And just as the fox paused, gathering itself for its leap, the harrier calmly stretched, muted, and flew, leaving a naturally foiled fox and a vindicated observer behind.

VESPERS FOR A FALLOUT

When I was little, all the neighborhood kids used to sit on our front steps and listen for the two sounds that would spark a summer evening. The first was the jingle of the ice-cream truck; the second was the sputter of the DDT fogger.

The ice-cream truck usually arrived first, and we'd fight for the privilege of squandering our allowances on smoking Popsicles and vanilla ice cream covered in dye-colored grit. The fogger usually arrived just before dark, just before the wood thrush, singing vespers, retired for the night. Popsicles in hand, we'd chase the fogger down the street, running in and out of the chemical cloud, laughing all the way.

It was harmless, after all. The grownups told us this; the government too! And we were children. We were obedient. And we had never been betrayed. We accepted the wisdom of grownups and governments on faith.

"There. Above the trees," wife Linda directed, bringing her Bausch and Lomb 8×42s to bear. We saw them immediately, a weary string of birds holding just above the trees.

"Or-i-oles," Judy Toups pronounced, studying the slim icterid lines, dragging out the syllables the way folks who live in Mississippi do.

"Orchard [orioles]," I added, noting the burnt orange plumage ignited by a rising sun.

"And a northern," Linda amended, picking the trailing odd-bird-out of the flock.

"GoOod," Judy intoned, assessing both Linda's skills and our fortune. As local expert and our guide, this was Judy's prerogative and privilege.

Behind the first group of birds was another, this one comprised of rose-breasted grosbeaks, wings flashing silver dollar–sized patches of white. Mixed in were scarlet tanagers, unmistakable at any distance. A wave of eastern kingbirds followed, blunt-headed birds whose fluttery wingbeat makes them look like they are perpetually trying to catch up.

Then another flock of orioles (sprinkled with tanagers).

Then tanagers sprinkled with orioles. Another.

Another.

More kingbirds.

More orioles.

Spring fallout on the Mississippi Coast.

We'd been birding the Gulf Coast for a week, hoping, praying for the great precipitation of wings that birders dream of. Praying for a second chance.

"You should have been here Thursday," Judy had announced upon our Saturday arrival. "ThOUSAnds of birds," she pronounced, letting the syllables climb in measure with the flight. "Thousands," she repeated, expressing both the wonder and injustice of it all.

"What's the weather picture look like for the rest of the week?" I asked, trying not to sound too hopeful (and fooling no one, least of all Judy).

"There's *supposed* to be another cold front coming through," Judy guardedly advised. "But not until later in the week. We'll keep an eye on the weather maps and play it by ear."

Front or no front, there would still be birds to enjoy, of course. Resident species like Swainson's warbler and swallow-tailed kites—birds that a couple of vagabond birders from New Jersey would be thrilled to see. And there would be migrants too. Birds traveling northbound on the Yucatán Express—the cuckoos, flycatchers, thrushes, vireos, warblers, tanagers, grosbeaks, and orioles—that vault the Gulf of Mexico every spring. But without a cold front and its daunting wall of rain, the mass of migrating birds would overshoot the coast and forage inland.

This is why, every spring, birders from Texas to the Tortugas head for the Gulf Coast, watch the weather maps, and pray for rain.

We prayed too and watched as the jagged-toothed line marked with a capital *H* marched down from Canada on the Sunday evening news. We cheered as the advancing line cleared the Dakotas on Monday and held our breath as it plunged into neighboring Arkansas on Tuesday.

But by Wednesday the front had crept no closer than northern Mississippi. The system was losing steam, and a typically diffident weather forecaster changed his earlier prediction from "rain Thursday," to "chance of showers in the northern part of the state." It sure sounded as though the system was going to stall.

Judy, hoping to flaunt the strategic riches of Mississippi, was vexed. Linda and I were bummed.

Sure enough, Thursday dawned uneventfully sunny or, as Judy put it, "There is nothing more boring than a blue sky." We skipped the news that night, opting instead to eat out at a neat little hole-in-the-wall ribs place, smothering our disappointment with barbecue sauce and a few beers.

On the way home, it started to sprinkle. Then it started to rain. Then it started to *pour*—poured so hard, in fact, that the windshield wipers bowed under the strain. Poured so hard that by the time we got back to our room, we didn't park the car so much as dock it.

The storms continued off and on all night, filling our room with lightning flashes and our dreams with sweet anticipation. Just offshore, over the stormy Gulf of Mexico, a drama was unfolding. Beneath a dark, directionless sky, weary birds were fighting for their lives and many were losing.

The story of the great masses of migrating birds that carpet the Gulf Coast has a tragic side, a dark irony that taints every fallout. The conditions that produce masses of birds for birders bring despair for the birds themselves. When the great storms lash out across the Gulf of Mexico, birds die. The coastal fallouts that birders dream of are comprised of weary survivors.

In the weeks before their cross-gulf journey, migrating songbirds prepare by feeding voraciously, putting on fat, the fuel that they will consume during their flight. Cargo restrictions are severe for birds whose weight is measured in grams. Fully loaded, a hooded warbler may top out at thirteen grams, one-third of which is fuel. It is enough to see them across the Gulf under normal, favorable conditions. But there is little excess to spare.

Every evening, from late March until early May, North America's long-distance migrants initiate their great leaps of faith. Despite the hardship and the risk, bird migration is a strategy for survival. It permits many kinds of birds to distribute themselves across northern reaches of the planet at a time when winter's retreat creates an abundance of food and space. Then, when winter begins closing its fist over the land, migration offers birds a means of escape.

Without migration, many of North America's nesting birds would never have extended their ranges northward. Without migration, the number and diversity of birds seen in North America on June 1 would differ little from what might be seen on January 1.

Leveling out at two to four thousand feet, the migrating birds travel all night, navigating, like all great voyagers, by the stars. If their fortune holds, they will reach the United States mainland. There they will seek out the habitat that meets their peculiar needs to rest and feed.

But often things do not go well. As all great voyagers know, great gains are bought at great risk. Cold fronts pushing offshore greet birds with a wall of clouds. Rain drags at their wings. Head winds slow their progress, adding hours to the flight, wasting fuel.

When the last of their fat reserve is spent, as the birds begin to metabolize the muscle tissue that holds them aloft, they weaken and lose altitude. Soon only desperation keeps them above the reach of the waves.

For thirty minutes, we watched as flock after straggling flock labored across the woodland clearing, putting distance between themselves and the Gulf of Mexico. The terrible night was over; the aquatic hurdle vaulted.

"Let's get over to Ansley," Judy coached. "If it's good here, it will be *great* over there." Ansley is a chenier (pronounced shin-ear)—a wooded hummock surrounded by open marsh, a migrant trap of the first magnitude.

We parked right on the road (inconveniencing no one). Without hesitation (or insect repellent), we entered the finger of trees reaching out into open marsh, and what we discovered was a surprise but hardly a disappointment. Yes, there were grosbeaks (and tanagers and orioles) at Ansley, but not in the saturation numbers we'd expected. The treasure of Ansley was measured in the number of thrushes seeking sanctuary beneath the trees. Dozens of thrushes. Scores! The woodland was alive with these denizens of the forest floor.

Prominent in the ranks were burly wood thrushes—the bird whose evening song was as much a part of summer as Popsicles and pop flies. Also racing beneath the chenier were other thrushes, slighter and slimmer, and veery, darker and secretive, and Swainson's.

The game in Mississippi (and in many other places) is to pan through the Swainson's thrushes and find the gremlin gray-cheeked, a thrush disguised as a shadow. Birding is not a spectator sport, thank God. If it was, we would have drawn the laughter of the gallery by trying to sneak up on birds whose evasive skills border on artistry. Every bird we approached responded by stalking directly away, avoiding sunlight with a finesse that would make any vampire proud to be an understudy. Coincidentally, running interference for the birds was a host of winged vampires—mosquitoes—who quickly ascertained that birders in pursuit of a possible gray-cheeked thrush are an easy mark.

By the time the game was over, the chenier covered end to end, we had collectively banked what even the stingiest among us would call 2½ countable gray-cheeks, approximately seventy veerys, as many wood thrushes, and two dozen Swainson's—more thrushes than I had ever seen in one place at one time. But the real winners in the event were the mosquitoes, who drew first blood and last and may have collectively banked as much as a quart and a half.

We didn't grudge the loss of vital fluids. Mosquitoes come with the turf, are part of a functioning, natural environment. Take away the mosquitoes, take away the insects, and starving birds have no recourse but to starve. A corner of the world as globally significant to migrating birds as the Mississippi Coast is worth a few mosquito bites.

We had almost reached Judy's car before we heard the sound of an approaching vehicle—a truck of some sort; a truck that sounded like it was running on about half its cylinders.

It was a sound that was vaguely familiar. A sound linked to memories of Popsicles and pop flies. But before memory could index it, the truck came into view—a country mosquito truck spraying the chenier with a chemical mist, killing insects in a strip of woods that serves only to house mosquitoes and preserve the lives of migrating birds.

For just a moment, I thought I heard, once again, the song of the wood thrush singing vespers in my parents' backyard. But it's certain I was mistaken. It's been many years of attrition since wood thrushes sang there. And the birds foraging in Ansley, on the coast of Mississippi, were too weary and too hungry for song.

AFTER THE COLD FRONT

After the cold front went through, the clouds were driven back and the stars crept out of hiding. The hosts of purple martins rose before the dawn and greeted the stars with the chuckles and scolding chortles of their ink-colored kind.

They would spend much of the day aloft, these largest of North America's swallows. They would soar on swept-back wings, feast upon the transient, spot-winged glider dragonflies who hitch their fortunes to the wind and use it to transport themselves hundreds of miles. In the afternoon, the martins would descend and sheath the utility wires in the town. Visitors walking the streets would wonder at the great numbers of swallows and marvel that any place could be so blessed.

After the cold front went through, the warblers, which had waited so long for the proper conditions, were carried far from breeding territories in the north. Some were older adult birds, but most were juveniles, apprentices making the South American run for the first time. At dawn, over the waters that surround the tip of the Cape May peninsula, they began to descend, seeking shelter for the day.

They passed over the heads of surf fishermen, joggers, and early morning strollers. They buried themselves in the hedges and woodlots and shrub-strewn meadows. It was early in the season and the morning free of hawks, so they fed in the open, moving like multicolored sparks among the leaves, darting out now and again to snatch some moth who mistakenly believed that there was safety in flight.

The fishermen, who cast their lines and their sights out to sea, were surprised to find so many small birds coming in off the water. They looked so fragile and so tired, and when the gulls closed in and snapped up many in their bills, they felt bad for the birds— or would have, except that the bluefish began a blitz; rods began to bend, and catching fish became more important than feeling sorry for birds.

After the cold front went through, the massed flocks of terns grew restless and flighty because they knew the day of departure was at hand. For weeks they had gathered on the beaches in harsh-voiced clusters—gray-backed adults and scallop-backed birds of the year. On the ground, they waddled more than walked and took flight only to feed and to avoid the charge of unleashed dogs.

Flushed, they rose like angry smoke, cursing the dog and its owner in the language of terns. Eventually they would settle or, turning the disruption to utilitarian use, would go offshore to feed. Just beyond the breakers or on the horizon far offshore, they would hover in killing clouds over the schools of baitfish that the bluefish massacred from below.

Among the flocks were diminutive least terns with petite yellow bills and larger common terns with bills the color of arterial blood. They sliced into the water, plucking small silver-sided fish from innocence, then hurried toward shore before the brigand gulls could catch them.

After the cold front went through, large numbers of monarch butterflies began moving down the beach, hugging the dunes, flying with stiff-winged determination. There were scores of the insects in view and, by simple extrapolation, thousands cleaving a path down the Cape May peninsula. The insects were engaged in the first leg of their relay race to Mexico. The first winds of autumn had given them both urgency and speed.

In the evening, when the wind stilled and cold air enfolded land, the monarchs sought shelter on the sunny side of wind-sculpted cedar trees. Wings closed, the insects appear to be nothing more than dead leaves. In this way they defeated all but the eyes of the sharpest onlookers. In this way they found passage through the night.

After the cold front went through, the hummingbirds that had been moving in small numbers since early August picked up the tempo of migration. At the observation platform at Cape May Point State Park, the lilliputian forms were zipping over the heads of onlookers at five-to-ten-minute intervals. In the evening, when the tiny wings wearied, townspeople who put up hummingbird feeders would be treated to a host of hungry birds. Along woodland edges, where the orange-blossomed trumpet vines flourished, the vagrants would compete with resident hummingbirds for nectar.

Cold makes hummingbirds hungry. The energetic demands of migration make them hungry too—hungry and incautious. Along a bushy edge, a young hummingbird drawn to a surfeit of flowers, blundered into the web of a large black-and-yellow garden spider. Its struggles brought the web's owner and, in time, exhaustion.

Hungry is as hungry does, and nature does not discriminate.

After the cold front went through, the first of the American kestrels began to move. Brown-backed females and harlequin-colored males, the small falcons swept over the dunes and along the water's edge in groups of three, four, and five, rising and falling like knotted streamers in the wind.

They appeared in pulses that quickened as the afternoon wore on. Each new group was greeted with enthusiasm by those assembled on the observation platform, until a shout brought all heads up. In moments, all optics were focused upon the large plank-winged raptor soaring overhead.

It didn't have a white head and it didn't have a white tail, but it was nonetheless a bald eagle. The kestrels and the eagles were the vanguard of what is one of the greatest concentrations of migrating birds of prey in North America. From mid-August until the end of November, it would be a rare moment when some bird of prey would not be visible over the platform—conditions permitting, of course (which is very much the point of this essay, in case you have not guessed).

After the cold front went through, sweeping summer before it and ushering a taste of autumn in behind, it kept on moving, traveling farther offshore. The winds that circle in a clockwise pattern around high-pressure centers went from northwest to northerly to northeasterly and then they slackened. As the center of the high passed, the winds turned southerly, pumping warm, moist air back into the region and bringing a return to summer.

Two days after the cold front went through, the people in the towns walked beneath empty utility wires, and the green-head flies that hatched after the purple martins left made life miserable for those wearing shorts.

The morning sky was empty of warblers; the beaches devoid of terns. Migrating monarch butterflies were only a vestige of their cold front–spurred numbers, and hummingbirds were hardly to be found except on the shady side of gardens, where summer lingered.

On the platform at Cape May Point State Park, those savvy watchers who knew the cause and effect relation between weather and wildlife were nowhere to be seen. They would return when the next cold front arrived. In fact, the only people around were casual visitors, who climbed the stairs lured by the optimistic promise of the sign that read Official Hawk Watch.

They'd stay a minute or two. Put a quarter in the pay-per-view optics and scan the horizon. Then, finding nothing to entertain them, they'd leave—wondering what perversity would prompt the state to establish a natural area in a place that clearly didn't have any wildlife.

BONDED TO THE WEST WIND

I am bonded to the West Wind—and its ally the North Wind (and the East and South Winds, and all the hybrid winds that lie between). But mostly I follow the West Wind. When the axis of the earth inclines toward autumn, I follow it to mountain peaks and peninsula points as surely as migrating birds are driven before it.

In July and August, the West Wind ferries shorebirds my way. Dowitchers and yellowlegs, plovers and peep—fresh from the Arctic tundra, deposited daily on tidal flats and reservoir shores. For weeks on end, mud and mud-colored birds are the focus of my life. Even my name (when I arrive two hours late for work) is Mudd.

Then it's September and my windy liege shakes down the branches of northern forests, sending a storm of passerines my way. Warblers that move like multicolored sparks, thrushes that cloak themselves in shadows by day and whose nocturnal passage is heralded by a nasal yelp in the night.

But October and November are the months when the West Wind really shows its stuff. That is when the wind masters themselves, the birds of prey, surf its currents south. Important tasks turn to trifles when buteos mount the skies and falcons cruise the coast. If there is a sight to surpass an eagle pinned to a ridge, I've never dreamed it. (And if anyone has ever run a correlation between northwest winds and worker absenteeism, I'll bet its pretty direct.)

Worshiping the West Wind has a price. Every morning before dawn, my faith obligates me to sit in front of the TV and tune in to that great oracle of our time: the weather channel. Coffee in hand, eyes fused to the screen, I study the meteorological battle lines and pray.

If things auger well (i.e., if the front has cleared), one sitting through the local forecast is all that faith asks. But if the meteorological priests warn of a stalled front or raise the specter of a series of lows forming along the frontal boundary, I'll sit through coffee cup after cup, watching the local radar, trying to boost the barometric reading with longing and hope.

Wife Linda says I'm addicted. She claims she can't understand how a grown man can sit (within twenty feet of a sink full of dishes) and stare at simulated thundershowers crawling across a TV screen at ten-minute intervals. She doesn't comprehend how a front stalled over the Great Lakes or wind a few degrees east of north can make all the life-and-death difference in the world.

Actually she does understand. She just refuses to admit it while there are dishes in the sink.

If washing dishes could jump-start a stalled front, I'd be up to my elbows in suds. If wearing a lucky charm could affect the weather, I'd dress like a Christmas tree.

But I am charmed by the wind, not the charmer. I go where it goes, when it directs me. To pinnacles and peninsula points. Where I stand with other followers amid the wind-driven stream of birds, grateful for whatever fortune the West Wind blows my way.

MY PERFECT UNIVERSE

The wind almost took the car door out of my hands, would have if I hadn't been prepared for it. It cut like a cold-edged file and flayed exposed portions of my anatomy—not that there were many.

"Thank heavens I don't have to live out here," I thought. "There couldn't be any survivors," I added.

With this heavy thought to motivate me, I started for the meadows. Despite the cold, despite my certainty, I still hoped fervently to find at least one of the flock of tree swallows still alive.

There had been forty or so tree swallows at Cape May Point before temperatures took the plunge. They'd been here all winter, fortunate beneficiaries of an uncommonly warm season. Most of these emerald-backed insect-eating birds don't linger farther north than the outer banks of North Carolina. Along the Gulf Coast, where winters are mild, they accumulate in hordes.

But like many creatures, the winter's mild temperatures had seduced them. Why, in Cape May there were even butterfly sightings in mid-January: an orange sulphur and a mourning cloak!

Then the jet stream took a dive. Then things began to die.

The day after the temperatures dropped into the single digits, the number of tree swallows had been halved. Yesterday, three days after the cold front hit town, the numbers were halved again.

The frayed flock sat on the ice for the most part. Sometimes they would take wing and flutter like candle flames in the wind. Then they would settle. It was clear they were starving. It was futile to try to save them. And they were just the visible tip of the iceberg. All around me in the frozen marsh, there were creatures succumbing to the killing cold—rails, bitterns, herons, even some hardy ducks and geese. It tried my humanity. It called my truce with the universe into question—a question I thought I had resolved long ago.

When I was younger, I was very much interested in understanding why nature was as it was. In particular, I wanted to know why it was that nature was a regular killing field. I wanted an accounting for why life was bounded by so much pain and death.

I'm not saying there isn't a dark, beautiful symmetry to it. Things live, things die, pain is the usher. I'm just saying why not . . . not death, just life?

It seemed a defensible alternative. And since I was young, and since I could not find a comparable solution among the answers handed down by the adults, I decided to do the universe over and this time do it right.

Not being as gifted at creating as the Creator, I found rather quickly that I could not envision a completely different universe than the one I was in. So I was forced to fall back on a plan that emphasized "new and improved" as opposed to "completely different."

I decided to take the universe as we know it and just start working backward. You know. Like a new manager coming into a botched operation. I'd assess the situation, salvage what I could, and do away with all the things that were bad.

The first thing I decided to do away with in this bold new universe was predators—those creatures that survive by killing other things. Nasty business, predation. Very hurtful.

There would be no more lions or tigers or polar bears in this perfect world I was creating. No killer whales or sharks or rattlesnakes.

Or hawks or owls (even though I really liked hawks and owls). Or worm-killing robins or insect-eating swallows. Or bats or krill-filtering whales or ladybugs or lap cats—at least lap cats that killed birds at feeders. No killers. That was the rule.

It would certainly mean a less diverse world. But if it meant a safer world—one in which no creature caused pain or death to another—it was worth it.

Then I concluded I'd have to do something about winter. Winter, after all, killed things too. Crickets that made music and butterflies that made gardens animate; fireflies that made nights come alive and sparrows who froze to their perches when the chilling winds crept out of the north.

It was settled. No winter. I righted the tilt in the earth's axis, fixing permanently the apportionment of warmth over the face of the planet. It meant, of course, that life couldn't distribute itself as far as it did under the old system when seasons moved across the earth. There could never be life at the poles, and everything would be more or less crowded around the planet's middle, but . . .

But that was certainly a small price to pay for a perfect world, particularly since we'd gotten rid of all the predators and had a lot more room than we used to have. We'd all be one big, happy family living in the fat middle of an agrarian planet.

Then it occurred to me that even plants have a right to exist. What if they had feelings and just couldn't express them? What if they felt pain and were as desperate to live as everything else? And even if they weren't conscious, they were, as living things, privileged. They had as much right to live as anything else.

So in my perfect world I decided to do away with the herbivores too. Anything that nibbled leaves or bored holes in stems or gnawed seeds—terminated. Out of here.

That really narrowed down the players in my perfect world. In fact, it seemed that I was left with a wonderful bunch of nectar-feeding creatures—hummingbirds, butterflies, and honeybees.

Then it occurred to me that there wasn't any need for flowers. Because in a perfect world in which nothing died there was no reason to procreate. Have a lot of unchecked procreation in a perfect world and pretty soon you have overcrowding—which is less than perfect.

So I did away with procreation. If nothing dies, nothing needs replacement, right?

Now I really had a lot of room. In fact, my perfect world seemed to exist solely for creatures that were able to convert sunlight into food—the process called photosynthesis. Plants can do this . . . and a few microscopic organisms too.

I'd just learned about photosynthesis in biology. We'd done experiments involving microorganisms too. Then I recalled one experiment where we had subjected a bunch of microscopic organisms to light. And how they had tried to get away from the light, seeking the shelter of some shadow.

We didn't call it light, of course. We called it a negative stimulus, but the result was the same. The critters skedaddled like they'd been burned.

So in my perfect world—my hurtless, harmless world—there could be no light, I decided. It would be like the womb. It would be like the universe before hurt. It would be perfect. And so I said the words.

"Let there be darkness." And in my mind, it was so.

It didn't take long before I started adding elements of imperfection back into my perfect universe. Perfection might be perfect, but it is also boring. And life might be painful, but take it from me, it sure seems better than perfection.

There might be other ways to put a universe together—one in which tree swallows do not die; one in which life exists without risk. But after having taken creation back to the big bang and having taken upon myself the grave privilege of putting my finger in the dike to save a priceless nothing, I have chosen instead to accept life's pattern as it has evolved and hope, even if I sometimes find it hard to believe, that there is reason.

I navigated the meadows quickly because it was cold. It was empty—at least it was empty of tree swallows. During the night, huddled together in the *Phragmites*, the last of them had died.

I hope it didn't hurt them too much. I hope that there is a reason. But even if there is no reason, there is life, which I accept as the foundation of my faith. Risk may be the price, and the price is high, but the alternative? The alternative is hollow.

SPRING OF WONDER, AUTUMN OF MASTERY

It seems to me (with apologies extended to Hermann Hesse) that human lives are trapped between opposing poles. We aspire to freedom but crave security. We work toward what is right and good, but our feet invariably wander off the path of righteousness and into the tangles.

My regard for birds has been this way too: two-sided. On the one hand, the appeal of birds is aesthetic and emotional. It puts the "Wow!" in cardinals and the "Isn't that sweet?" in a chick-a-dee-dee-dee. The other side of my focus is acquisitive and analytical. It imparts significance to things like anchor-shaped patterns on scapulars, and it prompts me to stand in 103-degree heat in search of some bird whose only real appeal is that I have never seen it before.

Aesthetic appeal and analytical/acquisitive interest—the twin poles of birding. In my life they are represented by two experiences. The first I dubbed the Spring of Discovery; the second, the Autumn of Mastery. Neither event, I am inclined to believe, could be replicated today.

The Spring of Discovery occurred in May 1962. I was eleven and enjoying ill health (which means I was *supposed* to be quietly convalescing from minor surgery but wasn't). Instead, I was busy running around my parents' backyard trying to gain fragmentary glimpses of tiny treetop birds.

My parents' backyard was pretty typical of Suburbia, U.S.A.—a postage-stamp patch of grass ringed by trees. I'd started watching birds at the age of seven, and I'd seen a lot of good birds in that yard. Blue jays of the brassy voices, nesting brown thrasher that go right for your nose, tufted titmice . . . white-breasted nuthatches . . . and a tidy swarm of robin nestlings whose forsaken lives begged saving. Oh, I was one hotshot backyard birder all right. The best in the neighborhood.

But whatever my assumed proficiency, I had no sense of migration, no grasp of the biannual drama that carries discovery to every suburban doorstep. That all changed in 1962. That's what the Spring of Discovery was all about.

I guess I conned Mom into letting me sit outside. I guess I must have gotten bored with whatever school assignments I'd been saddled with and looked up at the tops of the oaks, and seen all the activity up there.

I guess I must have sprin . . . that is, limped painfully . . . into the house. And got my father's 6×24 binoculars. And the National Geographic Society's book about song and garden birds that served as my field guide.

I can stop guessing from this point. I *know* what happened next. My eyes grew wide with discovery and a host of images poured in. Thirty-five years later I can still recall each vivid encounter.

There was the zebra-striped warbler that moved like a nuthatch and the white-bottomed one whose back—when you finally got to see the back—was the even color of cool, green jade. There were yellow-bellied ones with necklaces and yellow-bellied ones without necklaces—and there was one, one absolutely, unbelievably beautiful-beyond-expression *one* whose throat was the color of a flame trapped in amber.

That one was called the Blackburnian. That one was my favorite.

There were other birds too. Baltimore orioles that glowed like peeled orange crayons, scarlet tanagers that blazed within their leafy confines like fanned charcoal in a patio grill. There was also one beautiful black-and-white bird whose bill was chalky white and whose chest bore a crimson bib.

That one was the rose-breasted grosbeak. That one was my favorite too.

It is interesting to note that bird song played no part in the Spring of Discovery, although certainly birds were just as vocal in 1962 as they are today. I wasn't interested in song. I was captivated by color.

It is also interesting to note that the flood of birds was not fallout-dependent (as migration in the Northeast is today). The day-to-day number and diversity were as constant as a shifting kaleidoscope. Morning or afternoon, I could pass my eyes through the treetops and relish the feeling of wonder. And I did too.

That was the Spring of Discovery. It spanned two weeks and lasted a lifetime. There have been many wonderful moments of discovery since then, but no time when wonder has so dominated the world.

The Autumn of Mastery came a little over a decade later. I was just out of college, jobbing as a carpet installer, and I had once again discovered the lure of birds. But something in my regard was different. Something had changed. I wasn't merely interested in seeing birds and enjoying birds—not exactly. What I was really interested in was seeking out birds that I had never seen before and pinning names to them.

I was also frustrated and angry. Frustrated because the plumages of the "confusing fall warblers" were all so *confusing*. Angry because my marginal field identification skills were holding me back, preventing me from seeing the subtle distinctions that would add species to my list.

So one day in early September, on a morning so cool it brought a jacket out of the closet, I grabbed my binoculars and went into the woods—to a brushy clearing surrounded by second-growth forest that bordered a lake. I staked myself out in the center of the clearing vowing to "learn 'em or die." The outcome, for the first hour or so, was never certain.

All around the clearing, little green birds flickered and danced.

Dozens of them. Scores! They almost never sat in the open. They never took perches for long. And every time my binoculars were brought to bear some sixth sense seemed to warn them that their identities were in jeopardy. They reacted by boring little warbler-sized holes into the foliage.

As minutes passed and my angst mounted, the "confusing fall warblers" became those "frustrating fall warblers," became those "damned fall warblers." But just when my pique was reaching its peak, my binoculars chanced to fall upon one particular yellow-bellied bird—and the kaleidoscope stopped shifting.

In many respects, it was like all the rest of the birds in the clearing. Just another green and yellow bird with wing bars and white in the tail. But there was something different about its chest. The chest had a pale gray band across it, like the critter had been tie-dyed or something.

The band wasn't as sharply defined as wing bars and tail spots—those little building blocks of identification that I had dutifully learned and had come to count on. It was subtle, the mere shadow of a field mark. But it was nevertheless discernable, and it differentiated the bird from all the rest. The question was, *was* it a field mark?

I looked at the plate in the book. And there it was. The telltale mark. The tie-dyed warbler. An immature magnolia.

"*Gotcha,*" I whispered, and it came out a hiss. "Got you." And that's all it took. One catalytic bird. One bird to serve as a measure of comparison for all the rest. Gradually, one by cryptic one, the other denizens of the glen surrendered their identities—chestnut-sided warblers (without chestnut sides), yellow warblers (that weren't yellow), bay-breasted warblers (sans bay). One by one, I gathered them with my growing arsenal of skills.

There is something interesting about the phrase "got you." It denotes possession, and possession is a form of control. I didn't consciously realize this at the time. It wasn't, in fact, until years later that I was able to put the acquisitive side of birding into perspective. The catalyst was a work of fantasy written by Ursula Le Guin called *Earthsea Trilogy.* In this trilogy, Le Guin describes an elemental language, the language of the Beginning. In this language, all things are known by their true names. The language is secret, of course—known only to dragons and the odd wizard or two—and this is good. Why? Because anyone who knows the language and the true name of a thing has mastery over that thing. They control it.

That's what I was doing during the Autumn of Mastery. I was pinning names to birds and making them mine. For most of my adult birding life, my focus has been the naming and claiming of birds . . . and the acquisition of greater skills to apply to these ambitions.

The Spring of Discovery and the Autumn of Mastery—pivotal events that anchored my perspective and my life. Maybe other birders know a similar development; maybe not. But one thing I do know. Were I growing up in Whippany, New Jersey, today, it is unlikely that I would have the benefit of those experiences to anchor the poles of my life.

Why? Because now in spring there is no river of birds sweeping through the trees around my parents' house. There is not even a steady stream. What passes in May is hardly a trickle. The swarm of treetop birds who snared me in a net of color and WONDER during the Spring of Discovery are a vestige of what they once were and easily overlooked.

The clutch of confusing fall warblers that offered direct comparison and ushered in the Autumn of Mastery too are a shadow of their former abundance. In fact, I have never again seen so many assembled in the clearing by the lake as I did that day.

And if I were growing up in northern New Jersey today, and there was no Spring of Discovery or Autumn of Mastery, I wonder where else I would have planted the poles that define my life and what sort of life this would have defined.

But a greater part prompts me to wonder what this means to birding's future, if those young people growing up today can find no wonder and will never know mastery.

RIVER DIPPING

We were standing ankle-deep in frost-covered grass. Stripped down to T-shirts and shorts and shivering like poplar trees in a northwest gale. It was first-period gym class, third down, and long yardage (a condition that I have come to regard as a metaphor for my life). Facing off across the line of scrimmage were the fellow members of my high school senior class. On the sidelines, prodding us toward responsible, regimented adulthood, was Good Coach Teddy Bear.

Coach Teddy Bear, who could make a freshman lose bladder control with a glance.

Coach Teddy Bear, whose list of warm-up calisthenics would have exhausted Arnold Schwarzenegger merely to recite.

Coach Teddy Bear, who in the collective memory of Whippany Park High School students was never heard to utter anything more sentimental than "Shower up."

As my classmates took their positions, a sound lofted out of the sky that put the game and all within hearing on hold. It was the sound of geese, one of the most magical sounds on earth, and it was drawing closer.

First one, then another, linebacker, tight end, and offensive lineman (or if you prefer, future accountant, future car salesman, future chemical engineer) stopped what they were doing, straightened, and looked up. In seconds, not a person on the field didn't have his face raised.

It was a large flock, a hundred birds or more, and not very high—not as migrating flocks go. They were close enough to make out the things that birders call field marks, the things that distinguish Canada geese from other geese. But they were distant enough that nothing but our longing could reach them.

One minute passed, two. The sound receded and the great phalanx of birds moved out of sight. Suddenly and simultaneously the chill realization struck.

We'd delayed the game without sanction. We'd courted the wrath of the Teddy Bear and the price would be pain.

Some bravely, some timorously, my classmates and I turned to face our fate—only to discover that the coach seemed oblivious to our indiscretion. In fact, he seemed to have forgotten us. He was still watching the geese, and it seemed to those who stood closest that his eyes were wet.

After another minute, Whippany Park High School's Prince of Pain raised a paw, wiped it across his Marine recruitment poster face, and turned toward the class.

"Wasn't that just too purty?" he said.

It was all we could do to keep from comporting ourselves like freshmen.

I am middle-aged, well-traveled, and fortunate—fortunate to have seen many of the massed bird spectacles the planet has to offer. Flamingo-frosted Lake Borgoria in Kenya, corella clouds at Fog Dam, Australia, snow geese rising off Delaware Bay marshes like an ascending avalanche of white-hot sound.

But the greatest spectacles of all, the ones that mark my past and draw my future, are the ones that take *mass,* add *movement,* and divide it with a *horizon* line. Above all the things that I love about birds, I love migration best.

It's not just numbers because, as I have said, I've seen numbers. They are awe-inspiring, but they are not alluring.

It's not just movement either. I marvel at the falcon's flight and the sympatric precision of shorebird flocks. But I am not captivated. I know what tricks lie hidden beneath the magician's cape.

But when birds rise into the sky and set off to vault hemispheres, something rises in me. I do not know what it is. I scarcely know how to describe it. But I am confident my regard is shared and universal. Why? Two reasons.

First, because there are in this world birders, and I submit that without migration there would be no birders as we know them. There would be ornithologists, who study birds as a scientific endeavor. There would be backyard birdwatchers whose interest in aviforms might be likened to avian landscaping. There just wouldn't be questing, limit-pushing birders.

Quest, after all, needs more than objective: it needs gratification. If every walk through the woods reaped the same rewards (robin, towhee, chickadee) and offered no greater prize or promise (*Connecticut warbler!!!*), quest would have quit, enthusiasm would have succumbed, to ennui long before anyone's interest was piqued. What drives birders to grab binoculars and vault outdoors is the possibility of finding something new.

Migration rolls the dice.

My second reason for believing that migration enjoys near universal allure? Look, if migrating birds can wring rapport out of the impassive likes of Coach Teddy Bear, they can strum a responsive chord in any soul. Including *mine*.

Including *yours*. Go ahead. Look back. Do an accounting of your own great encounters with birds. Not just the exciting ones. Not just the "Oh boy! There it is!" ones. The great ones. I'll bet you'll find, as I did, that most fit the migratory equation: *mass* plus *movement* divided by the *horizon*.

It was binoculars and a book given to a friend in the summer of 1958 that oriented me toward birds—and made catbirds and cardinals the focus of my life. But it was a flood of migrants in the spring of 1962 that put me in touch with a world of color and song and made me aware of possibilities undreamed of.

I was oarless and rudderless in the fall of 1975. And then one day I watched as a river of raptors flowed by. On that day, my life found mooring on a stony hilltop above Kempton, Pennsylvania. A place called Hawk Mountain.

Among the things I love most in this world are fallouts in May;

waves of sharp-shinned hawks pulsing through trees in October; shorebird clouds rising, circling, and setting off toward the Arctic; and the yelp of thrushes on moonless nights.

The most desperate escape I ever witnessed involved a southbound sharp-shinned hawk. The bird was caught offshore, forced to run a gauntlet of herring and black-backed gulls from the horizon to the beach—and it won.

The greatest predator-prey encounter also involved a migrating sharp-shinned hawk. The bird was flying down the tree line north of the hawk watch platform at Cape May Point when it was blindsided by a peregrine, who ferried it from the world of the living to the world of the dead but no further. A northern harrier was on the falcon immediately. The surprised falcon released the sharpie right into the harrier's waiting talons.

Perhaps the most startling act of retaliation I ever witnessed involved a migrating bird and a migrating insect, a monarch butterfly. The young kingbird made a sortie in the insect's direction, snapped, missed, and returned to its perch. The butterfly doubled back and made repeated stoops on the kingbird's head—forcing the young tyrant flycatcher to duck each time.

But without question, the most moving thing I have ever witnessed involved an evening at Cape May Point and a host of migrating passerines. As evening darkened, a host of birds began rising out of the woods and fields of Cape May Point. First there were hundreds, then thousands—robins, waxwings, sparrows, hermit thrushes, and other late-season migrants. They poured from the trees in such numbers that it seemed the woodlands must deflate, and as they climbed they called, filling the air with the calls birds use to encourage each other across the long, dark miles.

It must take great courage to be a bird or it must take great faith, but whichever it is I have taken this moment and others to heart.

There was a Greek philosopher named Heraclitus who once observed that one can put one's foot in a river only once. His point being that a river is constantly changing, never the same, one moment to the next. And he was right.

He had a student who, in the spirit of student trying to outdo the master, carried Heraclitus' observation one step farther. He, the student, said one could not put one's foot in the river even once, because the very act altered the river. He was right too, but he missed something.

People who place themselves in the river's flow not only change the river, they change themselves. As I have changed. As you have changed. As we continue to change. We who stand on the bank of the great north-south river of birds, waiting to see what the next moment brings.

ST MARK'S GOSPEL

ST MARK'S
Gospel

A Commentary for Believers

THOMAS CREAN, O.P.

AROUCA
PRESS

ISBN: 978-1-990685-43-9 (pbk)
ISBN: 978-1-990685-44-6 (hc)

Arouca Press
PO Box 55003
Bridgeport PO
Waterloo, ON N2J 3G0
Canada
www.aroucapress.com
Send inquiries to info@aroucapress.com

DEDICATION

This book is dedicated to the Benedictine monks of
Silverstream Priory, in gratitude for their great hospitality

"If I say, 'Suppose the Divine did really walk and talk upon the earth, what should we be likely to think of it?' then the foundations of my mind are moved. So far as I can form any conjecture, I think we should see in such a being exactly the perplexities that we see in the central figure of the Gospels: I think he would seem to us extreme and violent; because he would see some further development in virtue which would be for us untried. I think he would seem to us to contradict himself; because looking down on life like a map he would see a connection between things which to us are disconnected. [...]

"I think there would be, in the nature of things, some tragic collision between him and the humanity he had created, culminating in something that would be at once a crime and an expiation. I think he would be blamed as a hard prophet for dragging down the haughty, and blamed also as a weak sentimentalist for loving the things that cling in corners, children or beggars. I think, in short, that he would give us a sensation that he was turning all our standards upside down, and yet also a sensation that he had undeniably put them the right way up.

"So, if I had been a Greek sage or an Arab poet before Christ, I should have figured to myself, in a dream, what would actually happen if this earth bore secretly somewhere the father of gods and men." (Gilbert Chesterton, *The Hibbert Journal*, April 1910)

CONTENTS

PREFACE

IN THESE NOTES ON ST MARK'S GOSPEL, AS in my notes on St Luke, I have mostly put down such thoughts, and tried to answer such questions, as came to my own mind on reading these familiar words once more. As seasoning, I have added a few quotations from ancient writers and a few suggestions from modern ones. I have not always multiplied footnotes to indicate my sources, not wanting to give too scholarly an appearance to a book offered mainly as spiritual reading.

Since almost all the teachings and events narrated in the second gospel are also found either in St Matthew or St Luke, I have not tried to comment on everything, but rather to look especially at the many places where this evangelist adds some detail or vivid touch that is unique to himself. I have assumed the truth of the very widespread and early tradition that St Mark drew his gospel from the preaching of St Peter at Rome. The Pontifical Biblical Commission, in the days when it was still an organ of the Church's magisterium, affirmed that there were no good grounds for doubting this tradition. I suggest in various places that recognising Peter as the evangelist's source sheds light on details within the story.

St Albert the Great, if the book *On Cleaving to God* is from him, said that 'a man prays by what he is.' In the same way, a man comments on the gospels by what he is: what strikes us as worth saying will depend on our pre-existing interests and convictions. In this sense, the authors who influence a commentary will be far more numerous than those who have been immediately consulted in the writing of it. But the present notes have made use of St Bede's *Commentary on St Mark,* the *Catena Aurea* of St Thomas Aquinas, and the *Great Commentary* of Cornelius à Lapide. Among modern writers I am particularly indebted, like many other people, to Scott Hahn, both for the excellent *Ignatius Catholic Study Bible* annotated by him and Curtis Mitch, and for some of his other presentations. I have also benefitted from the expertise of my confrere, Fr Richard Ounsworth.

As well as other 19th to 21st century commentaries on this gospel, both Catholic and Protestant, I have consulted the second volume of the *Sacra Pagina* series, but despite its erudition can hardly recommend it, on account of the Modernism that disfigures it. These present notes, for all their limitations, seek at least to be faithful not only to Pope St Pius X's definitions of the duties of the exegete, but also to the solemn teaching of the 2nd Vatican Council that "the four gospels, whose historical character the Church unhesitatingly asserts, faithfully hand on what Jesus Christ, while living among men, really did and taught for their eternal salvation until the day He was taken up into heaven."

Holy Cross Priory,
Feast of St Bede,
AD 2022

ABOUT THE AUTHOR
ANCIENT TESTIMONIES

ST LUKE

"Peter coming to himself, said: Now I know in very deed, that the Lord hath sent his angel, and hath delivered me out of the hand of Herod, and from all the expectation of the people of the Jews. And considering, he came to the house of Mary the mother of John, who was surnamed Mark, where many were gathered together and praying" (Acts 12:12)

"Barnabas and Saul returned from Jerusalem, having fulfilled their ministry, taking with them John, who was surnamed Mark [. . .] being sent by the Holy Ghost, went to Seleucia: and from thence they sailed to Cyprus. And when they were come to Salamina, they preached the word of God in the synagogues of the Jews. And they had John also in the ministry [. . .] When Paul and they that were with him had sailed from Paphos, they came to Perge in Pamphylia. And John departing from them, returned to Jerusalem" (Acts 12:25, 13:4–5, 13).

"And after some days, Paul said to Barnabas: Let us return and visit our brethren in all the cities wherein we have preached the word of the Lord, to see how they do. And Barnabas would have taken with them John also, that was surnamed Mark. But Paul desired that he (as having departed from them out of Pamphylia, and not gone with them to the work) might not be received. And there arose a dissension, so that they departed one from another; and Barnabas indeed taking Mark, sailed to Cyprus" (Acts 15:36–39).

ST PAUL

"Aristarchus, my fellow prisoner, saluteth you, and Mark, the cousin german of Barnabas, touching whom you have received commandments; if he come unto you, receive him: and Jesus, that is called Justus: who are of the circumcision: these only are my helpers in the kingdom of God; who have been a comfort to me" (Col. 4:10–11).

"There salute thee Epaphras, my fellow prisoner in Christ Jesus; Mark, Aristarchus, Demas, and Luke my fellow labourers" (Philemon 23–24).

"Only Luke is with me. Take Mark, and bring him with thee: for he is profitable to me for the ministry" (2 Tim. 4:11).

ST PETER

"The church that is in Babylon, elected together with you, saluteth you: and so doth my son Mark" (1 Pet. 5:13).

PAPIAS *(bishop of Hierapolis in Anatolia, writing around AD 100)*

"Mark, having become the interpreter of Peter, wrote down accurately, though not in order, whatsoever he remembered of the things said or done by Christ. For he neither heard the Lord nor followed him, but afterward, as I said, he followed Peter, who adapted his teaching to the needs of his hearers, but with no intention of giving a connected account of the Lord's discourses, so that Mark committed no error while he thus wrote some things as he remembered them. For he was careful of one thing, not to omit any of the things which he had heard, and not to state any of them falsely" (recorded by Eusebius of Caesarea, *Ecclesiastical History*, bk. 3.39).

ST IRENAEUS *(C. 130–202)*

"Matthew also issued a written Gospel among the Hebrews in their own dialect, while Peter and Paul were preaching at Rome, and laying the foundations of the Church. After their departure, Mark, the disciple and interpreter of Peter, did also hand down to us in writing what had been preached by Peter [. . .] He commences with the prophetical spirit coming down from on high to men, saying, *The beginning of the Gospel of Jesus Christ, as it is written in Esaias the prophet*, pointing to the winged aspect of the Gospel;[1] and on this account he made a compendious and cursory narrative, for such is the prophetical character" (*Against the Heresies*, bk. 3.11.8)

---

1 He is interpreting the four living creatures of the Apocalypse, and sees the eagle as representing St Mark. St Augustine offers another interpretation.

CLEMENT OF ALEXANDRIA *(c.150–215)*

"So greatly did the splendour of piety illumine the minds of Peter's hearers that they were not satisfied with hearing once only, and were not content with the unwritten teaching of the divine Gospel, but with all sorts of entreaties they besought Mark, a follower of Peter, and the one whose Gospel is extant, that he would leave them a written monument of the doctrine which had been orally communicated to them. Nor did they cease until they had prevailed with the man, and had thus become the occasion of the written Gospel which bears the name of Mark.

"And they say that Peter—when he had learned, through a revelation of the Spirit, of that which had been done—was pleased with the zeal of the men, and that the work obtained the sanction of his authority for the purpose of being used in the churches. (*Hypotyposes,* book VIII, recorded by Eusebius of Caesarea, *Ecclesiastical History*, bk. 2.15).

TERTULLIAN *(c.155–220)*

"The gospel which Mark published may be affirmed to be Peter's, whose interpreter Mark was" (*Against Marcion*, bk. 4.5)

ST HIPPOLYTUS OF ROME *(c. 170–c. 235)*

"Whenever Marcion or any of his dogs shall bay against the Creator, bringing forward arguments from the comparison of good and evil, they should be told that neither the apostle Paul nor Mark of the maimed finger[2] reported these things (*The Refutation of All Heresies,* bk. 7, chapter 3).

---

2 *Kolodaktulos*, a rare Greek word that means 'mutilated in regard to one's finger'. A prologue to St Mark's gospel that appears in some ancient Latin manuscripts says that his fingers were short in comparison to the size of the rest of his body. A later story or legend was that he had cut off his thumb in order to be ineligible for the Jewish priesthood. Some people have ingeniously suggested that the Greek word is a metaphorical reference to his having left St Paul (Acts 13:13), by comparison to those who cut off a thumb in order to be ineligible for military service. No one knows the truth of the matter.

ORIGEN *(c. 184–255)*

"The second gospel is by Mark, who composed it according to the instructions of Peter, who in his Catholic epistle acknowledges him as a son" (recorded by Eusebius of Caesarea, *Ecclesiastical History*, bk. 6.25)

EUSEBIUS OF CAESAREA *(c. 260–340)*

"They say that this Mark was the first that was sent to Egypt, and that he proclaimed the Gospel which he had written, and first established churches in Alexandria" (*Ecclesiastical History*, bk. 2.15–16).

ST EPIPHANIUS *(c. 310–403)*

"Mark was ordered by St Peter at Rome to issue the gospel, and after writing it was sent by St Peter to Egypt. He was one of the seventy-two who had been dispersed by the Lord's saying, 'Unless a man eat my flesh and drink my blood, he is not worthy of me', as is proved to the readers of the gospels. Still, after his restoration by Peter he was privileged to proclaim the gospel by the inspiration of the Holy Ghost" (*Panarion*, 51.6).[3]

ST JEROME *(c. 345–419/20)*

"Taking the gospel which he himself composed, Mark went to Egypt. First preaching Christ at Alexandria, he formed a church so admirable in doctrine and continence of living that he constrained all followers of Christ to his example. Philo, a learned Jew, seeing the first church at Alexandria still Jewish in a degree, wrote a book on their manner of life, as something creditable to his own nation. Just as Luke recounts how the believers had all things in common at Jerusalem, so Philo recorded what he saw done at Alexandria, under the teaching of Mark. Mark died in the eighth year of Nero and was buried at Alexandria" (*On Famous Men*, 8).[4]

---

3 St Epiphanius's statement that St Mark had been one of the seventy-two is not compatible with Papias's much earlier testimony as reported by Eusebius. At this distance of time it seems impossible, again, to know who was right.

4 The identity of the community about whom Philo wrote is disputed.

"Mark is the second, the interpreter of the apostle Peter and the first bishop of the Alexandrian church, who indeed did not himself see the Lord and Saviour, but he narrated the things which he had heard his master preaching, following the historical truth of the events more than their sequence" (*Commentary on St Matthew*, preface).

ST AUGUSTINE *(354–430)*

"Mark, who chose neither to speak of Christ's kingly lineage, nor of the priestly stock or priestly consecration, and who treats instead of the things which the man Christ did, appears to be symbolised among those four living creatures {of the Apocalypse} by the figure of the man" (*On the Agreement of the Gospel-writers*, I.6).

ST BEDE *(672/3–735)*

"They say that he was of the Israelite nation, and sprang from priestly stock" (*Commentary on the gospel of St Mark*, prefatory letter).

The 8th year of Nero was around AD 62. Some authors think that this was in fact the date when St Mark appointed a successor at Alexandria before going to Rome.

COMMENTARY
on the
GOSPEL OF ST. MARK

1 The beginning of the gospel of Jesus Christ, the Son of God.

2 As it is written in Isaias the prophet: Behold I send my angel before thy face, who shall prepare the way before thee.

3 A voice of one crying in the desert: Prepare ye the way of the Lord, make straight his paths.

4 John was in the desert baptizing, and preaching the baptism of penance, unto remission of sins.

5 And there went out to him all the country of Judea, and all they of Jerusalem, and were baptized by him in the river of Jordan, confessing their sins.

6 And John was clothed with camel's hair, and a leathern girdle about his loins; and he ate locusts and wild honey.

7 And he preached, saying: There cometh after me one mightier than I, the latchet of whose shoes I am not worthy to stoop down and loose.

8 I have baptized you with water; but he shall baptize you with the Holy Ghost.

9 And it came to pass, in those days, Jesus came from

vv. 1–3

ST MARK STARTS WITH THE WORDS *THE beginning of the gospel*: this means both the beginning of his book, and the beginning of the public proclamation of the good tidings that he is recording. The Greek word for gospel, *euangelion*, was used of oracles from the Roman emperor that were supposed to gladden his people.

He introduces his quotation from Isaias by adapting one from Malachias. God had said through Malachias: *Behold I send my angel, and he shall prepare the way before my face.* St John the Baptist is *the angel*, both because he is a messenger and because of his purity of life. But St Mark changes the prophet's words to *before thy face*, to reveal the Father speaking to the Son. The evangelist makes this free use of the Old Testament to show that the Son is also the God who spoke through the prophets. At the same time, he is evoking a passage in Exodus, where God said to the people *I send my angel before thy face*. In this way, he suggests that Christ will accomplish, but more perfectly, that which Israel did in its exodus: but only by reading to the end of the gospel shall we understand this.

v. 4–11

By virtue of his distinctive garb and penitential life, St John is reckoned the patron of monks and other religious. In saying that he is *not worthy to stoop down and loose the latchet* of Christ's sandals, he is perhaps recalling a rite of the law of Moses, whereby a man separated himself from his claim on the bride whom he would otherwise have espoused by allowing his sandal to be removed. His words are thus a particularly apt way for the Baptist to deny that he is himself the Messiah, since as he says elsewhere of Jesus: *He who has the bride is the bridegroom.*

Since Christian baptism is also done *with water*, why does John contrast it with his own? His words make sense only if Christian baptism has also the power to infuse *the Holy Spirit*.

3

Nazareth of Galilee, and was baptized by John in the Jordan.

10 And forthwith coming up out of the water, he saw the heavens opened, and the

Spirit as a dove descending, and remaining on him.

11 And there came a voice from heaven: Thou art my beloved Son; in thee I am well pleased.

12 And immediately the Spirit drove him out into the desert.

13 And he was in the desert forty days and forty nights, and was tempted by Satan; and he was with beasts, and the angels ministered to him.

14 And after that John was delivered up, Jesus came into Galilee, preaching the gospel of the kingdom of God,

15 And saying: The time is accomplished, and the kingdom of God is at hand: repent, and believe the gospel.

When our Lord is baptised, the Father is fittingly revealed by the *voice from heaven*, since He speaks the Word from eternity. The Holy *Spirit* is revealed by the *dove*, since He proceeds in eternity by way of love, and it is by love that man is made innocent. Christ Himself did not need to learn that He is the Father's *beloved Son*; the voice comes to reward the Baptist's faith. God the Father thus becomes the first preacher of the gospel.

vv. 12–13

Does the Holy Spirit have authority over Christ, since He *drove him out into the wilderness*? In His humanity, Christ was subject to the Holy Spirit; but this verse refers especially to the intense charity of His human soul, infused by the Holy Ghost, by which He was impelled to go to the wilderness to pray and fast for mankind.

Only St Mark mentions *the wild beasts* who were with Him there. Abba Paul of the Thebaid, one of the desert Fathers, said: "If a man has obtained purity, everything is in submission to him, as it was to Adam when he was in Paradise before he transgressed." How much more were these beasts tame toward Christ, the new Adam.

vv. 14–15

What would His hearers have understood, when He preached that *the kingdom of God* was *at hand*? They would have spontaneously thought of the kingdom of David, which had been briefly glorious a thousand years before, under David himself and Solomon his son. This was the kingdom that had continued, though weakened, for another four hundred years after Solomon's time, but which had now been in abeyance for longer than it had stood. This is the kingdom that the prophets had said would return, transformed, when *the time* was *accomplished*.

Christ delays his preaching in *Galilee* until John has been *delivered up* to Herod, lest He seem to be competing with His cousin.

16 And passing by the sea of Galilee, he saw Simon and Andrew his brother, casting nets into the sea (for they were fishermen).

17 And Jesus said to them: Come after me, and I will make you to become fishers of men.

18 And immediately leaving their nets, they followed him.

19 And going on from thence a little farther, he saw James the son of Zebedee, and John his brother, who also were mending their nets in the ship:

20 And forthwith he called them. And leaving their father Zebedee in the ship with his hired men, they followed him.

21 And they entered into Capharnaum, and forthwith upon the sabbath days going into the synagogue, he taught them.

22 And they were astonished at his doctrine. For he was teaching them as one having power, and not as the scribes.

23 And there was in their synagogue a man with an unclean spirit; and he cried out,

24 Saying: What have we to do with thee, Jesus of Nazareth? art thou come to

destroy us? I know who thou art, the Holy One of God.

25 And Jesus threatened him, saying: Speak no more, and go out of the man.

26 And the unclean spirit tearing him, and crying out with

vv. 16–20

Speaking through the prophet Jeremias, the Lord had predicted a new exodus that would cause the old exodus from Egypt to be forgotten, and had said: *Behold, I will send many fishers, and they shall fish them.*[1] He now begins to fulfil this by calling the first four apostles. In the same place He had told Jeremias that he must remain unmarried, unusually for those times. This was to show that the preaching of the new exodus would supersede carnal ties; and so here also *James and John left their father.*

They also leave *the hired servants*: the word may also be translated as 'hireling', as in the parable of the Good Shepherd. This shows that the preachers of the new exodus must not be motivated by hope of a temporal reward, or else they will flee when the wolf comes.

The Lord calls one pair of brothers who are *casting nets*, and another pair who are *mending the nets*, perhaps to show that He calls men of both active and contemplative character for His service.

vv. 21–22

Christ begins His teaching *immediately on the Sabbath*. Since He will die on a Friday afternoon, the whole of His ministry takes place symbolically within a single week. Of course, really it took much longer: but symbolically, our Lord appears as one bringing about a new creation, foreshadowed by the week of creation in the beginning. Hence St Mark's repeated use of the word *immediately*, creating the impression of many events happening in a brief time.

vv. 23–28

Why are the devils called *unclean*? A thing becomes unclean when something of less value than itself so clings to it as to remove its proper beauty. The angelic spirits were created beautiful; those who fell chose inordinate self-love as their end, which now sticks to them irredeemably.

---

1 Jer. 16:16.

a loud voice, went out of him.

27 And they were all amazed, insomuch that they questioned among themselves, saying: What thing is this? what is this new doctrine?

for with power he commandeth even the unclean spirits, and they obey him.

28 And the fame of him was spread forthwith into all the country of Galilee.

29 And immediately going out of the synagogue they came into the house of Simon and Andrew, with James and John.

30 And Simon's wife's mother lay in a fit of a fever: and forthwith they told him of her.

31 And coming to her, he lifted her up, taking her by the hand; and immediately the fever left her, and she ministered unto them.

32 And when it was evening, after sunset, they brought to him all that were ill and that were possessed with devils.

33 And all the city was gathered together at the door.

34 And he healed many that were troubled with divers diseases; and he cast out many devils, and he suffered them not to speak, because they knew him.

vv. 29–34

This simple episode is a miniature of Christ's earthly mission: He teaches *with authority*, overcomes the devil, and passes from the synagogue to the *house of Simon* Peter.

Since a bishop is thought of as the spouse of his Church, Peter, as the first pope, will in a sense be the spouse of the universal Church. His *mother-in-law* is thus symbolically Eve, the mother of all the living. Christ's first day of ministry therefore seems like an overcoming of the first sin in Eden: He has overthrown the devil and *lifted up* the woman. But why is there is no one to symbolise Adam? He is Himself the new Adam.

St Matthew and St Luke say that Christ went from the synagogue into Simon Peter's house. St Peter, preaching to the Romans, recalls that the house was also that of his brother *Andrew*.

In a detail not found in the other gospels, St Peter recalls how that night, *the whole city was gathered together about* his front *door*. They are also gathered together about the One who said *I am the door of the sheep*.

How is it that *many* people are possessed by *demons* in one town? Perhaps the demons had been drawn to the region in their desire to discover Jesus's identity, and being frustrated had taken their revenge on His neighbours. *They knew him* to be a man without sin, but they did not know if He could be the Word incarnate. *If they had known*, says St Paul, *they would never have crucified the Lord of glory*.

9

35 And rising very early, going out, he went into a desert place: and there he prayed.

36 And Simon, and they that were with him, followed after him.

37 And when they had found him, they said to him: All seek for thee.

38 And he saith to them: Let us go into the neighbouring towns and cities, that I may preach there also; for to this purpose am I come.

39 And he was preaching in their synagogues, and in all Galilee, and casting out devils.

40 And there came a leper to him, beseeching him, and kneeling down said to him: If thou wilt, thou canst make me clean.

41 And Jesus having compassion on him, stretched forth his hand; and touching him, saith to him: I will. Be thou made clean.

42 And when he had spoken, immediately the leprosy departed from him, and he was made clean.

43 And he strictly charged him, and forthwith sent him away.

44 And he saith to him: See thou tell no one; but go, shew thyself to the high priest, and offer for thy cleansing the things that Moses commanded, for a testimony to them.

45 But he being gone out, began to publish and to blaze abroad the word: so that he could not openly go into the city, but was without in desert places: and they flocked to him from all sides.

vv. 35–39

Since the previous day had been the Sabbath, by telling us that the Lord went to pray next morning *a great while before day*, St Mark shows Him as sanctifying the Sunday.

When He says *that is why I came out*, He is speaking not only of His leaving Nazareth but also intimating His eternal origin. And since He came forth in eternity as the Word, what else would He do in time but *preach*?

vv. 40–45

Though the *leprosy* of New Testament times may have included what is called by that name today, it refers to a wider range of diseases of the skin. Why does our Lord speak *sternly* to this man for whom He had also felt *pity*? The word might also be translated 'peremptorily'. He wanted to cut short public expressions of gratitude, not only from humility and to set an example but also so that the man might immediately fulfil his own legal duty of offering *what Moses commanded*.

Jesus could no longer openly enter a town, in the sense that people were so excited by the sudden availability of miracles that they were not ready to receive what was more important to Him, His teaching.

1 And again he entered into Capharnaum after some days.

2 And it was heard that he was in the house, and many came together, so that there was no room; no, not even at the door; and he spoke to them the word.

3 And they came to him, bringing one sick of the palsy, who was carried by four.

4 And when they could not offer him unto Jesus for the multitude, they uncovered the roof where he was; and opening it, they let down the bed wherein the man sick of the palsy lay.

5 And when Jesus had seen their faith, he saith to the man sick of the palsy: Son, thy sins are forgiven thee.

6 And there were some of the scribes sitting there, and thinking in their hearts:

7 Why doth this man speak thus? he blasphemeth. Who can forgive sins, but God only?

8 Which Jesus presently knowing in his spirit, that they so thought within themselves, saith to them: Why think you these things in your hearts?

9 Which is easier, to say to the sick of the palsy: Thy sins are forgiven thee; or to say: Arise, take up thy bed, and walk?

10 But that you may know that the Son of man hath power on earth to forgive sins, (he saith to the sick of the palsy,)

11 I say to thee: Arise, take up thy bed, and go into thy house.

12 And immediately he arose; and taking up his bed, went his way in the sight of all; so that all wondered and glorified God, saying: We never saw the like.

13 And he went forth again to the seaside; and all the multitude came to him, and he taught them.

14 And when he was passing by, he saw Levi the son of Alpheus sitting at the receipt of custom; and he saith to him: Follow me. And rising up, he followed him.

vv. 1–12

WHEN OUR LORD RETURNS TO PREACH IN Capharnaum, the crowds are even greater, so that this time, there is *no longer room even about the door*. This is a lesson to preachers, that they will find more hearers by shunning popularity.

Since He is the image of the invisible Father, His mission has a paternal character, and so He calls the one whom He heals, *Child*.

He *perceived in his spirit* what the scribes were saying *within themselves*. This is an example of prophetic knowledge, since by natural knowledge not even the angels can know the thoughts of our heart.

Only St Mark specifies that it was *four men* who brought the paralytic. The Book of Wisdom tells us that there are four great moral virtues: *temperance, and prudence, and justice, and fortitude*. Having these, we are better able to bring others to Christ.

He calls Himself *Son of man* for the first time when speaking of the *power to forgive sins*. The prophet Daniel saw as it were *a Son of man* being presented to the Ancient of days, that is, to God, and receiving from Him *power, and glory, and a kingdom*. Christ thus shows that His kingdom is founded on His power to forgive sins, a power which He brought from heaven by the incarnation and which now exists permanently *on earth*.

vv. 13–17

Were these *scribes and the Pharisees* truly *just*? No, since no one can be just in the sight of God without that faith in His Son which is called 'justifying faith'. Without this faith it is impossible even to fulfil the ten commandments for long. These scribes

15 And it came to pass, that as he sat at supper in his house, many publicans and sinners sat down together with Jesus and his disciples. For they were many, who also followed him.

16 And the scribes and the Pharisees, seeing that he ate with publicans and sinners,

said to his disciples: Why doth your master eat and drink with publicans and sinners?

17 Jesus hearing this, saith to them: They that are well have no need of a physician, but they that are sick. For I came not to call the just, but sinners.

18 And the disciples of John and the Pharisees used to fast; and they come and say to him: Why do the disciples of John and of the Pharisees fast; but thy disciples do not fast?

19 And Jesus saith to them: Can the children of the marriage fast, as long as the bridegroom is with them? As long as they have the bridegroom with them, they cannot fast.

20 But the days will come when the bridegroom shall be taken away from them;

and then they shall fast in those days.

21 No man seweth a piece of raw cloth to an old garment: otherwise the new piecing taketh away from the old, and there is made a greater rent.

22 And no man putteth new wine into old bottles: otherwise the wine will burst the bottles, and both the wine will be spilled, and the bottles will be lost. But new wine must be put into new bottles.

23 And it came to pass again, as the Lord walked through the corn fields on the sabbath, that his disciples began to go forward, and to pluck the ears of corn.

24 And the Pharisees said to him: Behold, why do they

on the sabbath day that which is not lawful?

25 And he said to them: Have you never read what David did when he had need, and was hungry himself, and they that were with him?

26 How he went into the house of God, under Abiathar the

14

and Pharisees simply had some outward justice, as regards the more obvious parts of the law, which the *publicans and sinners* had lacked up till now.

The *children of the marriage* is a Hebrew idiom for 'the wedding-guests'. But the *sinners* sanctified by justifying faith are also His bride, the Church.

We *fast* since the Ascension, since the *Bridegroom* has been *taken away* as regards His visible presence. But He is present in the sacrament of the altar, and so those who recognise Him there *cannot fast*, but feast on His flesh and blood.

vv. 18–22

The imperfect justice of the Pharisees is compared to *an old garment*. They are not yet ready to hear the gospel, which is compared to a *new piecing*. If they adopted the gospel in the same spirit in which they sought to obey the law of Moses, as a means to establish their justice, the *rent*, or 'schism', that separates them from God would grow even *greater*. Christ is thus the *man* who will not put the *new wine* of the gospel into the *old bottles* who are the Pharisees, lest swelling with pride they *burst* and be *lost* for good. The former publicans like *Levi*, however, have become *new bottles* by their faith.

vv. 23–28

The reference to how David and his men ate the *loaves of proposition* or 'bread of the presence' *in the house of God* is first of all, an argument *a fortiori*. If in an emergency it was lawful to use even sacred food that the Law explicitly reserved to the priests, then how much more is it lawful to use food that only an excessively severe interpretation of the Law had forbidden. More than this, Christ is implicitly presenting Himself as the new David, that is, the Messiah. Since David on that occasion was fleeing from

high priest, and did eat the loaves of proposition, which was not lawful to eat but for the priests, and gave to them who were with him?

27 And he said to them: The sabbath was made for man, and not man for the sabbath.

28 Therefore the Son of man is Lord of the sabbath also.

the murderous king Saul, who had been rejected by God, Christ is implicitly warning the Pharisees that by making themselves His enemies, they risk being rejected as Saul was.

Although Abiathar was a priest at that time, his father Achimelech was still alive and therefore was high priest. Again, the Old Testament itself states that it was Achimelech to whom David spoke. Why then did Christ speak of these events as occurring *under Abiathar the high priest*? As we see later on, St Mark uses the word 'high priest' rather broadly to mean any priest of great importance. But there is more to it: Abiathar, like Saul, was also later rejected by God, and his priestly line was annulled, when he sought to enthrone a false heir as David's successor. The use of his name, which must have struck the Pharisees as odd, thus serves as a further warning of the risk they run by opposing the true Davidic heir, Jesus.

Since *the sabbath was made for man,* that he might learn how to worship God, *the Son of man,* in whom is the fullness of grace and truth, and therefore worships God perfectly, has the right to declare what the Sabbath requires. Perhaps only later would it strike the Pharisees that *the Lord of the Sabbath* is a phrase that can apply only to God.

1 And he entered again into the synagogue, and there was a man there who had a withered hand.

2 And they watched him whether he would heal on the sabbath days; that they might accuse him.

3 And he said to the man who had the withered hand: Stand up in the midst.

4 And he saith to them: Is it lawful to do good on the sabbath days, or to do evil? to save life, or to destroy? But they held their peace.

5 And looking round about on them with anger, being grieved for the blindness of their hearts, he saith to the man: Stretch forth thy hand. And he stretched it forth: and his hand was restored unto him.

6 And the Pharisees going out, immediately made a consultation with the Herodians against him, how they might destroy him.

7 But Jesus retired with his disciples to the sea; and a great multitude followed him from Galilee and Judea,

8 And from Jerusalem, and from Idumea, and from beyond the Jordan. And they about Tyre and Sidon, a great multitude, hearing the things which he did, came to him.

9 And he spoke to his disciples that a small ship should wait on him because of the multitude, lest they should throng him.

10 For he healed many, so that they pressed upon him for to touch him, as many as had devils.

11 And the unclean spirits, when they saw him, fell down before him: and they cried, saying:

12 Thou art the Son of God. And he strictly charged them that they should not make him known.

vv. 1–6

ONLY ST MARK TELLS US THAT OUR LORD looked *round about on* these people *with anger*, and it is the only time when this word, 'anger', is applied to Him. The object of the anger is a compound of various sins: especially unbelief, called *blindness*; but also unkindness, the making of religion hateful, and the abuse of authority. Although Christ's anger was the same in essence as our own, it was not the same in manner, since with us anger, or any other keen emotion, tends to overcome or at least to disturb reason. It was also inspired by charity for the souls of those with whom He was angry, since otherwise He would not have also been *grieved* on their account.

The Pharisees and the Herodians are respectively the anti-Roman and the pro-Roman party. They sink their differences to *destroy* Jesus. Today also we see strange alliances forming against His body the Church.

vv. 7–12

Could the Lord not have prevented the *multitude* from thronging or crushing Him, without the use of *a small boat*? Yes, but since the boat signifies the Church, He wished in this way to show that His presence in the Church will be beyond the power of disorderly men to disturb it. The Church is called *small*, either in comparison to the number of those who do not enter it, or because it is held in low esteem.

13 And going up into a mountain, he called unto him whom he would himself: and they came to him.

14 And he made that twelve should be with him, and that he might send them to preach.

15 And he gave them power to heal sicknesses, and to cast out devils.

16 And to Simon he gave the name Peter:

17 And James the son of Zebedee, and John the brother of James; and he named them Boanerges, which is, The sons of thunder:

18 And Andrew and Philip, and Bartholomew and Matthew, and Thomas and James of Alpheus, and Thaddeus, and Simon the Cananean:

19 And Judas Iscariot, who also betrayed him.

20 And they come to a house, and the multitude cometh together again, so that they could not so much as eat bread.

21 And when his friends had heard of it, they went out to lay hold on him. For they said: He is become mad.

22 And the scribes who were come down from Jerusalem, said: He hath Beelzebub, and by the prince of devils he casteth out devils.

23 And after he had called them together, he said to them in parables: How can Satan cast out Satan?

24 And if a kingdom be divided against itself, that kingdom cannot stand.

25 And if a house be divided against itself, that house cannot stand.

26 And if Satan be risen up against himself, he is divided, and cannot stand, but hath an end.

27 No man can enter into the house of a strong man and rob him of his goods, unless he first bind the strong man, and then shall he plunder his house.

28 Amen I say to you, that all sins shall be forgiven unto the sons of men, and the

vv. 13–20

St Mark emphasises the freedom of our Lord's choice of the Twelve, when He *called unto him whom he would himself.* This may reflect St Peter's insistence that he had not been chosen for his own merits.

Why do the brothers James and John receive the title *sons of thunder*? Perhaps because of their natural ardour. Yet thunder in the Scriptures is often an image for preaching. All the apostles were born from Christ's preaching and will preach in their turn, and so they are all sons of thunder. But St James and St John will be respectively the first and last of the apostles to die. Their title thus suggests the apostolic confession that will resound from the martyrdom of the one to the death of the other, at which point public revelation ended.

They could not so much as eat bread. "Would, O Lord Jesus," wrote St Bede, "that in our days too, Thou wouldst give such grace to Thy faithful that in their eagerness to learn, they might hinder their teachers not only from the desire for bodily pleasures but even sometimes from taking their daily bread!"

vv. 21–30

His friends, or more literally, 'those connected to Him', judge foolishly that Christ *is become mad*: but since the Greek word could also be translated 'is outside himself', or 'is in ecstasy', they speak more truly than they know. Love places a person outside himself, writes St Thomas Aquinas, so that he reckons whatever is good or evil for the one loved, as the good or evil of himself.

His opponents accuse Him on several occasions of being possessed. *Beelzebub* means 'the lord of the flies'; in the Old Testament the angel of the Lord uses the word in speaking to Elias about a demon worshipped by the Philistines whom the Jews were sometimes tempted to invoke.

Israel itself has also become a *kingdom* that *cannot stand*, now that the Jews are so divided about Christ's mission.

Since the forgiveness of sins comes from the Holy Spirit, and since we can only receive Him by recognising Him as the Spirit

blasphemies wherewith they shall blaspheme:

29 But he that shall blaspheme against the Holy Ghost, shall never have forgiveness, but shall be guilty of an everlasting sin.

30 Because they said: He hath an unclean spirit.

31 And his mother and his brethren came; and standing without, sent unto him, calling him.

32 And the multitude sat about him; and they say to him: Behold thy mother and thy brethren without seek for thee.

33 And answering them, he said: Who is my mother and my brethren?

34 And looking round about on them who sat about him, he saith: Behold my mother and my brethren.

35 For whosoever shall do the will of God, he is my brother, and my sister, and mother.

of Christ and the Father, anyone who thinks that Christ's spirit is *unclean* cannot receive the Holy Spirit and hence can *never have forgiveness.* Does this mean simply that they can never be forgiven for as long as they hold on to this malicious opinion, or that once having embraced this opinion, they will never in fact relinquish it? It is not certain; but Scripture gives us no example of anyone repenting of this sin.

vv. 31–35

That the one who does *the will of God* is called the *brother* or *sister* of Christ may not seem surprising, but how is such a person his *mother*? St Bede answers that he becomes such by preaching, as it were bringing Him forth in the soul of the one who hears the word with faith. We could also say that there is a veiled reference to our Lady; since all the other people who do the will of God would be sufficiently identified as Christ's 'brother' or 'sister' according as they are male or female, the addition of 'mother' implies that she also is among the people who do God's will.

1 And again he began to teach by the seaside; and a great multitude was gathered together unto him, so that he went up into a ship, and sat in the sea; and all the multitude was upon the land by the seaside.

2 And he taught them many things in parables, and said unto them in his doctrine:

3 Hear ye: Behold, the sower went out to sow.

4 And whilst he sowed, some fell by the wayside, and the birds of the air came and ate it up.

5 And other some fell upon stony ground, where it had not much earth; and it shot up immediately, because it had no depth of earth.

6 And when the sun was risen, it was scorched; and because it had no root, it withered away.

7 And some fell among thorns; and the thorns grew up, and choked it, and it yielded no fruit.

8 And some fell upon good ground; and brought forth fruit that grew up, and increased and yielded, one thirty, another sixty, and another a hundred.

9 And he said: He that hath ears to hear, let him hear.

10 And when he was alone, the twelve that were with him asked him the parable.

11 And he said to them: To you it is given to know the mystery of the kingdom of God: but to them that are without, all things are done in parables:

12 That seeing they may see, and not perceive; and hearing they may hear, and not understand: lest at any time they should be converted, and their sins should be forgiven them.

13 And he saith to them: Are you ignorant of this parable? and how shall you know all parables?

14 He that soweth, soweth the word.

15 And these are they by the way side, where the word is sown, and as soon as they have heard, immediately Satan cometh and taketh away the word that was sown in their hearts.

16 And these likewise are they that are sown on the stony

VV. 1–20

THOSE WHO RECEIVE THE SEED OF *THE word* into *much earth*, that is, into a thorough-going humility help not only themselves but many others to yield the *fruit* of good works. Why does Christ assign three different yields, of *thirty, sixty,* and *a hundred*? Perhaps these represent the three states of life: active, contemplative, and the union of both. But then why is the third state not represented by ninety? To combine the two successfully is itself an excellence.

Why does being *ignorant* of *this parable* cause one not to *know all parables*? Couldn't one understand the parable of the Prodigal Son, say, without understanding this one of the Sower? A person needs to know this parable at least practically, that is, he must have the humility to receive the divine word, or else none of the other parables will help him.

Why does our Lord characterise riches as *deceitful*? They are often acquired and maintained by dishonesty; but even more, because they confer an illusion of omnipotence.

Only St Mark describes the desires which choke the corn as *lusts after other things*. But is this not vague? No: for one of the things that can distract man from his proper work is novelty for its own sake.

ground: who when they have heard the word, immediately receive it with joy.

17 And they have no root in themselves, but are only for a time: and then when tribulation and persecution ariseth for the word they are presently scandalized.

18 And others there are who are sown among thorns: these are they that hear the word,

19 And the cares of the world, and the deceitfulness of riches, and the lusts after other things entering in choke the word, and it is made fruitless.

20 And these are they who are sown upon the good ground, who hear the word, and receive it, and yield fruit, the one thirty, another sixty, and another a hundred.

21 And he said to them: Doth a candle come in to be put under a bushel, or under a bed? and not to be set on a candlestick?

22 For there is nothing hid, which shall not be made manifest: neither was it made secret, but that it may come abroad.

23 If any man have ears to hear, let him hear.

24 And he said to them: Take heed what you hear. In what measure you shall mete, it shall be measured to you again, and more shall be given to you.

25 For he that hath, to him shall be given: and he that

hath not, that also which he hath shall be taken away from him.

26 And he said: So is the kingdom of God, as if a man should cast seed into the earth,

27 And should sleep, and rise, night and day, and the seed should spring, and grow up whilst he knoweth not.

28 For the earth of itself bringeth forth fruit, first the blade, then the ear, afterwards the full corn in the ear.

29 And when the fruit is brought forth, immediately he putteth in the sickle, because the harvest is come.

VV. 21–29

Having spoken of His own role as the first Sower of the word, Christ passes to the duties of preachers. Now that His word has *come in* to the world like a *candle*, God will not allow it to be placed *under a bushel*, or man-made measure, as happens when preachers avoid speaking of the truths that the prejudices of their age reject. Nor will He allow it to be placed *under a bed*, concealed by the idleness of those meant to preach.

Since God would not have spoken to man had He not wished to be understood, the very fact that He has *hid* His meaning in parables is proof that it will later *be made manifest*. The apostles and their successors will do this. Just as Jesus had said of His own preaching: *He that ears to hear, let him hear*, He repeats the words in regard to this future preaching: for whoever assents to the teaching of the Church is literally believing God, an act that is not possible without the infused habit of faith, any more than it is possible to hear sound without the organs of hearing.

Since the apostles and their successors are also bound to believe the message in order to preach correctly, they are told to *take heed what* they *hear*. The more assiduous they are to *mete* out the divine word, the *more* of it in proportion *shall be given to* them to understand. Above all, *he that hath* the knowledge that comes by faith *shall* one day *be given* the clear sight of the mysteries. But the bishop who *hath not* a living faith in what he

30 And he said: To what shall we liken the kingdom of God? or to what parable shall we compare it?

31 It is as a grain of mustard seed: which when it is sown in the earth, is less than all the seeds that are in the earth:

32 And when it is sown, it groweth up, and becometh greater than all herbs, and shooteth out great branches, so that the birds of the air may dwell under the shadow thereof.

33 And with many such parables, he spoke to them the word, according as they were able to hear.

34 And without parable he did not speak unto them; but apart, he explained all things to his disciples.

preaches will find that the honour *which he hath shall* one day *be taken away from him.*

However assiduous a preacher may be, he is only a dispositive and not an efficient cause of the spiritual growth of his hearers, just as a farmer cannot himself cause a single blade of wheat to grow. Thus, after he has *cast seed into the earth* by his words, and then goes on both to *sleep* in prayer and to *rise* again to new tasks, *he knoweth not* why in some cases it *bringeth forth* the fruit of conversion and perseverance, since this comes from the freedom that each soul has *of itself,* and not from the preacher. The hierarchy, *as if a* single *man,* continues a single work through *the night* of adversity and *the day* of prosperity, whilst three ages of the Church pass on earth, called here *the blade, the ear,* and *the full grain.* Perhaps these are the early, Jewish church; the nations of the world; and finally, just before the *harvest,* all Israel.

vv. 30–34

Why does our Lord only now ask *what parable* we should use for *the kingdom of God,* when He has already used two parables to *liken* it to the sowing of seed? His question evokes one put by the prophet Ezekiel, who asked to what he should liken the mighty Egyptian pharaoh.[1] Ezekiel went on to compare him to a tall tree, in whose branches the birds of the air made their nests, and under whose branches the beasts of the field brought forth their young, referring in this way to the princes and to the humble folk; but then he warned Pharaoh that he was a tree who would be cut down. Hence, by this new parable, our Lord implies that His kingdom, also, will be a mighty and visible empire. But what He omits is also significant: since all in the Church are called to reach the heights, He does not speak of beasts of the field, but only of *the birds of the air,* who rest in the *great branches,* which are the many churches spread throughout the world; and this tree is not to be cut down. Why such a difference between the two trees? Only the second has sprung from *a mustard seed,* that is from Christ Himself, in whom the

---

1 See Ezekiel 31, especially verses 2 and 18.

35 And he saith to them that day, when evening was come: Let us pass over to the other side.

36 And sending away the multitude, they take him even as he was in the ship, and there were other ships with him.

37 And there arose a great storm of wind, and the waves beat into the ship, so that the ship was filled.

38 And he was in the hinder part of the ship, sleeping upon a pillow; and they awoke him, and said to him: Master, doth it not concern thee that we perish?

39 And rising up, he rebuked the wind, and said to the sea: Peace, be still. And the wind ceased: and there was made a great calm.

40 And he said to them: Why are you fearful? have you not faith yet? And they feared exceedingly, and they said one to another: Who is this (thinkest thou) that both wind and sea obey him?

Holy Ghost was concealed like the fire that is hidden within this grain. By the abjection of His death, He became *less than all the seeds that are* buried *in the earth*.

vv. 35–40

The disciples *take him even as he was in the ship*; this seems to mean that He took no rest after a whole day teaching the crowds, which perhaps explains why He would later be *sleeping* in the boat. St Peter's nautical eye is apparent here, since only this gospel mentions the *other ships* that were with this one. Allegorically, only the ship of the Church possesses the Lord *even as he* is, since her teaching does not lessen either His divine or His human nature.

He was *in the hinder part of the ship*, perhaps because it is from here that the ship was steered, and so He is shown as the helmsman of the Church. He was *sleeping upon a pillow*, or literally, 'upon the pillow'. An ancient commentator called Theophylact says that this 'pillow' was a part of the ship, and was made of wood.

Only this evangelist includes the apostles' reproachful words: *Does it not concern thee?* By replying to their question by asking: *Have you not faith yet,* Christ therefore implies that they lack faith not only in His power but also in His friendship.

1 And they came over the strait of the sea into the country of the Gerasens.

2 And as he went out of the ship, immediately there met him out of the monuments a man with an unclean spirit,

3 Who had his dwelling in the tombs, and no man now could bind him, not even with chains.

4 For having been often bound with fetters and chains, he had burst the chains, and broken the fetters in pieces, and no one could tame him.

5 And he was always day and night in the monuments and in the mountains, crying and cutting himself with stones.

6 And seeing Jesus afar off, he ran and adored him.

7 And crying with a loud voice, he said: What have I to do with thee, Jesus the Son of the most high God? I adjure thee by God that thou torment me not.

8 For he said unto him: Go out of the man, thou unclean spirit.

9 And he asked him: What is thy name? And he saith to him: My name is Legion, for we are many.

10 And he besought him much, that he would not drive him away out of the country.

11 And there was there near the mountain a great herd of swine, feeding.

12 And the spirits besought him, saying: Send us into the swine, that we may enter into them.

13 And Jesus immediately gave them leave. And the unclean spirits going out, entered into the swine: and the herd with great violence was carried headlong into the sea, being about two thousand, and were stifled in the sea.

14 And they that fed them fled, and told it in the city and in the fields. And they went out to see what was done:

15 And they came to Jesus, and they see him that was troubled with the devil, sitting, clothed, and well in his wits, and they were afraid.

16 And they that had seen it, told them, in what manner he had been dealt with who had the devil; and concerning the swine.

VV. 1–20

ST MARK ALONE TELLS US THAT THIS DEMO-niac was in the habit of *crying* out and *cutting himself with stones*. Though people sometimes harm themselves for other reasons, a demon who possesses a man will take pleasure in causing him to do such harm to himself, since the demons despise the human body. Perhaps it is because they therefore delight in the body's corruption that they caused this man to dwell *in the tombs* and *monuments* of the dead.

Christ sets an example for the exorcists of His Church by asking the demon for his *name*. Exorcists tell us that when they are able to force a possessing spirit to state his name, they gain more power over it. *Legion* appears to be both the proper name of the presiding spirit, and an indication that many others are present. Only St Mark gives an estimate of the number of the swine who are drowned, *about two thousand*. Two in Scripture is sometimes used to denote division, because it is the first number to depart from unity: thus, the waters are divided from the waters on the second day of creation. Here it may suggest the power of the demons to divide the possessed man from the community of his fellows.

Why did the demons ask permission to *enter* the pigs, if they were immediately going to destroy them in the water, and then need some new habitation? Perhaps the demons panicked at the presence of Christ. Was it not hard on the owners to lose such an immense herd? They may themselves have been respon-sible for the demonic activity in the area: this region of *Decapolis* beyond the Sea of Galilee was populated by gentiles, many of whom would have invoked pagan gods, that is, demons.

Like St Luke, St Mark implies the divinity of Christ at the end of this episode: the man is told to relate *how great things the Lord hath done* for him, and he relates *how great things Jesus* has done.

17 And they began to pray him that he would depart from their coasts.

18 And when he went up into the ship, he that had been troubled with the devil, began to beseech him that he might be with him.

19 And he admitted him not, but saith to him: Go into thy house to thy friends, and tell them how great things the Lord hath done for thee, and hath had mercy on thee.

20 And he went his way, and began to publish in Decapolis how great things Jesus had done for him: and all men wondered.

21 And when Jesus had passed again in the ship over the strait, a great multitude assembled together unto him, and he was nigh unto the sea.

22 And there cometh one of the rulers of the synagogue named Jairus: and seeing him, falleth down at his feet.

23 And he besought him much, saying: My daughter is at the point of death, come, lay thy hand upon her, that she may be safe, and may live.

24 And he went with him, and a great multitude followed him, and they thronged him.

25 And a woman who was under an issue of blood twelve years,

26 And had suffered many things from many physicians; and had spent all that she had, and was nothing the better, but rather worse,

27 When she had heard of Jesus, came in the crowd behind him, and touched his garment.

28 For she said: If I shall touch but his garment, I shall be whole.

29 And forthwith the fountain of her blood was dried up, and she felt in her body that she was healed of the evil.

30 And immediately Jesus knowing in himself the virtue that had proceeded from him, turning to the multitude, said: Who hath touched my garments?

31 And his disciples said to him: Thou seest the multitude thronging thee, and sayest thou who hath touched me?

32 And he looked about to see her who had done this.

33 But the woman fearing and trembling, knowing what

vv. 21–43

It may have been the woman cured of the *issue of blood* who herself made known later that she had seen *many physicians* and only grown *worse* for their treatments, and also that *she felt in her body* that she was instantly cured on touching Christ's garment. By her impurity, she represents the gentiles, aware that they are deteriorating from the natural virtues of their forefathers, but growing worse despite all the exhortations of their doctors.[1]

Some Protestant commentators, hostile to the cult of relics, have supposed that this woman was guilty of a magical way of thinking, in seeking a cure by touching Christ's garment. But He praises her *faith,* finding no fault with it.

Why does our Lord bring three, but only three, of the apostles when He goes to raise the dead girl? Such a miracle is worthy to have witnesses, but He does not want her parents to be over-whelmed by a crowd.

St Peter, who was standing by when the dead girl arose, mentions the Aramaic words that our Lord used to awaken her. This suggests that at least in Galilee, Christ habitually spoke in Greek, which in that region was a common, public language, understood by both Jews and Gentiles. Aramaic might naturally

---

1 "Here, then, is this Roman republic, which has changed little by little from the fair and virtuous city it was, and has become utterly wicked and dissolute. It is not I who am the first to say this, but their own authors, from whom we learned it for a fee, and who wrote it long before the coming of Christ" (St Augustine, *City of God*, Bk. II.19).

was done in her, came and fell down before him, and told him all the truth.

34 And he said to her: Daughter, thy faith hath made thee whole: go in peace, and be thou whole of thy disease.

35 While he was yet speaking, some come from the ruler of the synagogue's house, saying: Thy daughter is dead: why dost thou trouble the master any further?

36 But Jesus having heard the word that was spoken, saith to the ruler of the synagogue: Fear not, only believe.

37 And he admitted not any man to follow him, but Peter, and James, and John the brother of James.

38 And they come to the house of the ruler of the synagogue; and he seeth a tumult, and people weeping and wailing much.

39 And going in, he saith to them: Why make you this ado, and weep? the damsel is not dead, but sleepeth.

40 And they laughed him to scorn. But he having put them all out, taketh the father and the mother of the damsel, and them that were with him, and entereth in where the damsel was lying.

41 And taking the damsel by the hand, he saith to her: Talitha cumi, which is, being interpreted: Damsel (I say to thee) arise.

42 And immediately the damsel rose up, and walked: and she was twelve years old: and they were astonished with a great astonishment.

43 And he charged them strictly that no man should know it: and commanded that something should be given her to eat.

be used when speaking to those who, having few or no public dealings, did not know Greek: people such as this young girl, or the deaf-and-dumb man cured in chapter eight.

St Peter has likewise passed on the detail that the girl *walked* when she returned to life; perhaps she ran to her parents. Why does our Lord command that *something be given her to eat*? It is a way of teaching the parents that she has returned to her ordinary life, and that she is neither a ghost nor endowed with superhuman powers. It is also, says St Bede, because whoever is raised from spiritual death needs to be fed with bread from heaven.

1 And going out from thence, he went into his own country; and his disciples followed him.

2 And when the sabbath was come, he began to teach in the synagogue: and many hearing him were in admiration at his doctrine, saying: How came this man by all these things? and what wisdom is this that is given to him, and such mighty works as are wrought by his hands?

3 Is not this the carpenter, the son of Mary, the brother of James, and Joseph, and Jude, and Simon? are not also his sisters here with us? And they were scandalized in regard of him.

4 And Jesus said to them: A prophet is not without honour, but in his own country, and in his own house, and among his own kindred.

5 And he could not do any miracles there, only that he cured a few that were sick, laying his hands upon them.

6 And he wondered because of their unbelief, and he went through the villages round about teaching.

vv. 1–6

THIS VISIT TO THE *SYNAGOGUE* IN HIS *OWN country* of Nazareth appears to be the same as that described by St Luke after the forty days in the wilderness. The humble origin of Christ, which would normally be incompatible with great *wisdom* and *doctrine,* is an argument in favour of His divine mission, but these Nazarenes perversely treat it as a disqualification. Their guilt is heightened by the fact that they are aware of the *mighty works wrought by his hands* elsewhere.

It is only here in the New Testament that Jesus is referred to as a *carpenter*, and since the word is used by those wishing to discredit Him, its accuracy is not guaranteed. Yet St Justin Martyr in the second century reports a tradition that He had made ploughs and yokes.[1] Since the disgruntled people in the synagogue don't mention St Joseph, it seems that he has already died.

The *James and Joseph* mentioned here seem to be the same as the sons of the Mary mentioned in chapter fifteen as mother of *James and Joseph.* She may also be the *Mary of Cleophas* mentioned by St John as *sister*, that is, kinswoman, of the Blessed Virgin. St Hegesippus, a second century martyr, states that this Cleophas had a son called Simeon, who would then be the same as the *Simon* mentioned here.

That *a prophet is not without honour except in his own country*, is one of the rare sayings of Christ reported by all four evangelists. But was He not honoured within *his own house*? He was by our Lady and St Joseph, but not by every chance visitor. Or more likely, 'house' here refers to the house of Israel, that is, to the nation considered as forming a single family.

He could not do many miracles in Nazareth, not for lack of power, because of the divine decree that makes faith a condition for miracles to be worked.

---

1 *Dialogue with Trypho,* LXXXVIII.8.

7 And he called the twelve; and began to send them two and two, and gave them power over unclean spirits.

8 And he commanded them that they should take nothing for the way, but a staff only: no scrip, no bread, nor money in their purse,

9 But to be shod with sandals, and that they should not put on two coats.

10 And he said to them: Wheresoever you shall enter into an house, there abide till you depart from that place.

11 And whosoever shall not receive you, nor hear you; going forth from thence, shake off the dust from your feet for a testimony to them.

12 And going forth they preached that men should do penance:

13 And they cast out many devils, and anointed with oil many that were sick, and healed them.

How is it that He *wondered because of their unbelief,* when He had known the state of their souls for many years? Perhaps because like faith, unbelief can grow; or perhaps they had had implicit faith until this moment in a Saviour who was to come, but have now lost this faith by rejecting Him when He came.

vv. 7–13

Our Lord's instructions to the twelve raise a famous, if minor, puzzle. St Matthew and St Luke include the *staff* as one of the accoutrements forbidden to the apostles, whereas St Mark declares that a staff alone was permitted. Some authors suggest that what is forbidden is 'acquiring' a staff, not taking one that they happened already to have. This explanation would fit with the verb used by St Matthew. But St Mark and St Luke use the same verb, which means more simply 'take'. Some other authors think that different kinds of staff are in question: the apostles are forbidden to take a staff that would be a sign of authority, but not a mere support for the journey. Yet the same Greek word for staff is used by all the evangelists. So, we should note that St Matthew and St Luke quote our Lord's words, whereas St Mark reports them in indirect speech. Perhaps, then, Christ forbade the disciples to take even a walking-staff first of all, but some of them protested or looked dismayed at this, and so He allowed them to take one after all, as an example to religious superiors to be willing to modify their instructions because of the weakness of their subjects. Thus, St Dominic told some of his sons to take no money with them for a journey to Paris, but one of them complained so much that he relented.

By using *sandals,* the apostles not only practise asceticism but also exemplify the prophecy of Isaias: *How beautiful are the feet of him that bringeth good tidings.* By wearing only one *coat,* or tunic, they practise trust in divine providence and signify that preachers should show themselves the same at all times, preaching a consistent doctrine.

Authors tell us that it was the custom for Jews living in Palestine to *shake off the dust from* their *feet* when they returned from abroad; by commanding the apostles to do the same when men do *not receive* them, Christ implies that those who do heed their

14 And king Herod heard, (for his name was made manifest,) and he said: John the Baptist is risen again from the dead, and therefore mighty works shew forth themselves in him.

15 And others said: It is Elias. But others said: It is a prophet, as one of the prophets.

16 Which Herod hearing, said: John whom I beheaded, he is risen again from the dead.

17 For Herod himself had sent and apprehended John, and bound him in prison for the sake of Herodias the wife of Philip his brother, because he had married her.

18 For John said to Herod: It is not lawful for thee to have thy brother's wife.

19 Now Herodias laid snares for him: and was desirous to put him to death, and could not.

20 For Herod feared John, knowing him to be a just and holy man: and kept him, and when he heard him, did many things: and he heard him willingly.

21 And when a convenient day was come, Herod made a supper for his birthday, for the princes, and tribunes, and chief men of Galilee.

22 And when the daughter of the same Herodias had come in, and had danced, and pleased Herod, and them that were at table with him, the king said to the damsel: Ask of me what thou wilt, and I will give it thee.

23 And he swore to her: Whatsoever thou shalt ask I will give thee, though it be the half of my kingdom.

24 Who when she was gone out, said to her mother, What shall I ask? But she said: The head of John the Baptist.

preaching will form a new Israel.

Only St Mark tells us that the apostles *anointed with oil many that were sick*. The Council of Trent teaches that they thereby indicated that the new Law of Christ would contain the sacrament of extreme unction. "It is thus plain", writes St Bede, "that from the time of the Apostles themselves, it has been the tradition of holy Church that those possessed by demons or afflicted with any disease should be anointed with oil consecrated by a high-priestly blessing."

vv. 14–29

Herod, here, means Herod Antipas, who rules in Galilee under Roman authority, and is the son of the Herod who massacred the innocents. How could he have supposed that our Lord was *John the Baptist risen again from the dead*, when John was Christ's cousin? Herod has only heard stories of miracles done by Christ, and hasn't looked into the question closely. Herod's brother *Philip* is still alive, and so Herod is committing adultery by living with *Herodias*. Herod, being less bad than Herodias *kept* John safe from her malice. *He did many things*: this could mean that he made some attempts to amend his life. However, other manuscripts contain a slightly different Greek phrase, which means, 'he was much perplexed'.

The scene at Herod's party is a diabolical parody of the banquet in the book of Esther, where King Assuerus was moved to promise Esther whatever she asked, even *the half of* his *kingdom*. She asked for the salvation of the Jews, whereas Salome asks for the beheading of *a just and holy* Jew. Herod was not bound in God's sight by his *oath* to *give* Herodias's *daughter whatsoever* she would *ask,* since an oath must be about something lawful, in order to be binding.

Theodoret, a learned fifth century bishop, reports that St John the Baptist was buried in Sebastia, where Herod had a palace, but that his tomb was opened in the days of Julian the apostate emperor, and his bones burned by the pagans.[2] The place of his head is disputed to this day.

---

2 *Ecclesiastical History,* Bk. III.3. Julian reigned from 361 to 363.

25 And when she was come in immediately with haste to the king, she asked, saying: I will that forthwith thou give me in a dish, the head of John the Baptist.

26 And the king was struck sad. Yet because of his oath, and because of them that were with him at table, he would not displease her:

27 But sending an executioner, he commanded that his head should be brought in a dish.

28 And he beheaded him in the prison, and brought his head in a dish: and gave it to the damsel, and the damsel gave it to her mother.

29 Which his disciples hearing came, and took his body, and laid it in a tomb.

30 And the apostles coming together unto Jesus, related to him all things that they had done and taught.

31 And he said to them: Come apart into a desert place, and rest a little. For there were many coming and going, and they had not so much as time to eat.

32 And going up into a ship, they went into a desert place apart.

33 And they saw them going away, and many knew: and they ran flocking thither on foot from all the cities, and were there before them.

34 And Jesus going out saw a great multitude: and he had compassion on them, because they were as sheep not having a shepherd, and he began to teach them many things.

35 And when the day was now far spent, his disciples came to him, saying: This is a desert place, and the hour is now past:

36 Send them away, that going into the next villages and towns, they may buy themselves meat to eat.

37 And he answering said to them: Give you them to eat. And they said to him: Let us go and buy bread for two hundred pence, and we will give them to eat.

38 And he saith to them: How many loaves have you? go and see. And when they knew, they say: Five, and two fishes.

39 And he commanded them that they should make them all sit down by companies upon the green grass.

vv. 30–44

For the second time in a few chapters, St Mark records that the apostles *had not so much as time to eat.* The fact seems to have stuck in St Peter's memory!

Let us go to buy bread for two hundred pence. Given that this sum was more than half a year's wages for the working man, it sounds sarcastic. The words could also be translated 'Are we to go to buy?', which would then sound incredulous.

Christ tells them to *Go and see* how much bread they already have, so that they will be the more certain that a miracle has taken place.

St Luke tells us that He bade the apostles make the crowds sit down in groups of fifty, St Mark that *they sat down in ranks, by hundreds and by fifties.* The Fathers remark that fifty, in the Scriptures, is the number associated with the forgiveness of sins and other debts, which is why a jubilee year occurred every fifty years, and why, according to St Thomas Aquinas, the Church makes more use of psalm 50, the *Miserere,* than of any of the other psalms.[3] Our Lord therefore commands them to sit down in fifties before receiving the miraculous bread as a sign that those who are to partake of the Eucharist must first have had

---

3 *Commentary on the Psalms,* 'On Psalm 50'. It is traditionally used, for example, at Lauds when no feast is being kept, after meals in religious houses, and as one of the seven penitential psalms.

40 And they sat down in ranks, by hundreds and by fifties.

41 And when he had taken the five loaves, and the two fishes: looking up to heaven, he blessed, and broke the loaves, and gave to his disciples to set before them:

and the two fishes he divided among them all.

42 And they all did eat, and had their fill.

43 And they took up the leavings, twelve full baskets of fragments, and of the fishes.

44 And they that did eat, were five thousand men.

45 And immediately he obliged his disciples to go up into the ship, that they might go before him over the water to Bethsaida, whilst he dismissed the people.

46 And when he had dismissed them, he went up to the mountain to pray.

47 And when it was late, the ship was in the midst of the sea, and himself alone on the land.

48 And seeing them labouring in rowing, (for the wind was

against them,) and about the fourth watch of the night, he cometh to them walking upon the sea, and he would have passed by them.

49 But they seeing him walking upon the sea, thought it was an apparition, and they cried out.

50 For they all saw him, and were troubled. And immediately he spoke with them, and said to them: Have a good heart, it is I, fear ye not.

their sins remitted. Some sit down by hundreds, says St Gregory, to denote those who purify themselves more thoroughly, cleansing thoughts as well as deeds.

St Mark notes that the *grass* was *green*, that is, fresh. This fits with St John's statement that the miracle occurred shortly before Passover, in the spring.

He *immediately obliged his disciples to* take ship after the miracle, lest they be tempted by the crowd's desire of making Jesus their king. He also, unusually, *dismissed the people*, to calm their excitement and give them time to think about over what had happened before He spoke next day about the bread of life. This dismissal also foreshadows the priest's dismissal of the people at the end of the Mass.

Why does He send the apostles to *Bethsaida*, when they are going to hear Him speak next day in the synagogue at Capharnaum? Peter, Andrew and Philip were originally from Bethsaida, as we learn from St John, and so the apostles would have had somewhere to stay there; they would thus have been safe from the dangerous enthusiasm of the crowd, who would probably have gone to Capharnaum to look for them, since that was the apostles' normal base of operations.

vv. 45–52

In describing how the Lord walked upon the water, St Mark does not mention that St Peter did the same, albeit briefly. Probably St Peter didn't mention it in his preaching, from humility. Only St Mark records that Christ *would have passed by them*, if they had not *cried out* in fear; for although they were *labouring in rowing*, they were not in danger from the sea as on a previous occasion. We thus learn that by crying out, that is, praying, the Church receives even more help than she needs to survive.

What is it that the apostles *understood not concerning the loaves*? They cannot have failed to understand that He could work miracles, so why were they *far more astonished* by this new one? They have not yet, it seems, sufficiently understood that He is true God: they did not see that He gave them bread in the desert to show that it was also He who had fed the Jews in the desert with

51 And he went up to them into the ship, and the wind ceased: and they were far more astonished within themselves:

52 For they understood not concerning the loaves; for their heart was blinded.

53 And when they had passed over, they came into the land of Genezareth, and set to the shore.

54 And when they were gone out of the ship, immediately they knew him:

55 And running through that whole country, they began to carry about in beds those that were sick, where they heard he was.

56 And whithersoever he entered, into towns or into villages or cities, they laid the sick in the streets, and besought him that they might touch but the hem of his garment: and as many as touched him were made whole.

manna. Hence, perhaps, they are *troubled* when they see Him walking upon the waters, which the Old Testament presents as a divine act: Job speaks of God as the one *who alone spreadest out the heavens, and walketh upon the waves of the sea.* The theophany is completed when our Lord says to them: *It is I,* or more literally, 'I am', which in the context evokes the name by which God named Himself to Moses.

The hearts of the apostles are thus said to be *blinded*, or hardened. "They were amazed", says St Bede, "at the greatness of His virtue, but they could not yet recognise in Him the true divine Majesty."

vv. 53–56

Not just the woman with the haemorrhage, but many others also are *made whole* by touching *the hem of his garment.* This refers to the fringes that Moses commanded the Jews to wear on the edge of their garments, interlaced with blue or violet thread. These were meant to remind the Jews of the heavenly origin of their laws, so that *being mindful of the precepts of the Lord,* they might *do them and be holy to their God.*[4] Since the undivided tunic of Christ is a symbol of the Church, these tassels may be said to represent the sacraments of the new law, by which those who lay hold on them are healed.

---

4 Numbers 15:40.

1 And there assembled together unto him the Pharisees and some of the scribes, coming from Jerusalem.

2 And when they had seen some of his disciples eat bread with common, that is, with unwashed hands, they found fault.

3 For the Pharisees, and all the Jews eat not without often washing their hands, holding the tradition of the ancients:

4 And when they come from the market, unless they be washed, they eat not: and many other things there are that have been delivered to them to observe, the washings of cups and of pots, and of brazen vessels, and of beds.

5 And the Pharisees and scribes asked him: Why do not thy disciples walk according to the tradition of the ancients, but they eat bread with common hands?

6 But he answering, said to them: Well did Isaias prophesy of you hypocrites, as it is written: This people honoureth me with their lips, but their heart is far from me.

7 And in vain do they worship me, teaching doctrines and precepts of men.

8 For leaving the commandment of God, you hold the tradition of men, the washing of pots and of cups: and many other things you do like to these.

9 And he said to them: Well do you make void the commandment of God, that you may keep your own tradition.

10 For Moses said: Honour thy father and thy mother; and He that shall curse father or mother, dying let him die.

11 But you say: If a man shall say to his father or mother, Corban, (which is a gift,) whatsoever is from me, shall profit thee.

12 And further you suffer him not to do any thing for his father or mother,

13 Making void the word of God by your own tradition, which you have given forth. And many other such like things you do.

vv. 1–13

HAT KIND OF RITUAL IMPURITIES WERE the scribes and Pharisees worried about contracting from going to the market or using household goods? The book of Leviticus specified that the dead bodies of unclean animals would defile vessels by falling into them, and that various kinds of bodily discharge would render unclean until the evening not only the man or woman who experienced them but also anyone whom he or she touched. The scribes and Pharisees seem to have acted on the principle that anyone whom they didn't know to be ritually clean should be treated as unclean, and so they performed frequent *washings* of themselves and their possessions. Such strictness was not mandated by the Law of Moses, and Christ's reply show that it was unnecessary, though what He condemns is this strictness not in itself but used as a veil for breaking commandments that were found in the old Law, and even in natural law, such as honouring one's parents.

The *beds* mentioned as being washed may be the couches on which people reclined to eat.

The words that Jesus quotes from Isaias fall between one passage where the prophet declares that *the vision* he has reported is for the Jews like *the words of a book that is sealed*, which neither the learned nor the simple can read, and another passage where he foretells a day *when the deaf shall hear the words of the book*.[1] By quoting the words in between, therefore, He is not only revealing to the Pharisees their specific sin and the fact that it had been predicted, but also giving them to understand that despite their learning, the whole of divine revelation is for them like a sealed book, and that a day will soon come when the gentiles, who are currently deaf to the word of God, will come to understand it.

---

1 Is. 29:11–12 and Is. 29:18.

14 And calling again the multitude unto him, he said to them: Hear ye me all, and understand.

15 There is nothing from without a man that entering into him, can defile him. But the things which come from a man, those are they that defile a man.

16 If any man have ears to hear, let him hear.

17 And when he was come into the house from the multitude, his disciples asked him the parable.

18 And he saith to them: So are you also without knowledge? understand you not that every thing from without, entering into a man cannot defile him:

19 Because it entereth not into his heart, but goeth into the belly, and goeth out into the privy, purging all meats?

20 But he said that the things which come out from a man, they defile a man.

21 For from within out of the heart of men proceed evil thoughts, adulteries, fornications, murders,

22 Thefts, covetousness, wickedness, deceit, lasciviousness, an evil eye, blasphemy, pride, foolishness.

23 All these evil things come from within, and defile a man.

Corban is Aramaic for gift or offering. The person in question tells his needy parents that he is offering a sum of money to the temple rather than to them, and that they *shall profit* from this very fact. Possibly some sons dedicated this money to the temple only during the life-time of their parents, so that the temple could benefit from the interest on it, and then reclaimed it after their parents had died.

Christ gives as an example of a commandment of God the precept of Exodus that the one who *curses father or mother* must *die.* Hence, it is not possible for a Christian to claim that capital punishment is intrinsically wrong.

vv. 14–23

Someone might object: given the importance of divine worship, for which ceremonial purity was required, were the Pharisees not right to err on the side of caution in their application of the laws of uncleanness? Our Lord answers this objection by saying to the multitude: *There is nothing from without a man that entering into him, can defile him.* In other words, there is nothing intrinsic about touching a ritually unclean person or about using a plate on which a dead insect has fallen that can make one unfit to worship God; they render one unfit only insofar as God has declared that they shall. Hence, it is irrational to go beyond what God Himself has required when following the laws about these things. By contrast, a person's own sins have an intrinsic power to defile him. These are more than anything else *the things which come from a man,* since only sin is committed by man as first cause, without the concurrence of God.

The Jews had become so accustomed to treating certain foods and other things as unclean that they had come to think of them as being intrinsically and obviously so. Christ indicates that they are unclean only by a positive law of God, and hence only for as long as this law remains in force. But since this law and its abrogation can be known only by faith, He once more speaks of the *ears to hear,* that is, of the infused virtue of faith necessary to receive His words.

The phrase *purging all meats* fits best, from a grammatical point

24 And rising from thence he went into the coasts of Tyre and Sidon: and entering into a house, he would that no man should know it, and he could not be hid.

25 For a woman as soon as she heard of him, whose daughter had an unclean spirit, came in and fell down at his feet.

26 For the woman was a Gentile, a Syro-phoenician born. And she besought him that he would cast forth the devil out of her daughter.

of view, with the earlier words *he saith*; by what He says here, our Lord purges all foods, that is, declares them to be intrinsically clean, and therefore lawful to eat once the ceremonial laws of the Old Testament shall have lost their binding force at His death. Only in hindsight do the apostles fully grasp this: St Peter will require the vision of the sheet let down from heaven containing animals of every kind before he can realise that no creature is unclean in itself.

Evil thoughts give rise to twelve other evils. It is the only time in the gospel that our Lord gives a list of sins, like a physician telling a patient all that he has wrong with him, before offering the remedy. *An evil eye* is an idiom for *envy*. The word translated as *blasphemies* refers to evil speech against human beings as well as against God.

v. 24

We learn from St Matthew that the Pharisees took this teaching about ceremonial uncleanness badly. Perhaps for this reason, Christ leaves the Holy Land for a while; *Tyre and Sidon* were to the north, in Phoenicia. He also symbolically suggests by this action what His quotation from Isaias also indicated, that the word of God will pass to the gentiles. But since it is not yet time to preach to them, *he would that no man should know* that He is there. The prophet Elias also went to live for a while in secret in the region between Tyre and Sidon. Hence, just as He has honoured Moses by coming out of Egypt as a child, so now He honours Elias by retracing the route that that prophet took when exiled for the word of God. By thus reminding the apostles of this prophet, He is also preparing Peter, James, and John to see him very soon on the mount of transfiguration.

vv. 25–30

If it was *not good to take the bread of the children*, that is, the gifts that Christ had come to bestow upon the Jews, *and cast it to the dogs*, by working a miracle for a *Gentile*, why did He do it? Abstractly speaking, it was unfitting, but given the circumstance of her great faith, it became fitting. The Greek word translated

27 Who said to her: Suffer first the children to be filled: for it is not good to take the bread of the children, and cast it to the dogs.

28 But she answered and said to him: Yea, Lord; for the whelps also eat under the table of the crumbs of the children.

29 And he said to her: For this saying go thy way, the devil is gone out of thy daughter.

30 And when she was come into her house, she found the girl lying upon the bed, and that the devil was gone out.

31 And again going out of the coasts of Tyre, he came by Sidon to the sea of Galilee, through the midst of the coasts of Decapolis.

32 And they bring to him one deaf and dumb; and they besought him that he would lay his hand upon him.

33 And taking him from the multitude apart, he put his fingers into his ears, and spitting, he touched his tongue:

34 And looking up to heaven, he groaned, and said to him: *Ephpheta*, which is, Be thou opened.

35 And immediately his ears were opened, and the string of his tongue was loosed, and he spoke right.

36 And he charged them that they should tell no man. But the more he charged them, so much the more a great deal did they publish it.

37 And so much the more did they wonder, saying: He hath done all things well; he hath made both the deaf to hear, and the dumb to speak.

His own tongue was bound and so could not engage in any of these sins. It is *looking up to heaven* that our Lord sighs: He knows that by imparting His Father's gifts to this man, He will also be giving him the power to offend His Father, and to become aware of how others are offending Him. Surely this thought would touch the filial heart of Christ.

Finally, He is foreshadowing His own passion when, in St Paul's words, *with a strong cry and tears* He will merit for mankind the grace to receive and confess the true faith.

here as 'dogs' is translated in the next verse as *whelps*: both times, it is a diminutive form of the word, which may have the effect of softening the epithet.

vv. 31–37

He goes even further north, all the way to *Sidon*, before turning east and then south to reach *the sea of Galilee* and the *Decapolis*. From Sidon to the Decapolis would be a walk of a hundred miles or so.

Only St Mark describes the healing of the *deaf-and-dumb* man by these gestures and the word *Ephpheta*. It is a miniature of the redemption: the *finger* of God in Scripture is an image of the Holy Spirit, while spittle, since it comes from the mouth, is an image of the Word. By the visible missions of the Son and the Holy Spirit, man's *ears* are opened to hear the word of God, and *his tongued loosed* so that he may speak *right*, that is, declare the truth about God in a way that is free from error.

Only here is it said of Jesus that *he groaned*, or sighed, when working a miracle. Why did He do this? First of all, He may simply have been weary, and the act of working a miracle physically demanding: from another passage in the gospel, we seem to learn that in performing a miraculous cure, He habitually experienced a power passing from Himself into the person cured. He may have wished to intimate this here once and for all, as a sign of the reality of His human nature. Perhaps He was also teaching the apostles that their ministry and miracles would be demanding for them.

Then again, until now, this deaf-and-dumb man has been shielded by his very handicap from many sins that ravage God's creation. His ears were closed to the blasphemies, curses, lies, and flattery by which human beings dishonour their tongues.

1 In those days again, when there was a great multitude, and had nothing to eat; calling his disciples together, he saith to them:

2 I have compassion on the multitude, for behold they have now been with me three days, and have nothing to eat.

3 And if I shall send them away fasting to their home, they will faint in the way; for some of them came from afar off.

4 And his disciples answered him: From whence can any one fill them here with bread in the wilderness?

5 And he asked them: How many loaves have ye? Who said: Seven.

6 And taking the seven loaves, giving thanks, he broke, and gave to his disciples for to set before them; and they set them before the people.

7 And they had a few little fishes; and he blessed them, and commanded them to be set before them.

8 And they did eat and were filled; and they took up that which was left of the fragments, seven baskets.

9 And they that had eaten were about four thousand; and he sent them away.

vv. 1–9

COULD THE DISCIPLES HAVE FORGOTTEN the feeding of the five thousand, that they ask our Lord how the great crowd can be filled *with bread in the wilderness*? It hardly seems possible, despite the long walk to Sidon and back that has intervened. Perhaps we should imagine them asking the question with a smile, as if to say, "Will you do it for them again?"

Although all the evangelists narrate the first feeding, only St Matthew and St Mark narrate this feeding of the *four thousand*. Apart from the difference in the numbers of loaves, men, and baskets, there is also a difference in the fish. The first time it was two fishes, here it is *a few little fishes*. Nothing is said this time about sitting in companies of fifties or a hundred, or about there being much grass; but the people are once again *sent away* at the end.

In both miracles, *giving thanks, he broke and gave* the bread *to his disciples* to distribute. Christ called Himself *the living bread*. The first breaking of the loaves may therefore stand as a symbol for His passion. On the eve of His Passion, He gave thanks to His Father for the work accomplished on earth, before surrendering His body to be broken upon the Cross. He placed the merits of this Redemption into the hands of His Church, so that all might have *their fill*, as the broken bread becomes the nourishment of the people; and because these merits are inexhaustible, many *fragments* of the bread remain.

If the breaking of the bread represents the passion, we might expect it to occur just once. But though Christ suffered only once, He does not offer His body only once. Jesus has left to His Church the holy sacrifice of the Mass, and thereby continues to offer Himself till the end of the world. This is represented by the second multiplication of the loaves. If the first disciples sometimes spoke of the Mass as the 'breaking of bread', this was not only because the sacramental species are broken during

10 And immediately going up into a ship with his disciples, he came into the parts of Dalmanutha.

11 And the Pharisees came forth, and began to question with him, asking him a sign from heaven, tempting him.

12 And sighing deeply in spirit, he saith: Why doth this generation seek a sign? Amen, I say to you, a sign shall not be given to this generation.

13 And leaving them, he went up again into the ship, and passed to the other side of the water.

14 And they forgot to take bread; and they had but one loaf with them in the ship.

15 And he charged them, saying: Take heed and beware of the leaven of the Pharisees, and of the leaven of Herod.

16 And they reasoned among themselves, saying: Because we have no bread.

17 Which Jesus knowing, saith to them: Why do you reason, because you have no bread? do you not yet know nor understand? have you still your heart blinded?

the rite, but also, says St Robert Bellarmine, because 'breaking' here means 'immolation'.[1]

That explains why He worked two such similar miracles: the Mass is the image of the Passion. At every Mass, Christ the high priest gives thanks to the Father; He multiplies His presence by the miracle of transubstantiation, and distributes the food to *the people* through the hand of the priest, and yet He remains, however many may have received His body.

That is one explanation of the two miracles, both in their similarity and their difference. But it is not the only one, since in a little while He will intimate that the bread is also to be understood as a symbol for teaching.

vv. 10–13

The location of *Dalmanutha* is unknown. The *Pharisees* who come there ask for *a sign from heaven*, on the pretext that only signs that happen in the heavens, such the sun standing still or manna falling from the sky, would prove Christ's divine mission, and that wonders done on earth might be accomplished by the aid of an evil spirit. This was irrational, since only the Creator has the power to multiply bread, wherever it is done, and so He sighed *deeply*. Such a sign as they professed to desire would *not be given to* that *generation,* since, remarks Cornelius à Lapide, "even had He shown such a sign in heaven, they would immediately have sought a subterfuge, and required some other." Not even the sign in the sun at Fatima has convinced all those who were unwilling to believe.

vv. 14–21

The next episode, on the Sea of Galilee, is mysterious and humorous at the same time. For while it may be, as St Bede says, that when the apostles got on board, "in their eagerness to accompany our Lord, the very need of refreshing their bodies had escaped from their mind", now at any rate, they are

---

1 In the Liturgy of St Mark, used by Coptic Christians, the priest consecrates the bread with the words: "This is my body which is broken for you and given for forgiveness of sins."

18 Having eyes, see you not? and having ears, hear you not? neither do you remember.

19 When I broke the five loaves among five thousand, how many baskets full of fragments took you up? They say to him, Twelve.

20 When also the seven loaves among four thousand, how many baskets of fragments took you up? And they say to him, Seven.

21 And he said to them: How do you not yet understand?

wondering where their next meal will come from. He takes the opportunity to tell them about alien *leaven.* As St Matthew makes explicit when he recounts this episode, leaven here is an image for doctrine: just as a little yeast causes all the dough to rise, so whatever teaching men accept will shape their whole way of thinking and acting. If they listen to the *Pharisees,* they will become corrupters of the Law under the guise of zeal for it; if they listen to *Herod*, they will become openly irreligious.

The apostles interpret this image, easy though it is, in an unintelligent way, being *blinded* for the moment to anything but material bread, and so He responds with one of the most puzzling riddles of the gospel. It's as if He were saying: "Since you like misunderstanding Me so much, I'll give you something not to understand!"

It is clear that some mystery is hidden in the numbers, but what? Christ tells us to understand the bread that He broke as a symbol for the word of God. So, in what sense did He break such bread for a multitude twice? There have been two great, public revelations: the Old and the New Testament. The first time, He broke *five loaves*, because the old Law was contained above all in the five books of Moses. He distributed them through His disciples to *five thousand* men, since God taught the Law through the priests to the Jews: and the Jews are signified by the number five, the Jewish people being recognised by its allegiance to the Law. There were *twelve baskets full of fragments* left over, because the parts of the Old Testament that the Jews could not comprehend before the incarnation were received by the twelve apostles after the resurrection, when Christ *expounded to them in all the scriptures the things that were concerning him.*

The second time, He broke *seven loaves*. The new Law is not principally contained in books, but is rather the Holy Ghost Himself dwelling in the hearts of believers, enlightening us and guiding us how to act. This is why it is represented by the number seven, on account of His seven gifts. This bread is distributed among *four thousand* men: these are the believers in the New Testament. The Catholic people are signified by the number four, because the Church is recognised by being spread through the

22 And they came to Bethsaida; and they bring to him a blind man, and they besought him that he would touch him.

23 And taking the blind man by the hand, he led him out of the town; and spitting upon his eyes, laying his hands on him, he asked him if he saw any thing.

24 And looking up, he said: I see men as it were trees, walking.

25 After that again he laid his hands upon his eyes, and he began to see, and was restored, so that he saw all things clearly.

26 And he sent him into his house, saying: Go into thy house, and if thou enter into the town, tell nobody.

27 And Jesus went out, and his disciples, into the towns of Caesarea Philippi. And in the way, he asked his disciples, saying to them: Whom do men say that I am?

world, that is, by being Catholic: Scripture speaks of th
corners' of the world, as we still do today. Here, there are *seven
baskets of fragments* remaining, perhaps to symbolise the minds
of the angels: for the mysteries of grace that we cannot yet
understand are understood by the angelic host, whom Scripture
calls *the seven spirits which are before his throne*, to whom, says St
Paul, *the manifold wisdom of God* is *made known through the Church*.

If this is correct, it may be with ironic humour that He asks:
How do you not yet understand?

vv. 22–26

Our Lord wishes first to strengthen the confidence of the
blind man. So, He takes him *by the hand*, and they walk together
into the open country. Why does He cure him in two stages, a
unique event in the gospels? On a purely human level, it is an
overwhelming experience for someone who has gone blind to
recover his sight – this man could see in the past, since he knows
what trees look like. Christ therefore treats him gently, first giving him only an imperfect and blurred vision. The two stages of
the cure also suggest our own spiritual progress. To see *men as it
were trees, walking*, means that one recognises that they are men,
but cannot see their faces. When we have been regenerated by
word and sacrament, symbolised by the *spitting* and the *laying*
on of *hands*, we can for the first time recognise other men for
what they are, brothers, at least potentially, but we cannot yet
see their souls, as it were their spiritual countenances. Yet, as
St Thérèse of Lisieux remarked, "souls differ more than faces."
Some further divine gift, in this life or the next, is necessary to
see *all things clearly*.

This formerly blind man must *tell nobody* who has performed
the cure, perhaps lest the inhabitants of Bethsaida attribute it
to the devil and so increase their guilt: Bethsaida is one of the
towns over whose unbelief Christ laments elsewhere.

vv. 27–30

Caesarea Philippi was a city lying just over the northern border
of the holy land. When Jesus was a boy, it had been founded

28 Who answered him, saying: John the Baptist; but some Elias, and others as one of the prophets.

29 Then he saith to them: But whom do you say that I am?

Peter answering said to him: Thou art the Christ.

30 And he strictly charged them that they should not tell any man of him.

31 And he began to teach them, that the Son of man must suffer many things, and be rejected by the ancients and by the high priests, and the scribes, and be killed: and after three days rise again.

32 And he spoke the word openly. And Peter taking him, began to rebuke him.

33 Who turning about and seeing his disciples, threatened Peter, saying: Get behind me, Satan, because thou savourest not the things that are of God, but that are of men.

34 And calling the multitude together with his disciples,

he said to them: If any man will follow me, let him deny himself, and take up his cross, and follow me.

35 For whosoever will save his life, shall lose it: and whosoever shall lose his life for my sake and the gospel, shall save it.

36 For what shall it profit a man, if he gain the whole world, and suffer the loss of his soul?

37 Or what shall a man give in exchange for his soul?

38 For he that shall be ashamed of me, and of my words, in this adulterous and sinful

by the tetrarch Philip, whose wife was stolen by Herod. Philip called it simply 'Caesarea', in honour of the emperor, but people in general called it 'Philip's Caesarea' to distinguish it from other cities of the same name. The River Jordan had its source there.

Why does Jesus choose *the towns*, that is, the outskirts, of this foreign city to ask the disciples for the various opinions about Himself? St John Chrysostom suggests that the disciples would feel freer to speak their mind there, away from the Jewish authorities. It may also be to help the apostles see that *the Christ* will not be a king of the Jews only, but the founder of a new people, at once Jewish and Roman. One enters this people by baptism, symbolised by the Jordan.

St Peter must have related his confession in summary form and without including Christ's response: *Blessed art thou, Simon bar Jona* ... He does this no doubt from humility and perhaps because it was dangerous, especially in Rome, to say openly that he had been promised the keys of a kingdom.

vv. 31–38

What does St Mark mean by *the high priests*, since there was only one high priest in Israel? It is uncertain: the expression may include those who had formerly held this office, or those who were at the head of the twenty-four main priestly divisions.[2]

St Mark uses the same Greek verb three times in a few lines, translated respectively as *strictly charged, rebuked,* and *threatened.* The sense each time is 'warn so as to prevent something or to bring it to an end'.

The evangelist specifies that the instruction to *deny* oneself and *take the cross* is addressed to *the multitude* as well as to *the disciples*, since no one can be saved who refuses it. Christ briefly impresses on them the superiority of the eternal good of salvation over *the whole world*, then, lest they be too dismayed by talk of the cross, He declares that the kingdom of God will soon be seen *in power*, at least by some witnesses. This was variously

---

2   See 1 Paralipomenon 24.

generation: the Son of man also will be ashamed of him, when he shall come in the glory of his Father with the holy angels.

39 And he said to them: Amen I say to you, that there are some of them that stand here, who shall not taste death, till they see the kingdom of God coming in power.

fulfilled: a week later, at the transfiguration; less than a year later at the resurrection; after the resurrection, when the apostles worked miracles in His name; and a generation later, when the temple was destroyed and the old covenant publicly yielded place to the new.

1 And after six days Jesus taketh with him Peter and James and John, and leadeth them up into an high mountain apart by themselves, and was transfigured before them.

2 And his garments became shining and exceeding white as snow, so as no fuller upon earth can make white.

3 And there appeared to them Elias with Moses; and they were talking with Jesus.

4 And Peter answering, said to Jesus: Rabbi, it is good for us to be here: and let us make three tabernacles, one for thee, and one for Moses, and one for Elias.

5 For he knew not what he said: for they were struck with fear.

6 And there was a cloud overshadowing them: and a voice came out of the cloud, saying: This is my most beloved son; hear ye him.

7 And immediately looking about, they saw no man any more, but Jesus only with them.

8 And as they came down from the mountain, he charged them not to tell any man what things they had seen, till the Son of man shall be risen again from the dead.

vv. 1–8

THE OTHER APOSTLES MAY HAVE WON-dered whether St Peter had lost his special status among them after the Lord addressed him as *Satan*. Partly to show them that it is not so, He takes St Peter and the two sons of thunder to the *high mountain, apart by themselves.*[1] This recalls how Moses took Aaron and Aaron's two eldest sons to enter the presence of God on the summit of Mount Sinai. For though the apostles are all brothers, the eleven have also a filial relation to Peter.

In case they had been at all troubled by the two main accu-sations of His enemies, that He infringed the Law and unjustly assumed divine glory to Himself, these apostles are granted to see Moses the law-giver and Elias, famously zealous for God's honour, *talking with Jesus.*

Why is St Peter's first thought to *make three tabernacles?* Some people think that the transfiguration happened about the time of the feast of Tabernacles, when the Jews live for a week in booths made of branches, in commemoration of their forty years in the desert after the exodus: this is an autumnal feast. Hence, although *he knew not what he said*, he spoke in a way prophetically, since St Luke relates that Moses and Elias were speaking to our Lord about His exodus from this world.

One week previously, Jesus had accepted the title of *the Christ*, that is, the one anointed to be priest, prophet and king. Now, the Father's *voice* from *the cloud* speaks certain words that He had inspired a priest, a prophet, and a king to use in the Old Testament, thus intimating His Son's possession of these three offices. David, the king, had heard the words: *Thou art my Son*; Isaias, the prophet, had heard: *Behold my chosen, my soul delighteth in him;* and Moses, the priest, had said to the people, *The Lord shall*

---

1 Origen, born around AD 184, states that this was Mount Thabor, south-west of the Sea of Galilee (*Commentary on Psalm* 88.13). St Jerome says the same (Letter 46.13, *To Marcella*). Both men knew Palestine well.

9 And they kept the word to themselves; questioning together what that should mean, when he shall be risen from the dead.

10 And they asked him, saying: Why then do the Pharisees and scribes say that Elias must come first?

11 Who answering, said to them: Elias, when he shall come first, shall restore all things; and as it is written of the Son of man, that he must suffer many things and be despised.

12 But I say to you, that Elias also is come, (and they have done to him whatsoever they would,) as it is written of him.

13 And coming to his disciples, he saw a great multitude about them, and the scribes disputing with them.

raise up to thee a prophet of thy nation like unto me: him thou shalt hear.
At the baptism, the voice of the Father had already said: *This is my beloved Son.* Why are the words *Hear ye him* spoken only now? These two theophanies suggest the two stages of our adopted sonship: although we already become children of God at baptism, we are still *waiting for the adoption of the sons of God, the redemption of our body*, at our resurrection. The first adoption we receive without merit, and often even before we have the use of reason; the second adoption will be a reward for hearing the words of the Son and putting them into practice.

vv. 9–13

Why are the disciples uncertain what is meant by the Son of man's rising *from the dead*? The Jews knew about the general resurrection at the end of the age, but not yet about the resurrection of the Messiah before the end.

Our Lord does not reject the teaching of the Pharisees and scribes that *Elias must come first*, that is, before the Messiah, since this *is written* in the prophet Malachias. But He goes on to refer to prophecies that the scribes and Pharisees neglected, about the sufferings of the Messiah: His words here may also be translated as a question: How *is it that it is written of the Son of man that he must suffer?* He allows the three apostles to deduce the answer for themselves: if Elias is to come before the glorious coming of the Messiah, and yet the Messiah is to suffer, then the Messiah must come twice. Elias *shall restore all things*: this is usually understood to refer to a future conversion of the Jews, since Malachias had said that Elias would *turn the heart of the fathers to the children, and the heart of the children to their fathers*, as it were reconciling the ancient patriarchs with their descendants before the return of the Messiah.

Yet the scribes and Pharisees are not wholly wrong, since in a secondary sense, Malachias's words refer to St John the Baptist. The angel Gabriel had foretold to John's father that he would *turn the hearts of the fathers unto the children*, indicating by this partial quotation that the Baptist is a partial fulfilment of the old prophecy.

14 And presently all the people seeing Jesus, were astonished and struck with fear; and running to him, they saluted him.

15 And he asked them: What do you question about among you?

16 And one of the multitude, answering, said: Master, I have brought my son to thee, having a dumb spirit.

17 Who, wheresoever he taketh him, dasheth him, and he foameth, and gnasheth with the teeth, and pineth away; and I spoke to thy disciples to cast him out, and they could not.

18 Who answering them, said: O incredulous generation, how long shall I be with you? how long shall I suffer you? bring him unto me.

19 And they brought him. And when he had seen him, immediately the spirit troubled him; and being thrown down upon the ground, he rolled about foaming.

20 And he asked his father: How long time is it since this hath happened unto

him? But he said: From his infancy:

21 And oftentimes hath he cast him into the fire and into waters to destroy him. But if thou canst do any thing, help us, having compassion on us.

22 And Jesus saith to him: If thou canst believe, all things are possible to him that believeth.

23 And immediately the father of the boy crying out, with tears said: I do believe, Lord: help my unbelief.

24 And when Jesus saw the multitude running together, he threatened the unclean spirit, saying to him: Deaf and dumb spirit, I command thee, go out of him; and enter not any more into him.

25 And crying out, and greatly tearing him, he went out of him, and he became as dead, so that many said: He is dead.

26 But Jesus taking him by the hand, lifted him up; and he arose.

27 And when he was come into the house, his disciples

No one knows where Elias is now or whether he is to be seen again by many or by few. But it has been very generally supposed that he will resist the antichrist in some way.

vv. 14–29

Only St Mark tells us that *all the people were astonished and struck with fear* when they saw Christ after the transfiguration. The fact that He arrived at just the right time to solve the dispute between the *scribes* and the *disciples,* can hardly account for it. It is likely that some of the glory had not faded. Even Moses's face had 'horns of light' coming from it after he had received the Old Testament from God, which made the children of Israel afraid to come near him; and if *that which is done away was glorious, much more that which remaineth is in glory.*[2]

Each of the first three gospels tells the story of this man with his possessed son, but St Mark most vividly. Only he records the father's words that his son habitually *gnasheth with the teeth and pineth away*: this last phrase seems to mean 'becomes stiff and lifeless'. This instance of the devil's malice is reminiscent of Psalm 111, which contrasts the righteous man with the wicked. Of the latter, it says that he *shall gnash his teeth and pine away*. Of the righteous it says that *light is risen up in darkness* for him, and that *his horn shall be exalted in glory*: since the word for 'horn' also means 'ray of light', this phrase recalls the transfiguration that has just occurred, when Christ's face shone in the night.

Again, only this evangelist relates the conversation between Christ and the boy's father. By asking *how long* it was that the boy had shown signs of possession, He sets an example for exorcists, who work more expeditiously when they know when and how an evil spirit entered. Having witnessed the disciples fail, the father expresses himself with uncertainty, saying: *If thou canst do anything.* The Greek of our Lord's reply is difficult to translate succinctly, and it is also uncertain whether the word 'believe' in the first clause is originally part of it, since it is not found in all the manuscripts. If it is, then the first part

---

2   See Exodus 34:30 and 2 Cor. 3:7–11.

secretly asked him: Why could not we cast him out?

28 And he said to them: This kind can go out by nothing, but by prayer and fasting.

29 And departing from thence, they passed through Galilee, and he would not that any man should know it.

30 And he taught his disciples, and said to them: The Son of man shall be betrayed into the hands of men, and they shall kill him; and after that he is killed, he shall rise again the third day.

31 But they understood not the word, and they were afraid to ask him.

32 And they came to Capharnaum. And when they were in the house, he asked them: What did you treat of on the way?

of the reply means something like: "the real question is 'if you can believe'." If not, then it might be translated: "as for 'if you can' . . ." In either case, the point is the same: the exorcism is made doubtful not by a possible deficiency in Christ's power, but by the weakness of the man's faith.

This does not imply that lack of faith is always to blame when exorcisms are slow, just as lack of faith is not necessarily the reason why a prayer for bodily healing may not be granted. While on earth, there was always a reason why Christ should work such miracles for whoever asked with faith, namely, to prove His divine mission. Now that His divine mission has been sufficiently proved, prayers and exorcisms are effective when this will be for the spiritual good of those who ask.

What is the relevance of the fact that *the multitude* was running *together* to the place? Jesus does not perform His works with more publicity than necessary, nor does He want the father's distress to become a spectacle, and so when the crowds increase, He exorcises the boy without further delay. It is also a lesson to exorcists to work with as few people present as is compatible with safety. Could He not have prevented the spirit from *greatly tearing* the boy? Yes, but He wanted its malice to be fully manifested. Exorcists tell us that a possessing spirit is frequently most violent when on the point of being expelled.

It is not surprising that *prayer* should be necessary for expelling demons; but why are there some whose expulsion also requires *fasting*? Some demons are more wicked than others, and fasting lends strength to prayer by causing the mind to be less immersed in material things.

vv. 30–32

Why were the disciples *afraid to ask him* the meaning of His prophecy of death and resurrection? Perhaps because they remembered the sternness with which He had spoken to St Peter when the latter had remonstrated with Him after the previous prophecy.

33 But they held their peace, for in the way they had disputed among themselves, which of them should be the greatest.

34 And sitting down, he called the twelve, and saith to them: If any man desire to be first, he shall be the last of all, and the minister of all.

35 And taking a child, he set him in the midst of them.

Whom when he had embraced, he saith to them:

36 Whosoever shall receive one such child as this in my name, receiveth me. And whosoever shall receive me, receiveth not me, but him that sent me.

37 John answered him, saying: Master, we saw one casting out devils in thy name, who followeth not us, and we forbade him.

38 But Jesus said: Do not forbid him. For there is no man that doth a miracle in my name, and can soon speak ill of me.

39 For he that is not against you, is for you.

40 For whosoever shall give you to drink a cup of water in my name, because you belong

to Christ: amen I say to you, he shall not lose his reward.

41 And whosoever shall scandalize one of these little ones that believe in me; it were better for him that a millstone were hanged around his neck, and he were cast into the sea.

vv. 33–37

Rather as when dealing with sin in Eden, so when He has to deal with it among the apostles, our Lord begins not with an accusation but with a question, asking them what they had been talking about on the way to *Capharnaum.* Like Adam after his fall, *they held their peace.* Only St Mark tells us that Jesus sits down to speak to them: it is the posture of a master, with the twelve standing round, and so the circumstances of the lesson will reinforce its content. His words seem to carry a double meaning. Primarily, they are an invitation: one becomes great in the kingdom of heaven by serving as a humble *minister.* Secondarily, they contain a warning: he who desires worldly greatness will find that God makes use of him against his will, as minister *of all.* Again, only St Mark mentions that our Lord *embraced* the *child* whom He put *in the midst of* the apostles. Since they are in *the house* at Capharnaum, which belonged to St Peter, it has been suggested that it may have been Peter's child. But that is only a guess.

vv. 38–41

He tells St John not to *forbid* the exorcist from *casting our devils in* His *name,* for the sake of the good that was arising from his activity, at least for now. "He shows," says St Bede, "that no one is to be driven away from that partial goodness which he possesses already, but rather to be stirred up to that which he has not as yet obtained". But is it not dangerous to attempt an exorcism without due authority? The Jewish hierarchy, which for the time being still enjoyed its divine privileges, also had its appointed exorcists: probably he was one of these.

His next words explain more generally how such a person *who followeth not* the apostles may nevertheless be *for* them and not *against* them, that is, how someone who is not yet a member of the Church may be on the side of the Church. Two conditions are necessary: that the person acknowledge His *name,* and that He serve those *who belong* to Christ. Such people are similar to catechumens, whom St Robert Bellarmine says can be in the Church according to their soul, though not yet according to their body. "Not", adds St Augustine, "that they ought already to think themselves safe and secure on account of this good

42 And if thy hand scandalize thee, cut it off: it is better for thee to enter into life, maimed, than having two hands to go into hell, into unquenchable fire:

43 Where their worm dieth not, and the fire is not extinguished.

44 And if thy foot scandalize thee, cut it off. It is better for thee to enter lame into life everlasting, than having two feet, to be cast into the hell of unquenchable fire:

45 Where their worm dieth not, and the fire is not extinguished.

46 And if thy eye scandalize thee, pluck it out. It is better for thee with one eye to enter into the kingdom of God, than having two eyes to be cast into the hell of fire:

47 Where their worm dieth not, and the fire is not extinguished.

48 For every one shall be salted with fire: and every victim shall be salted with salt.

49 Salt is good. But if the salt became unsavoury; wherewith will you season it? Have salt in you, and have peace among you.

among themselves they grow *unsavoury*, they will not, once He has gone, find any other person who might *season* them.

The 'fire' that salts *everyone* may also be understood to refer to the tribulations of this life, which all, both good and bad, must experience. Our Lord would then be instructing us that we should not worry about what we lose here below, but endeavour by accepting sufferings wisely, to make of ourselves a 'victim', that is, an offering acceptable to God. "I suffer a lot", mused St Thérèse of Lisieux, "but do I suffer well?"

Jesus says all these things after having brought the child into the midst of them. This refutes the error of those today who say that children should not be taught about hell.

will which they have towards Christians, without being washed with His baptism, and incorporated in His unity, but that they are already being so guided by the mercy of God, that they may attain these also, and thus depart from this life in safety."

vv. 42–50

If Christ's identification of Himself with His Church allows one to gain an eternal *reward* by serving Christ's people, to separate anyone from His Church therefore merits a punishment worse than being drowned by a *mill-stone*. According to St Gregory the Great, the mill-stone, which is turned with toil, symbolises the repetitive round of worldly work. Better, explains the apostle of England, to go to hell after a life spent in such tasks, than to accept ecclesiastical office and by one's bad teaching or example to cause others to fall.

Not only is there a duty not to *scandalise* others, there is also a duty not to let oneself be scandalised, that is, led into sin by others. It is not worth incurring damnation either for the *hand*, that is, one's work, or the *foot*, one's inclinations, or for the *eye*, a person whom one holds dear; for the consciences of the lost are never at peace, as if they had a *worm* within.

But why is there an *unquenchable fire* to punish sin? We should not be surprised by this, since *everyone shall be salted with fire*: that is, the unchanging divine nature, which Scripture calls elsewhere *a devouring fire* on account of its unapproachability, like salt also preserves each soul in the state that it had at the moment of departing this world.

One aspect of the unchangeableness of God is His faithfulness to His covenant, to signify which He commanded that *the preserving salt of the covenant* must be offered with *every victim*.[3] Likewise, though who *have in* themselves the *salt* of wisdom, and know how to *cut off* and *pluck out* occasions, of sin will become acceptable offerings to Him. The apostles should have this salt more than anyone else, having been appointed as *the salt of the earth* to purify and instruct worldly men; but if by contending

---

3 See Leviticus 2:13.

1 And rising up from thence, he cometh into the coasts of Judea beyond the Jordan: and the multitudes flock to him again. And as he was accustomed, he taught them again.

2 And the Pharisees coming to him asked him: Is it lawful for a man to put away his wife? tempting him.

3 But he answering, saith to them: What did Moses command you?

4 Who said: Moses permitted to write a bill of divorce, and to put her away.

5 To whom Jesus answering, said: Because of the hardness of your heart he wrote you that precept.

6 But from the beginning of the creation, God made them male and female.

7 For this cause a man shall leave his father and mother; and shall cleave to his wife.

8 And they two shall be in one flesh. Therefore now they are not two, but one flesh.

9 What therefore God hath joined together, let not man put asunder.

10 And in the house again his disciples asked him concerning the same thing.

11 And he saith to them: Whosoever shall put away his wife and marry another, committeth adultery against her.

12 And if the wife shall put away her husband, and be married to another, she committeth adultery.

THIS IS A TURNING POINT IN THE STORY. Our Lord leaves Galilee and goes to *the coasts*, or territory, *of Judea*, in preparation for the end. The *Pharisees* already know about His teaching on marriage and divorce. They are probably trying to provoke against Him the hostility of Herod and Herodias, each of whom has divorced a spouse. Herod rules over this area *beyond the Jordan*, called Peraea.

By using the word *command*, Christ causes the position of the Pharisees to appear weaker: they are obliged to reply, not that anything was commanded but that something was *permitted*.

The old Law did not teach any right of divorce, but assumed that divorce would sometimes happen, and commanded ways by which it was to be limited: a divorce could not be effected verbally, or by proxy, nor revoked after a second marriage. But was divorce permitted in the old Law in the sense of simply not being forbidden under some specified penalty, to be inflicted by a human court, or was it permitted in the sense that the Jews would not be punished for it by God, even in the next life? Since divorce and remarriage is an intrinsic evil, it might seem that it was only the former. But then it would seem that the Jews had been hardly treated, if the Law had failed to tell them about something necessary for salvation. It seems therefore that by not explicitly forbidding it, God manifested His purpose of tolerating, that is, of not punishing divorce as such even in the next life; although if evil things such as anger or lust had prompted a given divorce, these would be punished. For those things were forbidden even in the old Law.

God *made male and female*, and this *from the beginning of creation*; this seems to contradict the opinion of those who think that they were made long ages afterwards.

The 'permission' or toleration of divorce in the old Law is here revoked, even before the positive precepts of that Law ceased to be binding on Good Friday. His words to the disciples *in the*

13 And they brought to him young children, that he might touch them. And the disciples rebuked them that brought them.

14 Whom when Jesus saw, he was much displeased, and saith to them: Suffer the little children to come unto me, and forbid them not; for of such is the kingdom of God.

15 Amen I say to you, whosoever shall not receive the kingdom of God as a little child, shall not enter into it.

16 And embracing them, and laying his hands upon them, he blessed them.

17 And when he was gone forth into the way, a certain man running up and kneeling before him, asked him, Good Master, what shall I do that I may receive life everlasting?

18 And Jesus said to him, Why callest thou me good? None is good but one, that is God.

19 Thou knowest the commandments: Do not commit adultery, do not kill, do not steal, bear not false witness, do no fraud, honour thy father and mother.

20 But he answering, said to him: Master, all these things I have observed from my youth.

21 And Jesus looking on him, loved him, and said to him: One thing is wanting unto thee: go, sell whatsoever thou hast, and give to the poor, and thou shalt have treasure in heaven; and come, follow me.

22 Who being struck sad at that saying, went away sorrowful: for he had great possessions.

23 And Jesus looking round about, saith to his disciples: How hardly shall they that

house explicitly state only that the spouse who initiates the divorce and marries *another, committeth adultery*; but since this is true only because the original marriage remains in existence in God's sight, it follows that even a spouse unwillingly divorced would also incur the same kind of guilt, though to a lesser degree, by attempting a new marriage. "If he had wished one wife to be put away and another to be brought in", remarks St John Chrysostom, "He would have created several women."

vv. 13–16

Since the primary end of marriage is to raise children for the kingdom of God, Christ completes His teaching about marriage by a blessing of children. The apostles' attempt to prevent *them that brought them* gives rise to the only occasion in the gospels when He was *much displeased*. Once again, only St Mark relates that He took the children in His arms before blessing them.

vv. 17–31

The story of the rich young man is told vividly by this evangelist. The man came *running up and* was *kneeling before him* when he asked his question. He is enthusiastic about perfection: but as a certain philosopher has said, enthusiasm for a virtue is not the same as the possession of it. *Jesus looking on him, loved him*, for who does not love enthusiasm for what is good?

This gospel also relates Christ's subsequent words to the disciples more fully than do the other gospels. The reason it is so hard for them *that have* riches to *enter into the kingdom of God* is because it is so hard for them not to *trust* in them. The human will, unlike other things in this world, has a power to resist the divine action on it, and so it is *easier for a camel to pass through the eye of a needle* than for the rich man to be saved, since the camel, unlike the rich man, cannot refuse its consent to the miracle.[1]

---

1 There is, incidentally, no evidence for the claim sometime heard that 'the eye of a needle' was the name of a narrow gate somewhere in Palestine.

have riches, enter into the kingdom of God!

24 And the disciples were astonished at his words. But Jesus again answering, saith to them: Children, how hard is it for them that trust in riches, to enter into the kingdom of God?

25 It is easier for a camel to pass through the eye of a needle, than for a rich man to enter into the kingdom of God.

26 Who wondered the more, saying among themselves: Who then can be saved?

27 And Jesus looking on them, saith: With men it is impossible; but not with God: for all things are possible with God.

28 And Peter began to say unto him: Behold, we have left all things, and have followed thee.

29 Jesus answering, said: Amen I say to you, there is no man who hath left house or brethren, or sisters, or father, or mother, or children, or lands, for my sake and for the gospel,

30 Who shall not receive an hundred times as much, now in this time; houses, and brethren, and sisters, and mothers, and children, and lands, with persecutions: and in the world to come life everlasting.

31 But many that are first, shall be last: and the last, first.

32 And they were in the way going up to Jerusalem: and Jesus went before them, and they were astonished; and following were afraid. And taking again the twelve, he began to tell them the things that should befall him.

33 Saying: Behold we go up to Jerusalem, and the Son of man shall be betrayed to the chief priests, and to the scribes and ancients, and they shall condemn him to death, and shall deliver him to the Gentiles.

34 And they shall mock him, and spit on him, and scourge him, and kill him: and the third day he shall rise again.

This is the first time that we hear our Lord addressing the disciples as *children*. The next time will be at the Last Supper after Judas has gone out, although then the word used will be a diminutive, *little children*. It seems that the shock of His teaching about money, especially after the teaching about the indissolubility of marriage, was so great that He needed, as it were, to soften the blow.

He mentions those who give up *father*, yet does not mention 'fathers' in the list of what is received *an hundred times as much*. This may be lest He seem to contradict what He says elsewhere: *Call none your father upon earth*, and also because He wants to direct their minds above all to their heavenly Father. Only St Mark records that Christ mentions *persecutions* along with the blessings to be received even *now in this time*. Perhaps St Peter was moved to include this in his preaching because he foresaw that his flock in Rome would soon be persecuted, as came to pass under Nero.

How do the words *Many that are first shall be last, and the last, first* relate to what comes before? The apostles will be last in this time, since they will not enjoy the hundred-fold in the manner of the wealthy of this world, but in the way suggested by the words of St Paul: *Having nothing and possessing all things.*

vv. 32–34

The evangelist does not explain the fact, which again only he records, that the disciples *were astonished* as Jesus *went before them* to Jerusalem. Were they astonished that having foretold how the chief priests would put Him to death, He was nonetheless going to meet them? Yet the request of St James and St John, which follows immediately, shows that at least some of the apostles were still hoping for a glorious manifestation of Himself as Messiah. Perhaps, then, this amazement was a sort of supernatural awe that fell upon them without their being able to explain it. Or perhaps they saw something glorious in His person, somewhat as at the transfiguration; this might also explain how James and John could so soon speak of sitting with Him in His glory.

35 And James and John the sons of Zebedee, come to him, saying: Master, we desire that whatsoever we shall ask, thou wouldst do it for us:

36 But he said to them: What would you that I should do for you?

37 And they said: Grant to us, that we may sit, one on thy right hand, and the other on thy left hand, in thy glory.

38 And Jesus said to them: You know not what you ask. Can you drink of the chalice that I drink of: or be baptized with the baptism wherewith I am baptized?

39 But they said to him: We can. And Jesus saith to them: You shall indeed drink of the chalice that I drink of: and with the baptism wherewith I am baptized, you shall be baptized.

40 But to sit on my right hand, or on my left, is not mine to give to you, but to them for whom it is prepared.

Only St Mark mentions, in this third of Christ's prophecies of the passion, the detail that they *will spit on him.* Maybe St Peter witnessed it.

vv. 35–40

How can *James and John* seek to sit on either side of Christ, in His *glory*? Don't they know that Peter was the first among the twelve? Perhaps they imagine that in the Messianic kingdom, Peter will be travelling about as Christ's vice-gerent, and that they will be able to stay in the court in the king's presence. If they had seriously intended to usurp his position, they would surely have received a sterner reply. Were they still thinking of an earthly glory, such as Solomon had possessed, only greater, given that Christ had just spoken to them of receiving *houses* and *lands* a *hundred time as much* as before? Or were they thinking of a supernatural glory *in the world to come,* after the general resurrection? Perhaps their notions of the future were too confused for they themselves to know exactly what they meant, since Christ replies: *You know not what you ask.* In any case, the only people who will be publicly placed *on* His *right hand and on* His *left* will be the two thieves on Calvary.

Why does Jesus speak to them of drinking *of the chalice* and of being *baptised with* His *baptism*, as if these were the necessary conditions for them to obtain their request, and then, when they declare that they are ready to do these things, refuse it? Could He not have said straightaway that *it* was *not* His *to give to* them? If He had done so, they might have supposed that they could nevertheless obtain it by some bold initiative. But why is it not His to give, since He says elsewhere: *All things whatsoever the Father hath, are mine*? Perhaps because that was said of His divine nature, and He is speaking now of His human will; or else, because He appropriates, that is, particularly attributes, to the Father the act of predestining the saints to glory, as in the creed we attribute to the Father the act of creating heaven and earth. Both predestining and creating are striking manifestations of power, and since the Father by His power is the source of the other two divine persons, it is fitting to appropriate these acts to Him.

41 And the ten hearing it, began to be much displeased at James and John.

42 But Jesus calling them, saith to them: You know that they who seem to rule over the Gentiles, lord it over them: and their princes have power over them.

43 But it is not so among you: but whosoever will be greater, shall be your minister.

44 And whosoever will be first among you, shall be the servant of all.

45 For the Son of man also is not come to be ministered unto, but to minister, and to give his life a redemption for many.

But since the saints merit their predestined glory through their actions, why could drinking the chalice, that is, accepting their predestined path, and being baptised with Christ's baptism, that is, sharing in His sufferings for the salvation of the world, not after all be a way for James and John to reach the two places in question? That is, why does the Father's predestining decree exclude their request? In predestining His Son as man to have the highest place in the kingdom, God the Father chose Mary and Joseph to be closest to Him in glory, and so these two thrones are taken.[2]

St James was beheaded by Herod, and so became the first martyr among the apostles. St John accepted martyrdom without undergoing it: Tertullian, who was born about fifty years after the end of St John's life on earth, recounts that the apostle was plunged into boiling oil in Rome, and that when he miraculously emerged unhurt, he was sent back into exile on Patmos.[3] The church of St John before the Latin Gate marks the spot. He was also a martyr of desire, remaining on earth long after the others; so, on his feast day, the Church sings in his person, "O Lord, receive me, that I may be with my brothers. Open to me the gate of life and lead me in to Thy festal meal."

vv. 41–45

Having previously healed the apostles of their ambition by the child He placed in their midst, He now does the same by the example of the *princes*, that is, the great ones, of the *Gentiles,* whose arbitrary or vulgar displays of power would be odious to God-fearing Jews. If He speaks of those *who seem to rule*, rather than of those who do rule, this is perhaps because 'rule' is an honourable word, applied to God Himself, and the activities of these pagans are rather a kind of misrule.

He repeats His earlier teaching with greater emphasis: previously, He had said that the one wishing to be first would be

---

2 "Since the bond of marriage united Joseph to the Blessed Virgin, doubtless he approached nearer than any other to the eminent dignity by which the Mother of God greatly surpasses all created things" (Pope Leo XIII, *Quamquam pluries*).

3 *On the Prescription of Heretics*, 36.

46 And they came to Jericho: and as he went out of Jericho, with his disciples, and a very great multitude, Bartimeus the blind man, the son of Timeus, sat by the wayside begging.

47 Who when he had heard, that it was Jesus of Nazareth, began to cry out, and to say: Jesus son of David, have mercy on me.

48 And many rebuked him, that he might hold his peace; but he cried a great deal the more: Son of David, have mercy on me.

49 And Jesus, standing still, commanded him to be called. And they call the blind man, saying to him: Be of better comfort: arise, he calleth thee.

50 Who casting off his garment leaped up, and came to him.

51 And Jesus answering, said to him: What wilt thou that I should do to thee? And the blind man said to him: Rabboni, that I may see.

52 And Jesus saith to him: Go thy way, thy faith hath made thee whole. And immediately he saw, and followed him.

minister of all; now He says that this one will be *servant*, literally, 'slave', *of all*. Lest this seem too much to accept, He is obliged to mention His own work, of becoming a *redemption*, or ransom, and hence lower even than a slave, since to obtain a slave, one will give away a ransom. The religious of the Order of our Lady of Ransom imitated Jesus in this, by adding to the vows of religion a fourth vow to become the property of pagans, if this was necessary to free a Christian slave.

Our Lord says that He will give Himself *for many*. He dies for all: "There is not, never has been, and never will be a single man for whom Christ did not suffer."[4] St Albert the Great therefore remarks that the word 'many' suggests how His power to redeem is not limited to the number of human beings who will in fact come into existence until the end of time, but would have sufficed also for an indefinitely greater multitude. Yet it also suggests, says St Bede, that not all will believe.

vv. 46–52

Is this blind man, Bartimaeus, the same as the one who is described by St Luke as being cured by Christ when *he drew nigh to Jericho*? St Mark says that this man is cured *as he went out of Jericho*. It is possible that St Luke gave a condensed version of events, and that although the man was asking for help as Christ entered the city, he was obliged to persevere in asking and was cured only when Christ left it. But that is not a natural reading of St Luke; and despite the similarities in the story, there is an apparent difference between the way the two men come to Christ. In St Luke, the blind man is *commanded to be brought*; here, the blind man is *commanded to be called*, and comes by himself, having *leaped up*. The similarity between the stories may also arise because the second beggar had heard how the first was cured by calling on Jesus as *Son of David*.

---

4 2nd Synod of Quierzy, AD 853.

1 And when they were drawing near to Jerusalem and to Bethania at the mount of Olives, he sendeth two of his disciples,

2 And saith to them: Go into the village that is over against you, and immediately at your coming in thither, you shall find a colt tied, upon which no man yet hath sat: loose him, and bring him.

3 And if any man shall say to you, What are you doing? say ye that the Lord hath need of him: and immediately he will let him come hither.

4 And going their way, they found the colt tied before the gate without, in the meeting of two ways: and they loose him.

5 And some of them that stood there, said to them: Why are you loosing the colt?

6 Who said to them as Jesus had commanded them; and they let him go with them.

7 And they brought the colt to Jesus; and they lay their garments on him, and he sat upon him.

8 And many spread their garments in the way: and others cut down boughs from the trees, and strewed them in the way.

9 And they that went before and they that followed, cried, saying: Hosanna, blessed is he that cometh in the name of the Lord.

10 Blessed be the kingdom of our father David that cometh: Hosanna in the highest.

11 And he entered into Jerusalem, into the temple: and having viewed all things round about, when now the eventide was come, he went out to Bethania with the twelve.

VV. 1–10

ONLY ST MARK INCLUDES THE DETAIL THAT the *two disciples* found the *colt tied before the gate without, at the meeting of two ways.* It may be that St Peter was one of these disciples, as he was one of the two sent a few days later to find the room for the Passover. St Ambrose sees in this colt, tied to the village gate, "with no fixed owner, without stall, or food, or stable" an image of mankind before the Redeemer came.

As well as fulfilling the prophecy of Zacharias about the king who would come to *Jerusalem,* as *the just and saviour, poor, and riding upon a colt, the foal of an ass,* Christ's entrance also recalls the beginning of the reign of Solomon. Solomon's older half-brother, Adonias, had tried to pre-empt the succession by having himself declared king as their father David lay dying, but David acted quickly to prevent this by ordering Solomon to be anointed and then placed on the king's mule. Seated thus on the royal beast, Solomon was acclaimed by the multitude, and Adonias's attempt to seize power failed. Whether or not the crowds on Palm Sunday saw an allusion to those ancient events, they evoked them by their acclamations, especially in some words reported only by St Mark: *Blessed be the kingdom of our father David that cometh.* It was for his part in the conspiracy that Abiathar, mentioned earlier in this gospel, was cast out of the priesthood.

V. 11

From St Matthew and St Luke, we might have supposed that the expulsion of the traders from the temple happened on Palm Sunday itself. St Mark makes it clear that although our Lord went to the temple on the Sunday, He reserved the expulsion for the following day: the day of the entrance was to be one of public celebration. Yet He *viewed all things round about,* without acting, as if to show that when He drove out the traders on the morrow, it would not be from a sudden impulse or emotion.

12 And the next day when they came out from Bethania, he was hungry.

13 And when he had seen afar off a fig tree having leaves, he came if perhaps he might find any thing on it. And when he was come to it, he found nothing but leaves. For it was not the time for figs.

14 And answering he said to it: May no man hereafter eat fruit of thee any more for ever. And his disciples heard it.

Since next morning He is *hungry,* we may presume that He was
not offered any food in Jerusalem, just as He was not given
any lodging there. "Such was the poverty of the Lord", writes
St Bede, "and so far was He from flattering anyone, that in so
large a city, He found no host, and no place to dwell."

VV. 12–14

He returns to Jerusalem on the Monday, and sees *a fig tree afar
off.* Hosea had compared the Jews when they came out of Egypt
to *the first-fruits of the fig tree.* Prophesying a time when the scribes
and the priests would become deceitful, and strangers would
invade the land, Jeremias had said: *There are no grapes on the vines
and there are no figs on the fig tree.* Lamenting that evil-doers were
plotting to shed the blood of their brother, Micheas said: *Woe is
me . . . there is no cluster to eat, my soul desired the first ripe figs.* Christ
continues and fulfils this prophetic tradition in looking to see
if perhaps he might find anything on this tree and cursing it because
it has borne no fruit. "Since He is good and gentle," asks St
Ephraim, "why did He command the fig tree to dry up?" The
same author replies: "The time of His sufferings was near, and
so, lest it be thought that He was captured because He was
unable to free Himself, He cursed the fig tree, as a sign for His
friends, and a miracle for His enemies."

We can also say that He is judging Israel, as represented and
shaped by its rulers, for having *nothing but leaves,* that is, only
words of allegiance to God, without faith, hope and charity.

But why does He symbolise all this by seeking fruit *when it was
not the time for figs*? As well as the main crop, which ripens in late
summer, fig trees may produce an early, though smaller, crop
in the spring. The relation between the two crops would have
been a suitable simile for Israel in comparison to the nations.

The result of its barrenness is that *no man* will *hereafter eat
fruit of* the tree *any more for ever,* or literally, 'unto the age'. This
is a prophecy that God will not receive the fruit that He desires
from Israel; or at least not until *the times of the nations* are fulfilled.

Since it was from *fig leaves* that our first parents sewed
together *aprons* in a rather pathetic attempt to hide their

15 And they came to Jerusalem. And when he was entered into the temple, he began to cast out them that sold and bought in the temple, and overthrew the tables of the moneychangers, and the chairs of them that sold doves.

16 And he suffered not that any man should carry a vessel through the temple;

17 And he taught, saying to them: Is it not written, My house shall be called the house of prayer to all nations? But you have made it a den of thieves.

18 Which when the chief priests and the scribes had heard, they sought how they might destroy him. For they feared him, because the whole multitude was in admiration at his doctrine.

19 And when evening was come, he went forth out of the city.

20 And when they passed by in the morning they saw the fig tree dried up from the roots.

21 And Peter remembering, said to him: Rabbi, behold the fig tree, which thou didst curse, is withered away.

22 And Jesus answering, saith to them: Have the faith of God.

23 Amen I say to you, that whosoever shall say to this mountain, Be thou removed

nakedness after the Fall, the withering of this tree also seems to be God's judgement on all human attempts to hide from Him. For the Passion is at hand, which alone can cover our shame. Hence God in Eden replaced Adam and Eve's aprons of leaves with *garments of skins*, symbolising that only the death of a victim would help them.

VV. 15–20

In speaking of the profanation of the temple, only this evangelist reports the phrase *for all the nations*. The trading must have been conducted in the outermost court, which was reserved for the gentiles. Those gentiles who believed in or who were looking for the true God were thus prevented from praying to Him.

Again, only St Mark relates that Christ's prophetic action in the temple included His forbidding anyone *to carry anything through* it. This may refer to carrying profane things, unrelated to worship. But since the evangelist expresses himself absolutely, it seems to include also the animals brought for sacrifice. He would thus be temporarily suspending the worship of Israel as a sign that it will fail altogether in a generation, as He prophesies later this week. In either case, Christ's actions in the temple appear not only prophetic but also miraculous, for how else could the great active throng be stilled, so as to be *in admiration at his doctrine*?

On the Tuesday morning, they see the *withered* fig tree. Only St Mark tells us that it is *from the roots* that it is *dried up*, just as only he tells us just before that the *chief priests and scribes sought* to kill Him when they were rebuked in the temple. This is not a coincidence. The chief priests and scribes are as it were the roots of the people, whose example will take away the sap from the rest.

VV. 21–24

There are three occasions in the first three gospels where our Lord speaks to the disciples about the power of faith. After the transfiguration, in Galilee, He tells them that if they have faith like a grain of mustard seed, they will *say to this mountain, remove from here to there, and it shall remove* (Matt. 17:19). 'This mountain'

and be cast into the sea, and shall not stagger in his heart, but believe, that whatsoever he saith shall be done; it shall be done unto him.

24 Therefore I say unto you, all things, whatsoever you ask when ye pray, believe that you shall receive; and they shall come unto you.

must be the mount of transfiguration: His words are a prophecy that just as three of them have seen His glory 'here', on earth, so by their preaching they will bring many to behold His glory 'there', that is, in heaven. This is the goal of all preaching, and since the goal comes first in intention, it is mentioned first.

Later, on the final journey to Jerusalem, He tells them that if they had faith like a grain of mustard seed, they could by their command uproot a mulberry tree and transplant it into the sea (Lk. 17:6). This tree, with its blood-red fruit, is a symbol for the Cross, while the sea in Scripture is often a symbol for the nations: His words are a prophecy that the apostles will cause the science of the Cross to pass from Israel to the Gentiles. As St Paul tells the Corinthians, the message of the cross is the beginning of preaching: *Brethren, when I came to you, I judged not myself to know anything among you, but Jesus Christ, and him crucified.*

Here, on the third and last occasion, He combines the two earlier sayings in a climactic image: *This mountain* is to be *cast in to the sea*. Since they are now approaching Jerusalem from the east, and the temple lay on that side, and since the previous episode was the expulsion of the traders, we may presume that this refers to the mount on which the temple stood. Having cast the mulberry tree into the sea by preaching the Cross among the gentiles, the apostles will also set up the new temple and the acceptable sacrifice among them. This is the culmination of preaching, the wisdom that St Paul says that the apostles speak *among the perfect*, concerning the divine liturgy and mystical prayer.

On this third occasion, the faith with which they are to speak is not said to be like a mustard seed, but rather it is called *the faith of God*. This means 'perfect, divine faith'. If faith like a mustard seed makes the apostles like Christ in His humanity, who compared Himself to a mustard seed thrown into the earth by the incarnation, the faith of God makes the apostles like Christ in His divinity.

25 And when you shall stand to pray, forgive, if you have aught against any man; that your Father also, who is in heaven, may forgive you your sins.

26 But if you will not forgive, neither will your Father that is in heaven, forgive you your sins.

27 And they come again to Jerusalem. And when he was walking in the temple, there come to him the chief priests and the scribes and the ancients,

28 And they say to him: By what authority dost thou these things? and who hath given thee this authority that thou shouldst do these things?

29 And Jesus answering, said to them: I will also ask you one word, and answer you me, and I will tell you by what authority I do these things.

30 The baptism of John, was it from heaven, or from men? Answer me.

31 But they thought with themselves, saying: If we say, From heaven; he will say, Why then did you not believe him?

32 If we say, From men, we fear the people. For all men counted John that he was a prophet indeed.

33 And they answering, say to Jesus: We know not. And Jesus answering, saith to them: Neither do I tell you by what authority I do these things.

vv. 25–26

Is it by a great effort of will that we must *believe that* we *shall receive whatsoever* we *ask when* we *pray*? This cannot be the meaning, especially since He literally says, 'Believe that you received.' He seems to be both recommending a general, child-like confidence that God our Father anticipates our needs, and also instructing us that if the Holy Spirit moves us to pray in this way for some precise thing it is because He wills that we should receive it by means of this prayer. Since rancour, or resentment, is a common obstacle to this child-like attitude, and so causes petitions to be unheard or only partly heard by God, He concludes the lesson by a reminder of the universal duty to *forgive*. He speaks of 'standing' to pray, and so we should understand the words not only of secret prayers, which are often made kneeling, but also of liturgical prayer. The Mass of a priest who forgives his enemies, if he has any, is more powerful than the Mass of a priest who does not, other things being equal.

vv. 27-33

Through the prophet Micheas, the Lord said to *the mountains and the hills and the strong foundations of the earth, 'Answer me'*. Here, He says the same thing to *the chief priests and the scribes and the ancients*. In both cases, what is in question is why the representatives of the people have responded ungratefully to the benefits given them from heaven. Micheas had prophesied that as a result, their city would become a desolation.

1 And he began to speak to them in parables: A certain man planted a vineyard and made a hedge about it, and dug a place for the winefat, and built a tower, and let it to husbandmen; and went into a far country.

2 And at the season he sent to the husbandmen a servant to receive of the husbandmen of the fruit of the vineyard.

3 Who having laid hands on him, beat him, and sent him away empty.

4 And again he sent to them another servant; and him they wounded in the head, and used him reproachfully.

5 And again he sent another, and him they killed: and many others, of whom some they beat, and others they killed.

6 Therefore having yet one son, most dear to him; he also sent him unto them last of all, saying: They will reverence my son.

7 But the husbandmen said one to another: This is the heir; come let us kill him; and the inheritance shall be ours.

8 And laying hold on him, they killed him, and cast him out of the vineyard.

9 What therefore will the lord of the vineyard do? He will come and destroy those husbandmen; and will give the vineyard to others.

10 And have you not read this scripture, The stone which the builders rejected, the same is made the head of the corner:

11 By the Lord has this been done, and it is wonderful in our eyes.

12 And they sought to lay hands on him, but they feared the people. For they knew that he spoke this parable to them. And leaving him, they went their way.

COMMENTARY

VV. 1–12

ST MARK RELATES THE PARABLE OF THE TENants in the Vineyard in greater detail than do the other evangelists. It continues the theme of the benefits done to Israel. The *vineyard*, as Isaias had said, *is the house of Israel.* The *man* who plants it is God, in whose image man was made. He *went into a far country*, because though close to the Jews, He remained outside His creation.

The *hedge about* the vineyard must be the law, by which God kept Israel separate from the nations; the *wine-vat* is the psalter, by which believers enjoy the sober intoxication of the Holy Ghost;[1] the *tower* is the prophets, whence things are seen from afar. Christ joined these three things when He told the disciples before His death: *All things must needs be fulfilled, which are written in the law of Moses, and in the prophets, and in the psalms, concerning me.* The *husbandmen* are those who held spiritual or temporal authority among the people down the centuries, and who more often than not persecuted God's *servants*, the prophets.

Since the prophets were persecuted because they resembled Christ, who was called *My servant* by the Father speaking through Isaias, He so describes their sufferings as to prefigure His own passion. The first servant is *beaten*; the second is *wounded in the head* (a detail peculiar to St Mark), and *used reproachfully*; the third is *killed.* Likewise, our Lord, the *heir*, was struck with fists during His midnight trial, then wounded by the crown of thorns and mocked by the soldiers, before finally being crucified.

Yet it is not only Jewish rulers but also Catholic ones, at least taken individually, both temporal and spiritual, who are capable of apostasy, and they too have sometimes mistreated or killed the servants of God. Thus, St John Nepomuk was killed by King Wenceslaus IV, and St Joan of Arc by Bishop Cauchon. What of the plot to destroy the *heir* himself? Could some baptised rulers

---

1 Cf. Eph. 5:18.

13 And they sent to him some of the Pharisees and of the Herodians; that they should catch him in his words.

14 Who coming, say to him: Master, we know that thou art a true speaker, and carest not for any man; for thou regardest not the person of men, but teachest the way of God in truth. Is it lawful to give tribute to Caesar; or shall we not give it?

15 Who knowing their wiliness, saith to them: Why tempt you me? bring me a penny that I may see it.

16 And they brought it him. And he saith to them: Whose is this image and inscription? They say to him, Caesar's.

17 And Jesus answering, said to them: Render therefore to Caesar the things that are Caesar's, and to God the things that are God's. And they marvelled at him.

18 And there came to him the Sadducees, who say there is no resurrection; and they asked him, saying:

19 Master, Moses wrote unto us, that if any man's brother die, and leave his wife behind him, and leave no children, his brother should take his wife, and raise up seed to his brother.

20 Now there were seven brethren; and the first took a wife, and died leaving no issue.

21 And the second took her, and died: and neither did he leave any issue. And the third in like manner.

22 And the seven all took her in like manner; and did not leave issue. Last of all the woman also died.

23 In the resurrection therefore, when they shall rise again, whose wife shall she be of them? for the seven had her to wife.

24 And Jesus answering, saith to them: Do ye not therefore err, because you know not the scriptures, nor the power of God?

25 For when they shall rise again from the dead, they shall neither marry, nor be

apostasise so far as to seek to destroy holy Church herself? "The literal body of Christ", says the angelic doctor, "and the things that were done in it, are a figure of His mystical body and of the things that are being done in that."[2]

vv. 13–17

Since Caesar, that is, a temporal ruler, is himself one of *the things that are* God's, he ought to render himself to God. This he does by putting his power at the service of God's word, as far as he may. "A king serves God in one way insofar as he is a man," notes St Augustine, "and in another insofar as he is a king."

vv. 18–27

In replying to the *Sadducees*, Christ does not only correct their error about the *resurrection*, but also alludes to the existence of *angels*, which they also denied. Only St Mark tells us that He concluded His reply by saying: *You therefore do greatly err*: a lesson to preachers not to be afraid to rebut false teaching firmly.

---

2   *Quodlibetal questions*, VII.6.2, ad 5.

married, but are as the angels in heaven.

26 And as concerning the dead that they rise again, have you not read in the book of Moses, how in the bush God spoke to him, saying: I am the God of Abraham, and the God of Isaac, and the God of Jacob?

27 He is not the God of the dead, but of the living. You therefore do greatly err.

28 And there came one of the scribes that had heard them reasoning together, and seeing that he had answered them well, asked him which was the first commandment of all.

29 And Jesus answered him: The first commandment of all is, Hear, O Israel: the Lord thy God is one God.

30 And thou shalt love the Lord thy God, with thy whole heart, and with thy whole soul, and with thy whole mind, and with thy whole strength. This is the first commandment.

31 And the second is like to it: Thou shalt love thy neighbour as thyself. There is no other commandment greater than these.

32 And the scribe said to him: Well, Master, thou hast said in truth, that there is one God, and there is no other besides him.

33 And that he should be loved with the whole heart, and with the whole understanding, and with the whole soul, and with the whole strength; and to love one's neighbour as one's self, is a greater thing than all holocausts and sacrifices.

34 And Jesus seeing that he had answered wisely, said to him: Thou art not far from the kingdom of God. And no man after that durst ask him any question.

35 And Jesus answering, said, teaching in the temple: How do the scribes say, that Christ is the son of David?

36 For David himself saith by the Holy Ghost: The Lord said to my Lord, Sit on my right hand, until I make thy enemies thy footstool.

37 David therefore himself calleth him Lord, and whence is he then his son? And a great multitude heard him gladly.

38 And he said to them in his doctrine: Beware of the scribes, who love to walk in long robes, and to be saluted in the marketplace,

vv. 28–34

The *scribe* who poses a question next is not trying to trap our Lord: he genuinely desires to know what Christ will pronounce to be *the first commandment*. As a reward for his sincerity, he is told also about *the second*. The second *is like to* the first, insofar as it commands us to love our neighbour insofar as he is like God, or at least is capable of becoming so by the gift of sanctifying grace. Only this gospel gives us the rest of their conversation. Though well-intentioned, this scribe is somewhat presumptuous in commending Christ's answer. The Lord therefore both checks and encourages him by telling him that he is *not far from the kingdom of God*; and hence not yet inside it.

vv. 35–43

[No commentary for these verses.]

39 And to sit in the first chairs, in the synagogues, and to have the highest places at suppers:

40 Who devour the houses of widows under the pretence of long prayer: these shall receive greater judgment.

41 And Jesus sitting over against the treasury, beheld how the people cast money into the treasury, and many that were rich cast in much.

42 And there came a certain poor widow, and she cast in two mites, which make a farthing.

43 And calling his disciples together, he saith to them: Amen I say to you, this poor widow hath cast in more than all they who have cast into the treasury.

44 For all they did cast in of their abundance; but she of her want cast in all she had, even her whole living.

1 And as he was going out of the temple, one of his disciples said to him: Master, behold what manner of stones and what buildings are here.

2 And Jesus answering, said to him: Seest thou all these great buildings? There shall not be left a stone upon a stone, that shall not be thrown down.

3 And as he sat on the mount of Olivet over against the temple, Peter and James and John and Andrew asked him apart:

4 Tell us, when shall these things be? and what shall be the sign when all these things shall begin to be fulfilled?

5 And Jesus answering, began to say to them, Take heed lest any man deceive you.

6 For many shall come in my name, saying, I am he; and they shall deceive many.

7 And when you shall hear of wars and rumours of wars, fear ye not. For such things must needs be, but the end is not yet.

8 For nation shall rise against nation and kingdom against kingdom, and there shall be earthquakes in divers places, and famines. These things are the beginning of sorrows.

COMMENTARY

vv. 1–4

I N THE PREVIOUS CHAPTER, THE SCRIBE *answered wisely* by speaking of the superiority of charity over *all holocausts and sacrifices* offered in the temple. As if to show that entering into the kingdom of God required the Jews to let go of those sacrifices, Christ now speaks of the coming destruction of this wonderful building.

The temple was designed to be among other things an image of the cosmos, like our churches: St Maximus the Confessor tells us that the distinction of sanctuary and nave that is found in every Catholic church represents the heavens and the earth.[1] Hence, our Lord speaks of the destruction of the temple in words that also presage the dissolution of the world as we know it at the end of time.

Only St Mark gives us the names of the disciples to whom Jesus reveals these future events. St Peter has recalled that his brother *Andrew* was there. Why on this occasion was Andrew added to the usual inner circle of Peter, James, and John? Perhaps because God has chosen him to be a patron of those who live in critical times of stress and persecution. This would fit with his name, which means 'manly'. *They asked him apart*, that is, privately, since to speak openly of the destruction of the temple would have sounded treasonous. Peter and James did not live to see the event, but John did. We do not know about Andrew.

vv. 5–31

St Mark seems to record some phrases of this discourse more literally than St Matthew. Instead of *such as hath not been from the beginning of the world,* we have, *as were not from the beginning of the creation which God created.* Instead of *for the sake of the elect those days shall be shortened,* we have *for the sake of the elect which*

---

1 *Mystagogy*, chapters 2–3. Hence the altar-rail in Latin churches represents the meeting of the two.

9 But look to yourselves. For they shall deliver you up to councils, and in the synagogues you shall be beaten, and you shall stand before governors and kings for my sake, for a testimony unto them.

10 And unto all nations the gospel must first be preached.

11 And when they shall lead you and deliver you up, be not thoughtful beforehand what you shall speak; but whatsoever shall be given you in that hour, that speak ye. For it is not you that speak, but the Holy Ghost.

12 And the brother shall betray his brother unto death, and the father his son; and children shall rise up against the parents, and shall work their death.

13 And you shall be hated by all men for my name's sake. But he that shall endure unto the end, he shall be saved.

14 And when you shall see the abomination of desolation, standing where it ought not: he that readeth let him understand: then let them that are in Judea, flee unto the mountains:

15 And let him that is on the housetop, not go down into the house, nor enter therein to take anything out of the house:

16 And let him that shall be in the field, not turn back to take up his garment.

17 And woe to them that are with child, and that give suck in those days.

18 But pray ye, that these things happen not in winter.

19 For in those days shall be such tribulations, as were not from the beginning of the creation which God created until now, neither shall be.

20 And unless the Lord had shortened the days, no flesh should be saved: but for the sake of the elect which he hath chosen, he hath shortened the days.

21 And then if any man shall say to you, Lo, here is Christ; lo, he is here: do not believe.

22 For there will rise up false Christs and false prophets, and they shall shew signs and wonders, to seduce (if it were possible) even the elect.

23 Take you heed therefore; behold I have foretold you all things.

24 But in those days, after that tribulation, the sun shall be darkened, and the moon shall not give her light.

he hath chosen, he hath shortened the days. This Jewish idiom helps to reassure the hearer that God is in charge of events.

The darkening of *sun and moon,* the *falling down* of the *stars,* and the shaking of the *powers* refer to a final ending of the cosmos as we know it; but in prophetic language they also refer to the blotting out of Old Testament Israel with its priests, rulers and institutions. Since Christ's teaching would remain intact amid this spiritual and temporal wreck, He says: *Heaven and earth shall pass away, but my word shall not pass away.*

The Son is said not to know *of that day or hour* not only in the sense that it is not part of His mission to make known precisely when these things will occur, but also because to 'know' about a time in Scripture means to have authority over it, as when Christ says to the apostles: *It is not for you to know the times or moments which the Father hath put in his own power.* But the acts of bringing the temple and the cosmos to a close, though common to the whole Trinity, are appropriated to the Father since they are acts of power, and the Father is the source of the other two divine Persons. Hence, Jesus says simply 'the Son', and not 'the Son of man' or 'the Son of God', since His statement is pertinent to both His human and His divine nature.

25 And the stars of heaven shall be falling down, and the powers that are in heaven, shall be moved.

26 And then shall they see the Son of man coming in the clouds, with great power and glory.

27 And then shall he send his angels, and shall gather together his elect from the four winds, from the uttermost part of the earth to the uttermost part of heaven.

28 Now of the fig tree learn ye a parable. When the branch thereof is now tender, and the leaves are come forth, you know that summer is very near.

29 So you also when you shall see these things come to pass, know ye that it is very nigh, even at the doors.

30 Amen I say to you, that this generation shall not pass, until all these things be done.

31 Heaven and earth shall pass away, but my word shall not pass away.

32 But of that day or hour no man knoweth, neither the angels in heaven, nor the Son, but the Father.

33 Take ye heed, watch and pray. For ye know not when the time is.

34 Even as a man who going into a far country, left his house; and gave authority to his servants over every work, and commanded the porter to watch.

35 Watch ye therefore, (for you know not when the lord of the house cometh: at even, or at midnight, or at the cockcrowing, or in the morning,)

36 Lest coming on a sudden, he find you sleeping.

37 37 And what I say to you, I say to all: Watch.

vv. 32–37

Only St Mark gives us the final parable of this chapter. Our Lord seems to allude to the two-fold life of those within the Church. Those who live the active life have *authority over every work.* Those who live the contemplative life must especially look toward heaven, by prayer and the reading of the Scriptures, like *the porter* who scans the road for signs of the return of his master. He mentions each of the four watches of the night, but not those of the day, since this life is night in comparison to the eternal day. Two of these watches are times of increasing gloom, two of increasing light; and so we cannot be sure whether His return will occur when the Church is declining or prospering.

He tells the parable *to you*, that is, to the generation that will live to see the temple fall, and *to all* Christians who will live from the time of His words until the end, and who must not be found *sleeping*. "For he who sleeps attends not to real bodies, but to phantoms, and awakes empty of what he had seen. So are they whom love of this world takes hold of in life; for afterward, they must leave what they had dreamed was real."

1 Now the feast of the pasch, and of the Azymes was after two days; and the chief priests and the scribes sought how they might by some wile lay hold on him, and kill him.

2 But they said: Not on the festival day, lest there should be a tumult among the people.

3 And when he was in Bethania, in the house of Simon the leper, and was at supper, there came a woman having an alabaster box of ointment of precious spikenard: and breaking the alabaster box, she poured it out upon his head.

4 Now there were some that had indignation within themselves, and said: Why was this waste of the ointment made?

5 For this ointment might have been sold for more than three hundred pence, and given to the poor. And they murmured against her.

6 But Jesus said: Let her alone, why do you molest her? She hath wrought a good work upon me.

7 For the poor you have always with you: and whensoever you will, you may do them good: but me you have not always.

8 She hath done what she could: she is come beforehand to anoint my body for burial.

9 Amen, I say to you, wheresoever this gospel shall be preached in the whole world, that also which she hath done, shall be told for a memorial of her.

10 And Judas Iscariot, one of the twelve, went to the chief priests, to betray him to them.

11 Who hearing it were glad; and they promised him they would give him money. And he sought how he might conveniently betray him.

12 Now on the first day of the unleavened bread, when they sacrificed the pasch, the disciples say to him: Whither wilt thou we go, and prepare for thee to eat the pasch?

13 And he sendeth two of his disciples, and saith to them: Go ye into the city; and

COMMENTARY

VV. 1–11

S T MARK FIRST RECORDS THE INTENTION OF the chief priests and the scribes, who found a means to execute it *two days before the Pasch,* but then goes back a few days to the Saturday before Palm Sunday, to describe the meal *in Bethania.* The *woman* with the *alabaster box of ointment* is Mary, the sister of Martha, as St John relates. Why is she is not named here or by St Matthew? The traditional identification of her with the woman who performed a similar action for Christ in the house of the pharisee would provide a good reason: the wish not to identify, during her life-time, a woman who had previously been a public *sinner.* From St John we learn that though the *spikenard* was *poured out upon his head,* it also flowed on His feet, and so His whole *body* was anointed *for the burial.* Only St Mark mentions that she broke the box, suggesting the intensity of her devotion. Again, only he gives us the words of Christ: *She hath done what she could,* filling the whole house, as St John relates, with the odour of the ointment. Therefore, Jesus promises to do what only He can, namely to fill *the whole world* with *a memorial* of her action.

Since this episode comes between the desire of the chief priests *to lay hold* on Christ and the reference to Judas going *to betray him to them,* it seems to have precipitated the betrayal. For while Judas had apparently lost faith some time before, he now finds that he cannot benefit even financially from his place among the apostles.

VV. 12–16

St Peter does not mention that he was one of the two disciples sent to prepare *the Pasch.* This word refers at once to the Passover lamb which *they sacrificed* and to the subsequent Passover meal, but also to the entire week that was inaugurated by

there shall meet you a man carrying a pitcher of water, follow him;

14 And whithersoever he shall go in, say to the master of the house, The master saith, Where is my refectory, where I may eat the pasch with my disciples?

15 And he will shew you a large dining room furnished; and there prepare ye for us.

16 And his disciples went their way, and came into the city; and they found as he had told them, and they prepared the pasch.

17 And when evening was come, he cometh with the twelve.

18 And when they were at table and eating, Jesus saith: Amen I say to you, one of you that eateth with me shall betray me.

19 But they began to be sorrowful, and to say to him one by one: Is it I?

20 Who saith to them: One of the twelve, who dippeth with me his hand in the dish.

21 And the Son of man indeed goeth, as it is written of him: but woe to that man by whom the Son of man shall be betrayed. It were better for him, if that man had not been born.

22 And whilst they were eating, Jesus took bread; and blessing it, broke it, and gave to them, and said: Take ye. This is my body.

23 And having taken the chalice, giving thanks, he gave it to them. And they all drank of it.

24 And he said to them: This is my blood of the new testament, which shall be shed for many.

25 Amen I say to you, that I will drink no more of the fruit of the vine, until that day when I shall drink it new in the kingdom of God.

this meal and during which *unleavened bread* was eaten. Christ's prophetic instruction to the two apostles, given after He has been anointed by Mary, is somewhat reminiscent of Samuel's prophecy to the young Saul, whom he had just anointed as the first king of Israel, about the three men whom he would meet carrying provisions.[1] But in the Old Testament, which is still imperfect, the prophet and the anointed king are distinct; here they are the same.

Given that the *large dining room* is already *furnished* – literally, 'furnished, prepared' – what is left for the two disciples to *prepare*? The most important thing: they must go the temple and have a lamb sacrificed, which will be eaten by them all after sunset. If none of the evangelists mentions the presence of the lamb during the supper itself, this is so as not to distract from the presence of the true Lamb, of the new Passover.

vv. 17–21

St Mark records our Lord's prophecy of the betrayal with especial vividness: *One of the twelve, who dippeth with me his hand in the dish.* But why are the apostles ignorant who it is, since Judas can hardly have concealed his true disposition infallibly? Venerable Mary of Agreda answers that they had had their suspicions of him, but had checked them when they saw the particular tokens of love and honour that Christ and Mary paid to him. Since it would be *better* for Judas if he *had not been born*, it is impossible to hope for his salvation.

vv. 22–25

The first three evangelists give slightly different versions of the words that Christ spoke over the bread and the wine. St Thomas Aquinas remarks: "The Evangelists did not intend to hand down the forms of the sacraments, which in the primitive Church had to be kept concealed." Yet we may suppose that the short form of words pronounced over the bread, lacking the words 'given for you' quoted by St Luke and St Paul, reflects the

---

1 1 Samuel 10:1–4.

26 And when they had said an hymn, they went forth to the mount of Olives.

27 And Jesus saith to them: You will all be scandalized in my regard this night; for it is written, I will strike the shepherd, and the sheep shall be dispersed.

28 But after I shall be risen again, I will go before you into Galilee.

29 But Peter saith to him: Although all shall be scandalized in thee, yet not I.

30 And Jesus saith to him: Amen I say to thee, today, even in this night, before the cock crow twice, thou shall deny me thrice.

31 But he spoke the more vehemently: Although I should die together with thee, I will not deny thee. And in like manner also said they all.

32 And they came to a farm called Gethsemani. And he saith to his disciples: Sit you here, while I pray.

33 And he taketh Peter and James and John with him; and he began to fear and to be heavy.

practice of the Roman church over which St Peter presided; the Roman rite of Mass, as far back as we can trace it, lacked these words, unlike the Eastern rites, which contain them.

What does it mean to say that He would drink *of the fruit of the vine new in the kingdom of God*? From the more detailed account of St Luke, it appears that Christ spoke these words at the sharing of the non-Eucharistic chalice during the meal, in which case these words were first of all an announcement of the new thing that He was about to do by changing the wine into His blood, as the greatest of the sacraments of the Church, that is, of the kingdom of God on earth. But St Mark is inspired to place these words after the consecration of the chalice, to suggest that the Holy Communions that we have on earth are themselves only a foretaste of the more perfect communion of heaven.

vv. 26–31

Why does our Lord specify that He *will go before* the apostles *into Galilee,* after quoting the prophecy of Zechariah about the shepherd and the flock? Zechariah's prophecy continued with these words: *There shall be in all the earth,* or the land, *two parts in it shall be scattered, and shall perish: but the third part shall be left therein.* Since the holy land was divided into three parts, Judaea, Samaria, and Galilee, Christ may be telling the apostles that Galilee will be the region where their preaching will be most acceptable. But in another sense, Zechariah's words suggest the main religious divisions of the world after the Passion: between paganism, the Judaism that rejected Christ, and the Church.

St Mark, relying on St Peter, records the prophecy of the latter's denial with greater precision than the other evangelists: it is not just before the cock crows, but *before the cock crow twice,* that he will deny three times. Likewise, only he records the fact that St Peter denied this *the more vehemently.*

vv. 32–42

They come to a farm, that is an estate or a piece of land, *called Gethsemani,* a word that literally means oil-press. The name suggests the agony that He will undergo in this place.

34 And he saith to them: My soul is sorrowful even unto death; stay you here, and watch.

35 And when he was gone forward a little, he fell flat on the ground; and he prayed, that if it might be, the hour might pass from him.

36 And he saith: Abba, Father, all things are possible to thee: remove this chalice from me; but not what I will, but what thou wilt.

37 And he cometh, and findeth them sleeping. And he saith to Peter: Simon, sleepest thou? couldst thou not watch one hour?

38 Watch ye, and pray that you enter not into temptation.

The spirit indeed is willing, but the flesh is weak.

39 And going away again, he prayed, saying the same words.

40 And when he returned, he found them again asleep, (for their eyes were heavy,) and they knew not what to answer him.

41 And he cometh the third time, and saith to them: Sleep ye now, and take your rest. It is enough: the hour is come: behold the Son of man shall be betrayed into the hands of sinners.

42 Rise up, let us go. Behold, he that will betray me is at hand.

The Greek word translated as *to fear* may also be translated as to be amazed or struck with awe, perhaps at the sins of men.

St Jerome says: "Our Lord, in order to prove the reality of the humanity that He had assumed was sorrowful in very truth; yet since passion held no sway over His soul, He is said to have begun to be sorrowful, by something that took the place of a passion. For it is one thing to be sorrowful, another to begin to be sorrowful." Yet although Christ's feelings were not passions in the sense of emotions overpowering reason, they were more intense than our own since He did not allow the pain of them to be lessened by any contrary considerations, for example about His future resurrection, and because the evil that caused His sorrow, namely sin, is greater than any other evil and was also recognised by Him alone for what it is. "Men know neither how to rejoice truly nor to sorrow truly," said St John of the Cross, "for they do not understand the distance between good and evil."

He was *sorrowful even unto death*, that is, with a sorrow that would have been great enough to have caused death, had it been allowed to produce its natural effect. "Not," says St Jerome again, "from a fear of suffering, since He had come in order to suffer, but because of the wretched Judas and the falling away of all the apostles, and the setting aside of the people of the Jews and the overturning of poor Jerusalem. Even so had Jonas been saddened at the drying up of the ivy, not wishing that his tabernacle should perish."

He prayed that if it might be, the hour might pass from him, not as if He wondered whether it might pass, but wanting by this spontaneous prayer to express the spontaneous desire of human nature.

In St Matthew's gospel, the question is addressed to Peter but phrased so as to include all three apostles: *Could you not watch one hour with me?* Here, St Peter seems to take the responsibility for them all upon himself by quoting our Lord's words in the singular: *Couldst thou not watch one hour?*

43 And while he was yet speaking, cometh Judas Iscariot, one of the twelve: and with him a great multitude with swords and staves, from the chief priests and the scribes and the ancients.

44 And he that betrayed him, had given them a sign, saying: Whomsoever I shall kiss, that is he; lay hold on him, and lead him away carefully.

45 And when he was come, immediately going up to him, he saith: Hail, Rabbi; and he kissed him.

46 But they laid hands on him, and held him.

47 And one of them that stood by, drawing a sword, struck

a servant of the chief priest, and cut off his ear.

48 And Jesus answering, said to them: Are you come out as to a robber, with swords and staves to apprehend me?

49 I was daily with you in the temple teaching, and you did not lay hands on me. But that the scriptures may be fulfilled.

50 Then his disciples leaving him, all fled away.

51 And a certain young man followed him, having a linen cloth cast about his naked body; and they laid hold on him.

52 But he, casting off the linen cloth, fled from them naked.

53 And they brought Jesus to the high priest; and all the priests and the scribes and the ancients assembled together.

54 And Peter followed him from afar off, even into the court of the high priest; and he sat with the servants at the fire, and warmed himself.

55 And the chief priests and all the council sought for evidence against Jesus, that they might put him to death, and found none.

56 For many bore false witness against him, and their evidences were not agreeing.

57 And some rising up, bore false witness against him, saying:

58 We heard him say, I will destroy this temple made with hands, and within three days I will build another not made with hands.

59 And their witness did not agree.

60 And the high priest rising up in the midst, asked Jesus, saying: Answerest thou

vv. 43–52

Were the disciples at fault when they *fled away*? No doubt, and yet after the resurrection Christ does not rebuke them for it, but only for having been to slow to believe in the message of the women. The former was a result of human frailty, the latter a doubt of the veracity of God.

Who is the *young man* who *fled from them naked*? Many answers have been proposed: a young man who belonged to the house where they had eaten the Passover; St James the Just, the cousin of our Lord; the beloved apostle, St John; the evangelist St Mark himself; the rich young man who had previously gone away sad; and someone from the house to which the garden of Gethsemani was attached. There seems to be no way of resolving the doubt.

Since linen is a priestly material, the episode prepares us for the denudation of the Jewish priesthood just about to occur. It is also a counterpoint to the resurrection, when Christ also cast off a *linen cloth*, and departed from soldiers seeking to retain Him, not naked but clothed in glory.

vv. 53–65

Jesus *held his peace* when accused, and thereby honoured the Law, since the very fact that *their witness did not agree* plainly showed that the requirement of Deuteronomy, *in the mouth of two or three witnesses every word shall stand*, had not been met. Only when directly adjured by the high priest does He respond, thus honouring the office which Caiaphas still holds until the rending of the temple veil. By giving Christ's answer simply as *I am,* St Mark shows that the answer given by St Matthew to the same question, *Thou hast said,* is to be understood as an affirmation.

Why does the high priest claim that it is *blasphemy* to speak of *sitting on the right hand of the power of God and coming with the clouds of heaven*, given that the psalm and the prophecy of Daniel indicated that these things would one day be true of some 'son of man'? Perhaps Caiaphas was imagining that the person to whom these things would apply would have even outwardly

nothing to the things that are laid to thy charge by these men?

61 But he held his peace, and answered nothing. Again the high priest asked him, and said to him: Art thou the Christ the Son of the blessed God?

62 And Jesus said to him: I am. And you shall see the Son of man sitting on the right hand of the power of God, and coming with the clouds of heaven.

63 Then the high priest rending his garments, saith: What need we any further witnesses?

64 You have heard the blasphemy. What think you? Who all condemned him to be guilty of death.

65 And some began to spit on him, and to cover his face, and to buffet him, and to say unto him: Prophesy: and the servants struck him with the palms of their hands.

66 Now when Peter was in the court below, there cometh one of the maidservants of the high priest.

67 And when she had seen Peter warming himself, looking on him she saith: Thou also wast with Jesus of Nazareth.

68 But he denied, saying: I neither know nor understand what thou sayest. And he went forth before the court; and the cock crew.

69 And again a maidservant seeing him, began to say to the standers by: This is one of them.

70 But he denied again. And after a while they that stood by said again to Peter: Surely thou art one of them; for thou art also a Galilean.

71 But he began to curse and to swear, saying; I know not this man of whom you speak.

72 And immediately the cock crew again. And Peter remembered the word that Jesus had said unto him: Before the cock crow twice, thou shalt thrice deny me. And he began to weep.

a heavenly appearance, rather than bearing *the likeness of sinful flesh*, and that to think otherwise was to attribute to God something unworthy of Him. Yet it is Caiphas and not our Lord who is revealed as the law-breaker, since Leviticus decreed that *the high-priest shall not rend his garments*.

Christ's words, *You shall see*, are in the plural, addressed to the Sanhedrin as such and not simply to Caiphas. Since the Sanhedrin was the highest council on earth, but has now become uniquely corrupt, He refers here to the last judgement, when all earthly miscarriages of justice will be exposed and corrected.

St Robert Bellarmine considered that the high-priests and councils of the old Law were not able to err on matters of faith before the coming of Christ. Once Christ had come, however, it was no longer necessary for them to be divinely protected from error, since He is Himself the supreme high-priest of the Church.[2] Hence, Caiphas errs by solemnly declaring the gospel a *blasphemy*.

According to Mary of Agreda, the joy that Christ felt in suffering for mankind caused His face to shine in a way that the accusers found intolerable, and so they made haste *to cover his face*.

vv. 66–72
[No commentary for these verses.]

---

2 *Controversies*, 'On Councils', book 2, chapter, 8.

1 And straightway in the morning, the chief priests holding a consultation with the ancients and the scribes and the whole council, binding Jesus, led him away, and delivered him to Pilate.

2 And Pilate asked him: Art thou the king of the Jews? But he answering, saith to him: Thou sayest it.

3 And the chief priests accused him in many things.

4 And Pilate again asked him, saying: Answerest thou nothing? behold in how many things they accuse thee.

5 But Jesus still answered nothing; so that Pilate wondered.

6 Now on the festival day he was wont to release unto them one of the prisoners, whomsoever they demanded.

7 And there was one called Barabbas, who was put in prison with some seditious men, who in the sedition had committed murder.

8 And when the multitude was come up, they began to desire that he would do, as he had ever done unto them.

9 And Pilate answered them, and said: Will you that I release to you the king of the Jews?

10 For he knew that the chief priests had delivered him up out of envy.

11 But the chief priests moved the people, that he should rather release Barabbas to them.

12 And Pilate again answering, saith to them: What will you then that I do to the king of the Jews?

13 But they again cried out: Crucify him.

14 And Pilate saith to them: Why, what evil hath he done? But they cried out the more: Crucify him.

15 And so Pilate being willing to satisfy the people, released to them Barabbas, and delivered up Jesus, when he had scourged him, to be crucified.

vv. 1–15

CHRIST ANSWERS PILATE'S QUESTION, *ART thou the king of the Jews*, since His kingship over mankind forms part of the gospel. He *answered nothing* about the *many things* of which the Jewish authorities accused Him, since they have already shown themselves incapable of establishing these charges when they had the opportunity; again, He is honouring the Law by treating as authoritative its norms for honest trials.

Why does the fact that *the chief priests had delivered up* Jesus *out of envy* cause Pilate to offer to release Him as *the king of the Jews?* It could be that Pilate is taunting the chief priests by using this title of one whom they disown. But his leading idea seems to be that they are envious of the favour that Christ has won among the common people, and he therefore hopes by appealing to *the multitude* to find support for his own wish to release Him.

All the evangelists mention the offer of Pilate to release *Barabbas* instead of Christ. From the different gospels we learn that Barabbas was a notorious prisoner, a robber, a murderer, and a revolutionary. His name means 'son of the father', and so he seems like a prefiguration of antichrist, who will be a parody of Christ. The separation of Barabbas from our Lord was prefigured in the ritual that took place each year on the Day of Atonement, when two buck-goats were brought to the court of the temple, one of which was offered to the Lord for the sins of the people, the other of which was allowed to go free, but *into the wilderness*.

When asked *what evil has he done,* the people *cried out the more*, no doubt angered by the consciousness, engendered by the question, of their own irrationality.

Whereas our Lord wished to make satisfaction to His Father, Pilate wished *to satisfy the people*.

16 And the soldiers led him away into the court of the palace, and they called together the whole band:

17 And they clothed him with purple, and plaiting a crown of thorns, they put it upon him.

18 And they began to salute him: Hail, king of the Jews.

19 And they struck his head with a reed: and they did spit on him. And bowing their knees, they adored him.

20 And after they had mocked him, they took off the purple from him, and put his own garments on him, and they led him out to crucify him.

21 And they forced one Simon a Cyrenian who passed by, coming out of the country, the father of Alexander and of Rufus, to take up his cross.

22 And they bring him into the place called Golgotha, which being interpreted is, The place of Calvary.

23 And they gave him to drink wine mingled with myrrh; but he took it not.

24 And crucifying him, they divided his garments, casting lots upon them, what every man should take.

25 And it was the third hour, and they crucified him.

26 And the inscription of his cause was written over: THE KING OF THE JEWS.

27 And with him they crucify two thieves; the one on his right hand, and the other on his left.

28 And the scripture was fulfilled, which saith: And with the wicked he was reputed.

29 And they that passed by blasphemed him, wagging their heads, and saying: Vah, thou that destroyest the temple of God, and in three days buildest it up again;

30 Save thyself, coming down from the cross.

31 In like manner also the chief priests mocking, said with the scribes one to another: He saved others; himself he cannot save.

32 Let Christ the king of Israel come down now from the cross, that we may see and believe. And they that were crucified with him reviled him.

33 And when the sixth hour was come, there was darkness over the whole earth until the ninth hour.

34 And at the ninth hour, Jesus cried out with a loud voice, saying: *Eloi, Eloi, lamma sabacthani?* Which is, being

vv. 16–41

Alexander and Rufus must have been two men prominent in the church at Rome. St Paul, writing to the Romans, says: *Salute Rufus, elect in the Lord, and his mother and mine.* If this is the same person, then Simon of Cyrene's wife must have been well known to him.

St Mark's description of the crucifixion contains almost no details that are not also found in St Matthew. This may reflect the fact that neither St Matthew nor St Peter had been eye-witnesses of it. However, only St Mark mentions that the crucifixion between thieves fulfils the prophecy of Isaias: *With the wicked he was reputed.* St Peter had heard Christ quote this prophecy the previous evening, as St Luke records. Again, only this gospel mentions that the centurion was induced to confess Christ as *the Son of God* by the *loud voice* with which He spoke, beyond the powers of nature, before dying. This confession by a centurion symbolically foreshadows the transition of Rome from a persecuting power to one that will uphold the gospel.

The veil of the temple was not only *rent in two*, but was rent *from the top to the bottom*, to show that it is by the descent of the Son into human nature that the barrier between mankind and the Trinity has been overcome. "The veil is rent," says St Gregory Nazianzen, "for the heavenly things have been laid bare."

interpreted, My God, my God, why hast thou forsaken me?

35 And some of the standers by hearing, said: Behold he calleth Elias.

36 And one running and filling a sponge with vinegar, and putting it upon a reed, gave him to drink, saying: Stay, let us see if Elias come to take him down.

37 And Jesus having cried out with a loud voice, gave up the ghost.

38 And the veil of the temple was rent in two, from the top to the bottom.

39 And the centurion who stood over against him, seeing that crying out in this manner he had given up the ghost, said: Indeed this man was the son of God.

40 And there were also women looking on afar off: among whom was Mary Magdalen, and Mary the mother of James the less and of Joseph, and Salome:

41 Who also when he was in Galilee followed him, and ministered to him, and many other women that came up with him to Jerusalem.

42 And when evening was now come, (because it was the Parasceve, that is, the day before the sabbath,)

43 Joseph of Arimathea, a noble counsellor, who was also himself looking for the kingdom of God, came and went in boldly to Pilate, and begged the body of Jesus.

44 But Pilate wondered that he should be already dead. And sending for the centurion, he asked him if he were already dead.

45 And when he had understood it by the centurion, he gave the body to Joseph.

46 And Joseph buying fine linen, and taking him down, wrapped him up in the fine linen, and laid him in a sepulchre which was hewed out of a rock. And he rolled a stone to the door of the sepulchre.

47 And Mary Magdalen, and Mary the mother of Joseph, beheld where he was laid.

vv. 42–47

What does it mean to say that St Joseph of Arimathea was *himself looking for the kingdom of God*? Were not all the Jews hoping for a descendant of David who would restore freedom to the chosen people? It must mean that he was already a disciple, though secretly, as we learn from the other gospels. His desire to take down the body of our Lord from the Cross springs both from his faith and from his wish to observe a precept of the Book of Deuteronomy, which forbade the body of an executed man from remaining exposed overnight. In saying that Pilate *gave the body to Joseph*, St Mark uses a slightly unusual word for 'give': it means 'gave freely', and not in return for money. The word for 'body' is also slightly unusual, and means 'dead body'. It is the same word that is used when Christ says: *Wheresoever the body shall be, there shall the eagles be gathered together.* The *noble counsellor* and the *governor* who gather round this body are inspired by divine providence to treat it with marks of reverence.

1 And when the sabbath was past, Mary Magdalen, and Mary the mother of James, and Salome, bought sweet spices, that coming, they might anoint Jesus.

2 And very early in the morning, the first day of the week, they come to the sepulchre, the sun being now risen.

3 And they said one to another: Who shall roll us back the stone from the door of the sepulchre?

4 And looking, they saw the stone rolled back. For it was very great.

5 And entering into the sepulchre, they saw a young man sitting on the right side, clothed with a white robe, and they were astonished.

6 Who saith to them: Be not affrighted; you seek Jesus of Nazareth, who was crucified: he is risen, he is not here, behold the place where they laid him.

7 But go, tell his disciples and Peter that he goeth before you into Galilee; there you shall see him, as he told you.

8 But they going out, fled from the sepulchre. For a trembling and fear had seized them: and they said nothing to any man; for they were afraid.

COMMENTARY

THE NARRATION OF THE RESURRECTION
and ascension is brief, hardly more than a summary.
It seems that St Peter wished in his gospel to highlight
the passion of our Lord, perhaps to atone for having tried to
dissuade Him from accepting it.

The sabbath was past on Holy Saturday evening, after sunset.
The stone in front of His tomb would have sat in a deep groove
in the ground, making it even harder to move.

The women in the tomb see two angels standing, as St Luke
records, and one *sitting*, as St Matthew and St Mark record. Why
does he take the form of *a young man,* rather than an old one?
Probably because he is announcing new life. He is *on the right
side*, which in Scripture signifies happiness as opposed to sorrow
and eternity as opposed to time. He is seated to lend authority
to his words; the other two stand to suggest the equality that
we may achieve with angels by the resurrection.

Only St Mark notes that St Peter was spoken of to the women
by name. Was it boastful of him to record this in his preaching in
Rome? No, it was humbling, since it recalled his denial of Christ:
his name is mentioned lest he should seem to have forfeited his
place at the head of the college of apostles. Why does the angel
say, *His disciples and Peter*, rather than 'Peter and the disciples',
given that Peter is over the others? Perhaps because Peter was
first a disciple before he was at the head of the apostles; or
perhaps it hints at the fact that Christ has not yet absolved him.

Why does St Mark say that *they said nothing to any man*, when
we read a few verses later that Mary Magdalen went to tell *them
that had been with him*, as also St John's gospel says? It may mean
that they said nothing to anyone in the city until they had made
their way back from the tomb to the place where the apostles
were. Or perhaps, that they said nothing at first of the vision
of angels and the message, but only told the apostles that the
stone was rolled away and the tomb empty. But from St Luke we

9 But he rising early the first day of the week, appeared first to Mary Magdalen, out of whom he had cast seven devils.

10 She went and told them that had been with him, who were mourning and weeping.

11 And they hearing that he was alive, and had been seen by her, did not believe.

12 And after that he appeared in another shape to two of them walking, as they were going into the country.

13 And they going told it to the rest: neither did they believe them.

14 At length he appeared to the eleven as they were at table: and he upbraided them with their incredulity and hardness of heart, because they did not believe them who had seen him after he was risen again.

15 And he said to them: Go ye into the whole world, and preach the gospel to every creature.

16 He that believeth and is baptized, shall be saved: but he that believeth not shall be condemned.

17 And these signs shall follow them that believe: In my name they shall cast out devils: they shall speak with new tongues.

18 They shall take up serpents; and if they shall drink any deadly thing, it shall not hurt them: they shall lay their hands upon the sick, and they shall recover.

learn that at least some of the women mentioned this angelic message before the end of the day.

vv. 9–10

He rises *early the first day of the week*, as also He did in the first chapter of the gospel. Hence comes the custom among Christians of rising to pray when it is still dark, since it is believed that special graces are given at that time.

St Bede remarks that by making St Mary Magdalen the herald of the resurrection, our Lord took away the reproach that the female sex had to bear for the original fall: "Woman having passed on guilt to men, she now passes on grace." She is a new Eve, albeit not in the same way as the Blessed Virgin.

vv. 11–18

Much though He loved them, or rather because He loved them, *he upbraided* the eleven for *their incredulity and hardness of heart*, since it would be their task to teach the world the duty of belief in the resurrection. He does this just before leaving them, so that these words may be the more deeply imprinted on their minds.

How is it possible to *preach to every creature*? Some say it means 'to all men', not just to the Jews. St Gregory the Great says that man is every creature, since he alone has something in common with angels, animals, plants, and minerals. Or again, the gospel is preached to all creation because the Church has blessings for animals and crops, and for whatever serves the use of man, and she affects even the weather by her prayers. Or, finally, because once the gospel has been fully preached, *the creation also itself shall be delivered from the servitude of corruption into the liberty of the glory of the children of God*, when the cosmos is transfigured. Since all these things are true, we can assume that the Lord intended them all.

The brief mention of *baptism* as necessary in order to be *saved* implies the necessity of the visible Church, into which a person is baptised, and of the other sacraments, of which baptism is the gateway. St Bernard speculates that, in speaking of those who *shall be condemned,* Jesus repeats only the reference to faith

and not that to baptism in order to allow us to hope that some may be saved by a sincere desire for this sacrament.

But why is a person *condemned* simply because *he believeth not*? No one can be freed of his sins unless he first believes that God wishes to take them away. Again, whoever hears the gospel and rejects it *makes God a liar*, as St John says: and no one can live at peace with one whom he believes to be a liar.

Our Lord does not say that the five *signs* that He mentions will be accomplished by all believers, but that they will *follow them that believe*, since miracles will always accompany the mission of the Church. His words have different layers of meaning. Exorcists *cast out devils* in the most direct sense, but all those who preach, or who pray and do penance for mankind, also expel them. A miraculous gift of speaking in *new tongues* was often given to neophytes in the earliest times to be *a sign to unbelievers*, as St Paul says; but the converted gentiles also fulfilled this prophecy when they learned to pray from the Jewish scriptures, as do those today who convert and spontaneously give up what the apostle calls *obscenity or foolish talking or scurrility*.

In the life of St Paul, and in the lives of the desert fathers, we find saints who were divinely immune to harm from serpents; but according to St Gregory the Great, they also *take up serpents* "who by good encouragement remove malice from the hearts of others". Joseph Barsabas, surnamed 'the Just', who was the disciple put forward along with Matthias as a possible replacement for Judas Iscariot, drank *deadly* poison without suffering *hurt*, according to Papias, a bishop who lived at the end of the first century;[1] but priests who hear about the sins of others in the sacrament of penance without being disturbed may be said to do the same. These two miracles are less frequent in their literal sense than the others, since they lack any intrinsic value.

Miracles of healing *the sick* have always been frequent; spiritually, as St Gregory writes, all those may be said to heal, who see another growing weak in good actions, and strengthen him by their own example. In the Scriptures, the *hands* are often a symbol for our acts.

---

1 Eusebius of Caesarea, *Church History*, III.39.

19 And the Lord Jesus, after he had spoken to them, was taken up into heaven, and sitteth on the right hand of God.

20 But they going forth preached everywhere: the Lord working with them, and confirming the word with signs that followed.

VV. 19–20

For the first time in this gospel, we find the phrase *the Lord Jesus*. Unimaginative commentators, lacking a sense of rhetoric, therefore ascribe this passage to some unknown author, whose words came in some unexplained way to be put on a par by the church of Rome with the preaching of St Peter and the writing of St Mark. But there is no need for this hypothesis, since the change in vocabulary and tone effectively suggests the passage from this world *into heaven*. Hitherto, this gospel has been the lowliest of the four, not mentioning our Lord's eternal existence or His miraculous conception and birth, and showing Him sighing, and experiencing the human emotions of anger, indignation and fear; now, as if to compensate for this, it ends more gloriously than all the rest. St Matthew and St John finish on earth; and while St Luke speaks of the ascension, St Mark goes further still and declares Christ's enthronement *on the right hand of God*.

* * *

WHETHER BY HUMAN DESIGN OR BY PROVIDEN-tial guidance only, this gospel thus shows our Lord as accomplishing in reality what the human Israel had done in figure. God had told Moses: *Israel is my son, my first-born,* and He had brought them through Jordan into the land of promise. God had kept His promises, but they had not kept theirs, and when Jesus came, the land had long been profaned by pagan occupation, beyond human hope of deliverance. But He came as the true Son and first-born, being declared so at the start and end of His public life by God the Father and by the voice of Rome, and His journey has taken Him from the Jordan into the true land of promise, heaven itself.

His exodus is thus complete: it remains only for the apostles *going forth* to preach *everywhere* so that we may accomplish ours. For as St Peter says in his first epistle: *Christ also suffered for us, leaving you an example that you should follow his steps.*

9 781990 685439